EUROPEAN DAZE

European Daze

A Model Memoir

Adventures in How Not to Become a Supermodel

Barbara von der Osten

TDSS Publishing,
A division of The Divine Saga Studios, LLC

Ponte Vedra, Florida

Copyright © 2019 Barbara von der Osten.

All rights reserved. No part of this publication may be reproduced, distributed or transmitted in any form or by any means, including photocopying, recording, or other electronic or mechanical methods, without the prior written permission of the author, except by a reviewer who may quote brief passages in a review .

TDSS Publishing, a division of The Divine Saga Studios, LLC
Ponte Vedra, Florida
www.thedivinesagastudios.net

First Edition, 2019

ISBN: 978-1-7321664-1-7

Library of Congress Control Number: 2019901741

This is a memoir. Some names have been changed, some events have been compressed, and some dialogue has been recreated.

To reprint a portion of this book, order review or bulk copies, or contact the author: info@tdsspublishing.com.

Cover and Book Layout by TDSS Publishing
Cover Illustration by Kevin Cantrell

10 9 8 7 6 5 4 3 2 1

For Mom

CONTENTS

Acknowledgements

The World's Most Famous Beach 1

Open Interviews – New York 9

New York: It Begins 17

Paris 43

Milan 119

Zurich 227

Munich 267

Hamburg 323

Munich II 357

1987: The Beginning of the End 385

Epilogue 399

Playlist 407

Recipes 411

Author Bio 425

Acknowledgements

Although this book is my story, of my experiences, it wouldn't have been possible without the cast of characters who joined me in the fashion world during those years. To them, I owe a great deal of thanks—Robbie, Kristen, Ava, Emily, Hetty, Sean, Janice, Karen, Lisa, Celine and many others. Above all, I thank my first agent, Lawrine Childers, for seeing something in me that I didn't even know was there.

This book would not have been possible without the encouragement of my father, so long ago, to keep a journal of my adventures and to take photos and collect postcards along the way, much like he did during his time in the US Navy during World War II. He promised that one day I would be glad I did. My only regret is that he is not here to read this book.

I also could not provide a full accounting of my adventures in Europe without my parents keeping every letter, postcard, and tear sheet I sent home to them. For those times I failed to note events in my journal, I surely wrote home about them. For this I thank my mom, along with her constant love and support.

It does take great effort to turn a box full of notebook journals, calendars, postcards and photos into a narrative that others can follow and understand. For assistance with this, I thank Patricia Charpentier and her editors at Writing Your Life. I also thank Jan Costello Johnson for reading the manuscript and providing feedback. Jan, you are a true Renaissance woman!

And finally, heartfelt thanks go to Kevin Cantrell, for his encouragement and incredible artistic eye. *Ich Liebe dich*.

Photo taken by Stephanie Pfriender Stylander, 1984, New York City.

If I were a supermodel, you would already know my name. But I'm not, and you don't, so my story begins where all such tales begin - at the beginning.

ON THE WORLD'S MOST FAMOUS BEACH

It was the spring break of 1984. Daytona Beach, Florida. Two things happened that spring that would change the direction of my future in the most inconceivable ways. I made out with a rock star, and I met Maria. Which of these more directly pushed me into the world, I can't say. Maybe it was just the right mix of both.

So maybe he shouldn't be called a rock star exactly, but he was British, and he did have a popular band, and a song that melts hearts still to this day. Robbie Grey, the lead singer for the band Modern English, was in Daytona Beach to perform for the spring break crowds. I met him and the band when they checked into the Pagoda Hotel, where I worked as a desk clerk. The hotel served as the sister property of the more popular Plaza Hotel which lay at the center of spring break nirvana. Bands performing there stayed at our hotel.

It started out as simple conversations at the desk. This led to a ride to my parent's house and a roll on the floor with Chivas, my brother's fluffy new puppy. Back at the hotel, we made out in the hallway, more kissing than I had ever done in all my nineteen years. A good little, mostly virgin, girl, it never entered my mind to go all the way with him, even if he was famous. Nevertheless, he would smile, wink, and tell me to always "Keep the Faith." What that meant I had no idea.

Maria was an exotic beauty with Russian in her mix. I met her through my older sister, Trudy. We all worked at hotels along the World's Most Famous Beach. Tall and shapely, Maria had long, thick black hair and porcelain white skin that mesmerized you the minute you met her. With looks like that, she could have been quite the snob, yet she turned out to be a gentle, kind soul, and I knew that in an instant. But Maria was different, different from anyone I had ever met. She had dreams far beyond a hotel front desk in Florida. Dreams of New York, of fashion, of posing, of photographs, of fame.

Eternally shy, my only experience with modeling had come at the end of my junior year in high school. Burdines, a department store in the local mall, advertised auditions for their first ever Teen Advisory Board. They were looking for girls from the local high schools to model in fashion shows in the store several times a year. I figured since I was tall, I might have a shot. Sporting permed hair, I made my way to an interview and was surprisingly selected. For our first fashion show, we wore clothes by the designer Fiorucci and walked down a makeshift runway in the Juniors Department to a crowd of about thirty people. The next year Burdines bid us farewell with one last show, in which we wore designs by OP, Santa Cruz, and Calvin Klein. We were all graduating from high school, and a new board had been selected to replace us.

Now, with my lackluster community college performance while still living at home with my parents, Robbie and Maria were an awakening. They were exciting! My world had been exposed to more than what I knew, and anything was possible. There was a much bigger world out there, far beyond this beach in Florida. Far beyond this desk in a hotel on that beach.

I can't say I recall the exact moment or conversation that sealed the deal to take a chance and test our luck in New York, but somehow the decision was made. For weeks my sister and I worked on compiling pictures to show agents in New York. She came up with the locations, the outfits, the hair, and makeup. I showed up, ready to pose. At the beach, in my eggplant-purple two-piece swimsuit, with its ruffled bandeau top, and my bright pink cover-shirt which draped down to my mid-back, I splashed through the water and sashayed on the sand. I laughed. I joked. I gazed out over the dunes. Meanwhile, my sister snapped away on our new Kodak disc camera.

Back at the house, Trudy caked on even more makeup, eyeliner, and mascara and together we sought out outfits, creating them from silky black slips, wraps, and odd pieces found in closets and drawers. With hair teased up, I easily played the part. From sexy to fun, including one with tight jeans and a button-down shirt, topped by a cowboy hat and grounded by a cheap pair of boots. And to round it all out, we invaded my mom's closet for a green silk blouse with buttons and a tied bow around the neck for a more professional, sophisticated look. We covered all the bases.

Then the day arrived.

EUROPEAN DAZE

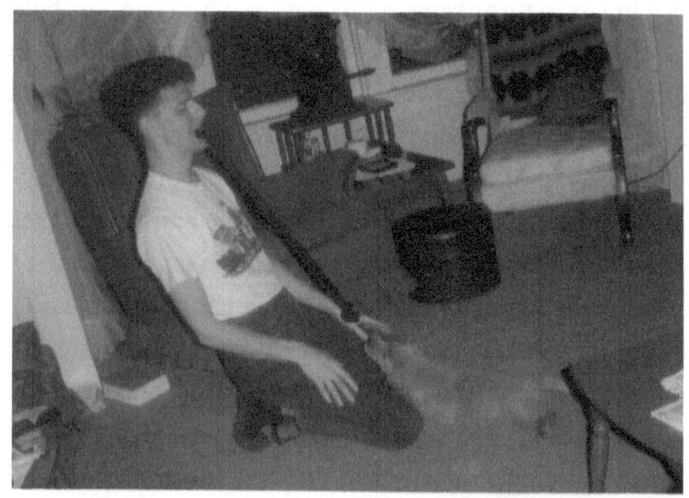

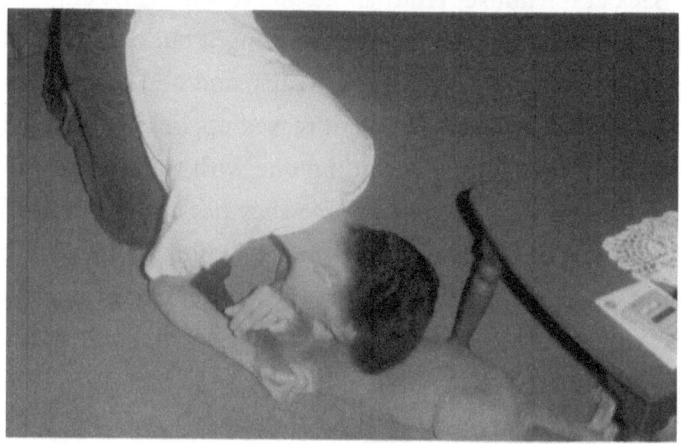

Robbie Grey, lead singer for the British band Modern English, playing with my brother's puppy in my parents' Florida living room (1984).

ON THE WORLD'S MOST FAMOUS BEACH

Snapshots to take to open interviews at modeling agencies in New York City (1984).
Photographer: Trudy H. VanBibber (my sister).

OPEN INTERVIEWS
NEW YORK CITY
JULY 1984

Our plan was simple. Maria and I would have pictures taken, then fly up to New York and go to open interviews at the different agencies. We excitedly boarded our flight and settled in. Shortly after take-off, Maria pulled out a large portfolio. Shocked, I suddenly grew quiet. While I had been running around the beach with my sister, Maria had been posing for real photographers, paying out good money for a book of professional-looking photos. In one of them, she wore nothing but a white fur coat. As in, her naked body with certain parts concealed by fur as she lay stretched out on a bed.

I had no idea this was what we were supposed to do! As I shuffled my deck of 3x5 photos, it suddenly dawned on me that we were complete opposites in how to approach New York. Yet, I continued on, proudly showing her my stack of blurry photos. I thought they were quite good and showed potential. They were fun. I had no expectations and didn't worry about what might or might not happen.

As the plane landed, I knew family would be at the airport to pick us up. Part of my family still lived on Staten Island, and we had arranged to stay one night with them. The next morning, we took the Staten Island Ferry over to Manhattan, making our way to the Barbizon-Plaza Hotel located on Central Park South. A thirty-eight-story hotel, it was a far cry from the seven-story hotel back on our beach in Florida. Our corner room sat high above the city, with floor to ceiling windows on two sides. With a list of agencies, addresses, and open interview times, we planned the days ahead.

On Monday the adventure began. Maria and I found our way to the infamous Ford Modeling Agency, arriving precisely at the start of their open interviews. We didn't even make it past the lobby. An agent came out to tell us personally that they wanted younger-looking girls to send to Europe. We apparently looked too sophisticated. Surprisingly, our spirits weren't dampened. We knew we had a few more chances.

The next morning, we overslept. Jumping out of bed, we hurriedly threw on clothes and did the best we could with makeup and hair in the few minutes we had to spare. Off we went to Elite Modeling Agency. They repeated what Ford had said about us looking too sophisticated. They did, however, pull me aside and encourage me to go to an agency called Prestige, their sister agency specializing in runway modeling.

As I turned to leave, the agent touched my arm and spoke. "A word of advice, never show unflattering pictures of yourself, no matter how much you like them."

Which ones were unflattering? I simply nodded and thanked her as I rejoined Maria, now staring in from outside the open door.

Still not feeling defeated, Maria and I continued on, trying our luck at a smaller agency called Legends. Interviews took

OPEN INTERVIEWS

so long, and by the time I got a chance at one, I forgot about being nervous. A beautiful, svelte black lady with a soft voice and a comforting smile came out to the lobby. Her smile was contagious, and I smiled back. She called my name and asked me to come back to talk with them.

This is how I first met Lawrine Childers. As she looked through my snapshots a number of times, we talked, her asking me about myself and my life in Florida. She asked me to wait while she took four of my pictures into another room to show other people. Shortly afterward, Louis, one of the bookers (someone who books jobs for models) came out to meet me. Shortly after that, I met another booker named Charlie. Finally, I met a woman by the name of Janelle who measured my height. This time agents and staff didn't just look me over, but actually talked to me as a person.

Janelle led me back out to the lobby and asked me to wait. Lawrine joined me a few minutes later, sitting down beside me.

"Barbara, our agency is interested in representing you. Are you okay with that?"

I slowly nodded, not really comprehending what she was saying.

"We are all, Louis, Charlie, Janelle and myself, in agreement. Will you consider signing with Legends?"

"Well, sure," I said. "Uh, what now?"

"We will draw up a contract and send it to you in Florida. If acceptable to you, then we ask that you return to New York in September."

"Oh, okay," I remember replying, less than eloquently. Feeling somewhat befuddled by the whole thing, I finally looked over at Maria. She didn't say a word.

When I called home that night, it began to sink in, and the shock and surprise turned into excitement.

"Guess what? A real modeling agency asked me to sign with them. I will have to move to New York in September!"

The phone went silent. For some unknown reason, my parents didn't seem too happy or excited. Little did I know at the time that to their way of thinking, this trip to New York and this crazy modeling fantasy would soon be over. It was just a trip to "get it out of my system," and then I would return to college.

On Wednesday, Maria and I headed out again, this time to Wilhelmina Modeling Agency on 37th Street. We remained silent as we rode the elevator up to the twelfth floor. Approaching the reception desk, we were asked to take a seat. Ten minutes or so later an agent came out to greet us, asking for our photos then disappearing into the back. We waited. And waited.

When the agent finally came back, she asked me to follow her to a back office.

"Uh, okay," I said which seemed to be the only available language I could muster during those days.

After a quick interview, she once again disappeared with a few of my photos. Shortly, two others accompanied her back into the room, walking around me, looking me over like a horse at auction. They talked to each other about me as if I wasn't there. Finally, the more matronly looking one concluded, out loud, "She's cute, but not cute enough." They showed me to the door. This didn't bother me because I was satisfied with Legends. I liked the people there, and I felt comfortable around them; more so than anywhere else we had been.

As our time in New York ended, Maria and I flew back to Florida with me still dazed and Maria quite sad. She had not fared as well as I had, and I felt bad for her. This was, after all, her dream originally, not mine. It felt awkward, my not wanting to say anything to upset her, but also filled with giddiness and excitement.

Once home, I began making plans to return to New York at the first of September.

NEW YORK
IT BEGINS
SEPTEMBER 10 - OCTOBER 19, 1984

September arrived almost before I could turn around, and I found myself back in New York. This time Maria and I were joined by my parents. The agency had requested they visit and meet the agents and bookers. Even though I was already nineteen years old, they wanted my parents to feel comfortable with the idea. No doubt they were also gauging my financial situation and my lifestyle up to that point.

The big day came, and we were up early, taking the Staten Island Ferry into Manhattan, a commute both my Mom and Dad had made many times during their earlier years. My Dad had been born and raised on Staten Island, and after World War II, he spent twenty years in the New York Police Department. Obviously, he was no stranger to the ways of the city.

My Mom bravely moved to Staten Island from Alabama in 1962 to be near her twin sister, finding work in the city and taking the same long commute every day. Then she met that police officer, my Dad, one night, and, after a few dates, as she tells it, she just knew he was the one. We only remained in Staten Island until 1968, when we moved to Alabama near my Mom's parents. Yet, the ways of New York and its boroughs stay with you, and Mom and Dad easily slipped back into the role of city commuter.

EUROPEAN DAZE

The three of us made our way to the 34th Street high-rise where Legends Modeling Agency was located. With no waiting, Lawrine introduced my parents to everyone in the agency, after which we sat with her as she explained the modeling business. I don't recall my parents saying much or asking many questions. I think maybe they were still in shock over the whole thing. Leaving the office, we quietly headed for the Port Authority on 42nd Street, catching the 5:00 p.m. bus back to Staten Island this time instead of taking the ferry.

In the following days, the paperwork and appointments became more urgent. I signed the agreement, not fully understanding what was in it, and what was expected of me. In short, I agreed to have Legends represent me and manage all aspects of my career as a professional model. I agreed to devote myself at all times to my career as a professional model. And, I agreed to pay to Legends twenty percent of any money received for modeling, acting, or other artistic activities.

With the contract signed, the agency began managing me right away by sending me to a dermatologist to remove two tiny bumps on my face, with my paying out $95.00 for the simple procedure. As far as I could tell, those bumps were hardly noticeable. Still, I didn't question expenses or obligations of who was to pay for what. Another appointment put me in a chair with a dentist who talked about his good friendship with actor-turned-president, Ronald Reagan. I can only imagine what a new crown or bleaching would cost there. I had entered a whole new world.

Meanwhile, while flitting about from dentist to dermatologist to the agency filling out forms, Maria continued to pursue her dream. She attended more open interviews at the modeling agencies, including Sue Charney. She didn't want to give up, but time soon ran out, and there were no more agencies to visit. Feeling despair, Maria flew back to Florida alone, and my new life began without her in the big city.

My family drove me to the Royalton Hotel, located just east of Times Square on 44th Street. We walked through the front door and into a lobby reminiscent of those old movies of the 1920s, not sleek and modern like I expected a city hotel to be. After checking in at the desk, we took my two suitcases up to Room #402, a surprisingly dull and lackluster room with mustard gold drapes, faded bedspreads, and unremarkable carpet and furniture. A lone window looked out over the street.

I stayed behind to unpack while my parents headed back to Staten Island. Shortly after they left, my roommate, Lily, walked through the door. She had short blond hair that bounced just above her shoulders. Glancing at her, she didn't appear to look like a model. But then again, neither did I.

Adapting to the city didn't take long. I had no problem adjusting to public transportation, and reading maps, even though I had never been alone in the city nor had to take buses or subways to get anywhere before. On my first day alone in the city, I took the #1 train going downtown, getting off at Sheridan Square and Christopher Street, and arriving at Scott Remple's apartment right on time. Charlie, a booker with Legends, had already arrived. He poured me a glass of wine and Scott commenced with not just cutting my hair but shaving it on the back and sides. I had no idea this was the look the agency had in mind for me. The new wave looks, not yet popular in my neck of the woods, appeared to be the new trend and the trendsetters knew something the rest of us didn't.

By all accounts, I started out in good form. I jumped right into the life of a model, traversing all over the city meeting all sorts of people. I spent the days darting to photographers' studios, to clients' offices, then back to the agency, and on to just one more go-see—an open interview where you go and see if they are interested in you, if they like your look, or if they think you might have the right look for a job they are casting for. Many times, these are more of a cattle call with so many models showing up that you wonder how in the world they can differentiate between everyone. Most of my time was spent on getting to the go-sees with only a few minutes in front of an actual person.

I needed to build my portfolio as quickly as possible. This became a kind of obsession to my agency, and soon to me as well. It became rather embarrassing to arrive at a studio and see all the other models with their portfolios containing professional photos. And here I was with a few xerox copies of my mostly amateur ones. Other models actually looked down on me, with a condescending little grin. I soon learned all about competition and arrogance. I always thought models should support each other, cheer each other on. Let the right person win the job. Apparently, I was mistaken.

Fortunately, there were more than enough photographers in New York willing to take photos of new models. Test photo shoots were quickly scheduled, many times with new photographers looking to build their own portfolios, or assistant photographers trying to move up the ladder and gain their own independent studios and clients.

Being naïve, and never asking questions, I soon found out that these test photo shoots were costing me. The charges were placed as debits on my account with the agency. Funny how they forget to mention all that to me beforehand. But then again, maybe if I had asked the smart questions, I might have been more knowledgeable about the process.

While constant attention focused on photos, the actual job of a model—to sell something through photos—received less attention. Posing in front of a camera may come naturally to many people, but not me. You want me to leap? You want me to sulk? Goofy I can do, but sexy? Self-confidence is something I faked, not felt. I rarely looked in the mirror at myself unless I had to apply a little makeup. I relied on others to tell me I was pretty, or model-like. It was my Canadian friend, Nadine, who upon seeing a few of my photos, told me she thought I looked like a cross between actresses Rachel Ward and Jennifer Beals. I never took that seriously or believed her when she said it. I didn't even believe it when my cousin Ann, who I always listened to and trusted, told me I should be a model. It seems many were pushing me in this direction without my truly believing in it or myself.

The agency set up my first test photo shoot, with booker-turned-photographer, Charlie. I gathered up what little clothes, shoes, and makeup I had and took the #1 train at Times Square, heading back to Christopher Street and Sheridan Square in the bohemian neighborhood of Greenwich Village, or, more precisely, the West Village. Here, where the 1960's counterculture movement centered, where the gay rights movement in the early 1970s gathered steam, I would learn a movement of my own—how to be a model.

As I entered Scott's apartment, another model, Stefanie, arrived. Scott quickly did my makeup, and Charlie himself styled my hair. I thought a lot of Charlie. He always seemed genuine, not something I had seen so far in New York or would see a lot of in the coming years when it came to photographers and agents. I didn't sense arrogance, power, or the like from him.

Stefanie and I traded off, one going outside on the street to shoot with Charlie, the other staying behind to change into another outfit. It didn't take long. Charlie knew what he was doing, and he knew what he wanted to coax out of us. After a few shots on the street, we headed up to the roof of Scott's building. Then it was time to find a new spot.

We grabbed all our things, hailed a cab, and headed to a place called Art on the Beach, a sandy stretch of land used for temporary art projects. After a short cab ride, we got out near the intersection of West and Chambers Streets. The four of us walked the short distance to a fenced area and, seeing no one around, climbed under the fence to get near the water. Leftover and abandoned sculptures stood straight and angled in the sand.

Taking off my jacket, and just wearing a white tank top, braless, I sat down on the sand and leaned against one of the leftover sculptures. Scott placed a sailor's cap on my head, and I turned to look out over the water. As I stared out into the Hudson River, I thought about my parents back in Florida

NEW YORK

First professional photo taken at Art on the Beach,
New York City, 1984. Photographer: Charlie L.

and how much I loved and appreciated them, and all their sacrifices through the years.

A few days later, Charlie asked me how I could move so well in front of the camera. I wasn't aware that I had but then responded that I just put myself in a different place in my mind. He would tell Lawrine and others at the agency about this. It didn't appear that any other models had ever expressed it this way and they seemed surprised but impressed. *Maybe I just might be cut out to be a model after all*, I thought

NEW YORK

The month of September flew by. Every day I ran all over the city, meeting all kinds of people. With so many crazy-busy days, I suddenly realized that my roommate Lily didn't have as many appointments as I did. The agency had been promoting me, pushing me out there in front of the fashion industry. Lily, however, had not been offered a contract with the agency yet. They were "testing" to see if any interest in her and her look developed. She wanted this, and she was trying with all she had.

Sitting at lunch one day at The Back Porch restaurant with my agent Lawrine, I asked her about it.

"So, why have I signed a contract with Legends and Lily still hasn't?"

Lawrine, always honest with me, didn't hesitate to answer. "Sometimes we just know when someone will be successful for us. Other times, we aren't so sure and need to wait to see what kind of response a prospect gets from certain photographers and clients."

"And what kind of response is Lily getting," I prodded.

"The response hasn't been all that good. So far no one seems to be excited about working with her."

Lawrine paused for a minute as I took this in, then added, "Lily may not be with Legends much longer."

I was quickly learning how harsh this business could be, first on Maria and now on Lily.

Towards the end of September, my schedule seemed daunting, but I continued on, determined to do my best. The first go-see of the day led me to 26th Street, where the photographer, Pat Hill, simply stared at me for a few minutes then picked up his Polaroid camera and took two photos. I got the impression he didn't know what to think of me. There was no time to obsess about it though as I had elsewhere to be.

Back on the street, I hailed a cab and headed to another test photo shoot. The photographer, Tim Lampson, was actually an assistant photographer ambitious to make his way to owning his own studio. He had his friends from Milwaukee do my makeup and hair, and we headed out on the street to shoot. A man stood on the corner watching. After we finished, he approached and handed me his card.

"I do films and videos, and I would like to work with you." I accepted his card and said I would mention it to my agent. Many times, I found that photographers and videographers, if that's what they truly were, hoped to skip around the agencies and have you work directly for them.

By this time, already running late to my next appointment. I did my best to calm my hair, and tone down my makeup. I raced to the address given by my agency and instantly realized something was amiss. Men and women roamed around the room in spandex tights and leotards. As I stared at them, a man entered the room with a clipboard in his hand, looked at me and said, "Change clothes and get ready for the next dance group." *Um, wait a minute*, I thought to myself. *I don't have anything to change into, one, and two, I'm not a dancer.*

NEW YORK

The appointment turned out to be a video casting for the music channel MTV. The concept of music videos was still pretty new to me, and I wasn't familiar with what needed to happen to make one of them. MTV had launched in August of 1981, and by this time, in 1984, the number of record companies and artists making videos for the channel had intensified. Everybody wanted to be on MTV.

As I stood there, in my dowdy clothes and caked on makeup, it suddenly dawned on me that my agency had not informed me this appointment was an audition, not a go-see. Singers, like Madonna, were beginning to add more dancers to their videos, and because of this, I found myself in a room full of dancers, some already successful, others pursuing their dream, the same as the aspiring actors and models in the city. Unlike me, though, they all seemed confident, like this was just another typical day in the city.

I asked to speak with Martin Kahan, the contact name the agency gave me. Kahan happened to be a top video director, and some of his most famous videos to date were for the band KISS, Michael Bolton, Eddie Money, and the band Scandal. And he had just recently been nominated for Best Video Direction at the inaugural MTV Video Music Awards for Ian Hunter's "All the Good Ones Are Taken." (He lost out to Tim Newman's "Sharp Dressed Man" video for ZZ Top, an American rock group.)

While others around me began to ready themselves, stretching their bodies in ways I had only seen in cartoons, I started to back away toward the door I had just come through. As I slowly began to turn, the man with the clipboard suddenly appeared, asking me where I was going. I babbled something about a very important meeting that I had to get to or else would be in hot water with my agency. This wasn't a lie, I did have an appointment, and, as it turned out, it was important. Scardy-cat that I was, I tucked my tail between my legs and ran out of there as fast as I could.

I climbed in a cab, jumped out at 1515 Broadway, and raced my way up to the 28th Floor to see someone by the name of Nancy Fields. Once again, I had no idea what the interview would be for. Turns out, it was an audition for two television commercials, one for Breck Mousse and one for Maybelline Mascara. When they called my name, I excitedly entered the studio and sat on a stool in front of a camera. Here I read my few lines for each product, tilting my head this way or that, smiling or not. I got the distinct impression that she, Nancy, liked me. But of course, what did I know.

Back at the hotel, Lily waited for me, and I quickly changed for our night out at the Red Parrot disco on 57th Street. The agency had invited us to attend a tribute to soap opera stars at the club.

The Red Parrot disco took up nearly an entire city block. The building had originally been a bus garage, turned roller disco, and now a theatrical dance club offering a diverse array of music. You had to hand it to New Yorkers—they sure knew how to surprise and shock. As we entered the grand room in the club, I felt like I was entering a stage, cued to perform.

I grew up watching soap operas such as *General Hospital*, *All My Children*, and *One Life to Live* with my grandmother. But as we mingled about the club, mixed with the daytime stars, I

NEW YORK

didn't recognize a single one of them. It was well after midnight when we finally called it a night and headed back to the hotel.

This day had been one of the long ones, starting with a go-see, followed by a test photo shoot, an MTV audition, two television commercial auditions, and finally, a social event at a local club. Exciting and exhausting at the same time, the pace of it all caused me to question whether this was the type of life I really wanted. It required non-stop movement, interactions, and energy. With no time to think, I just kept moving.

NEW YORK

After a month in New York, running all over the city day after day, my agency decided to show me to a Paris agency. I had heard talk of models being sent to Europe to build up their portfolios and gain experience in front of the camera. Europe had so many magazines and was always in need of models.

On a late Tuesday afternoon, the agency called, telling me to hurry in to see the agents from Paris. The two men, impeccably dressed, stared at me, speaking to each other in quick French as I sat there quietly. After what seemed like an hour, one of them touched my hand, and switching to English, asked: "Are you ready to come to Paris?"

Honestly, how does a girl respond to that? I believe I nodded confidently, saying something to the effect of, "Oh, Yes!"

The French agent continued, saying he would make all the arrangements with Lawrine and she would let me know the details. I simply nodded. Afterward, I wandered back to the hotel, making myself a peanut butter and jelly sandwich for dinner. Paris, France! It just hadn't sunk in yet.

The following day I arrived at 1515 Broadway again for a call-back for a television commercial. At first, I thought it was for the Breck Mousse, but it turned out to be for the Maybelline Mascara. They liked my face and my brown eyes. Another Legends model, sporting blonde hair and blue eyes, sat beside me, and we ran through our lines in front of the camera. I thought this to be much easier than posing in front of a photographer. Unfortunately, I would be on my way to Paris by the time they decided on which models to use.

Back at my hotel, I called home to Florida hoping to catch both my parents home from work. When they answered, we talked for a few seconds before I gave them the news. I was going to Paris, in France. Across the ocean. This time their silence only lasted a few seconds. Excitement filled their voices, at least at first. As apprehension began to fill the conversation, I knew what they were thinking. How could they afford to send me to Paris? I was ready for this though. Legends would advance the money for my plane ticket, and the agency in Paris would provide a place to stay. Everything had already been worked out. That night, Lily and I celebrated by going out to dinner, ordering French onion soup, and a half carafe of French wine.

Each night I performed the same ritual, calling into the agency to get my schedule for the next day. I continued building my portfolio by shooting with photographers around the city. On one particular shoot with a photographer by the name of Roland, we walked uptown, looking for a good spot. Stopping around 80th or 90th Street, he dared me to explode in front of the camera.

"When Paris sees those long legs, they'll expect you to fly."

This was his way of preparing me for Paris, daring me to jump around, get a little wild. Out on the street, with traffic and people everywhere. Within one hour, Roland had become the most helpful of all the photographers I had met up to this point. In essence, he told me that when in front of the camera, I needed to develop an attitude, and let my emotions come through. I could even pretend to be someone else for a while. Now I knew the secret to modeling.

With all the running around the city, I finally landed my first paying job. Not for print, not for a video, but for showroom modeling for ESPIRIT. For eight hours, I changed from outfit to outfit to show to representatives of various magazines, such as *Redbook*, *Mademoiselle*, and *Glamour*. Pay was only $15 an hour, amounting to $120 for the day. Regardless, I could now call myself a working model.

Meanwhile, travel plans were coming together. I would be leaving for Paris on October 19 along with two other Legends models, Kristen McMenamy, a tall, willowy redhead from Pennsylvania, and Ava Lewis, a classic southern beauty from Swainsboro, Georgia. With France in my future, anything seemed possible.

I had also recently met with an agency from Tokyo. The Japanese agent told me to keep in touch with him while in Europe, handing me a paper with his address, phone number, and something called a telex number. The thing I quickly learned about Japan is that you can make a lot of money in a very short amount of time there. From other models' accounts, the Japanese took incredible care of you, so there was no need to worry. I would keep that in mind going forward.

EUROPEAN DAZE

Even with the Paris planning, go-sees and appointments in the city didn't let up. The frantic pace continued. My agency believed I would only be gone a few months then be back in New York with a spectacular portfolio. At least, that was the plan.

By all accounts, I had a good start: an agent who was behind me all the way, a photographer who saw so much potential, a TV agent who got excited about my possibilities. Even MTV showed interest in me. I too was excited, and the world was mine to take. With all this backing, you would think nothing could go wrong; that I was destined for greater things. You would think.

Before traveling to Paris, I was scheduled to do a fashion show at a New York nightclub. Danceteria, a four-floor disco, was well-known as a center for new-wave music, with performances by such bands as Depeche Mode and even Madonna. With the show set for a Thursday evening (no one ever slept in New York City it seemed), I arrived before 6:00 p.m., finding over a hundred models and eleven designers and their racks of clothes crowding the backstage area. Garbage cans full of beer and bottles of liquor were everywhere. You just grabbed whatever you wanted. Drugs were available as well, but that wasn't my scene. I had smoked pot once during high school and promptly fell asleep.

While waiting my turn for hair and makeup, I glanced around, meeting the eyes of one male model sitting across from me. Kit, from South Carolina, bore chiseled facial features and a quiet southern drawl when he spoke. We sat comparing notes about New York and city life. He said he was glad to meet someone else from the South that he could relate to. I don't know if you really consider Florida the real South, but I knew where he was coming from. Besides, it felt refreshing to finally meet a nice guy who wasn't gay.

Soon I made my way to the hair and makeup chairs, then reported to my designer, Prudence, for my outfit, a beautiful black and purple dress. Fitted black lace hugged my torso, from my breasts to the top of my hips. From there flowed a deep purple taffeta skirt. I looked, and felt, spectacular. Pulling on a pair of black lace gloves all the way up to my elbows, I felt even more confident. This was a look I could pull off!

Tenth on the list for the show, our group of four female models and one cocky male model stood our place in line. Finally, we received the signal. The runway was ours. I went last, the finale for the designer. Cued to begin, I walked out on stage as massive applause erupted, with yelling and cheering, and cameras flashing. The audience loved the dress. Or maybe it was me.

Excitement about traveling to Paris escalated in the following days. So much needed to be done before we could leave, however. First, I needed a passport. In order to expedite this, the agency arranged for me to use a dummy plane ticket from a travel agency on 42nd Street. I had to pay $20 to use it, but it was worth $700. With the ticket in hand, I made my way straight to the passport agency, standing in line for over three hours. Afterward, I quickly returned the ticket and the next day I had my passport, just two days before I was scheduled to fly out.

Back at the agency, Kristen, Ava and I met with the owner, Kay Mitchell. Mitchell founded Legends Modeling Agency in 1981, and by the time I arrived in 1984, she was becoming a significant force in the modeling business. Kay went over what to expect in Paris and mentioned that we could travel on the weekends. The three of us were over the moon with excitement.

Returning to the hotel, I waited for Lily to return. I wanted to share my excitement with her but didn't dare as I knew it might hurt her feelings. As it turned out, the agency had dropped her this day. They told her she wasn't fresh enough, but that they would keep her on the books for two more weeks. Furious, and understandably upset, Lily packed her things up the next morning and left without saying a word to me. It began to seem that when something good happened for me, something bad was happening for someone else

NEW YORK

Professional test photo shoot on the streets of New York City, 1984.
Photographer: Roland

EUROPEAN DAZE

Professional test photo shoot on the streets of New York City, 1984.
Photographer: Roland

NEW YORK

Another test photo shoot on the streets of New York City, before flying off to Paris, 1984. Photographer: Roland

PARIS

OCTOBER 20 - DECEMBER 16, 1984

Orly Airport on an early French morning in late October gave off a laid-back and noncommittal vibe. The six-hour flight from New York had been the longest Kristen, Ava and I had ever taken, and the time change would take some getting used to. We slowly gathered our carry-ons and filed off the plane along with the other passengers. Just as we reached the passport control booth, the agent decided to close-up and take a break. Others in line behind us began yelling "Let's go" over and over, louder each time, but the French agent took her time getting back to the booth, seeming to hardly even notice the rest of us in the room.

We had been told a representative from the agency would be waiting for us in the baggage claim, holding up a sign with the words First Agency on it. We scanned the entire area. No such person could be found. After collecting our luggage, we decided to split up. I would stay with all the luggage and wait for the agency contact, Ava would find a phone, and Kristen would go back upstairs and look around for him. If nothing else, the three of us already knew how to work together.

Shortly after our split, a young man approached, speaking in French. My face quickly told him I didn't understand a word he said and he switched to English.

"First?"

I excitedly jumped up and started screaming, "Yes, yes! First." But then I quickly switched to "Oui, Oui," my only French vocabulary at this point.

He introduced himself as Eric, and I could tell communicating with him wasn't going to be easy. He spoke little English, and he wore a confused look on his face. We waited for Ava and Kristin to return, and you could see the relief wash over them as they approached. Gathering up our luggage, we followed Eric out of the airport. In the parking area, he stopped in front of the smallest car we had ever seen. Kristen, Ava and I stared, wondering how we were to fit in there with all our luggage. Fortunately, Eric had a plan. One of us would ride with him, and the other two would take a taxi.

Ava crammed into the front seat of Eric's car, and Kristen and I took the first taxi in line. Off we went on the eleven-mile trip to the small apartment the agency had arranged for the three of us to stay in during our time in Paris. Our cab driver spoke only French, and we quietly sank into the back seat. I couldn't tell you much about the ride or what our first glimpses of Paris were. The newness of the experience, the first time out of the States, the realization of where we were had not yet hit us.

Arriving outside the apartment, Kristen and I climbed out of the cab and waited to retrieve our luggage. The cabbie told us, in what little English he could muster, that the fare was 150 francs. Although we were no experts in the exchange rates and the fees, it did seem excessive to say the least. A man happened to be walking by and, overhearing the cabbie, he abruptly stopped and turned toward him. The two began speaking in

French, and it didn't seem like a friendly conversation. Turns out the cabbie did overcharge us, and this man told him to give us fifty francs back. We graciously accepted the returned money and thanked the other man profusely. He just nodded and kept walking. A duality of introduction to the French.

Our apartment was located on the rue Poncelet, a narrow street just off the Avenue des Ternes in the seventeenth arrondissement, or district, of Paris. The building sat nestled among various shops, which lined the full length of the street. We lugged our luggage up the two flights of stairs, and after a few tense moments of trying to unlock the door with the key Eric provided, we finally crammed ourselves into the apartment and shut the door tightly behind us.

The layout of the small apartment seemed rather odd. You entered the large, thick red front door and straight ahead sat the separate kitchen containing a gas stove, small refrigerator, and a few glasses and utensils. Proceeding down the hallway, you came to a tiny, angular room on the left which contained the toilet. Across the hall was the bathroom with a small sink and a split-level half tub with an attached shower wand (what we might call a shower massager in the years to come). From there, you enter the combined dining and living room, which contained a table, three chairs, and a plush red sofa. Three closets rounded out the room with two for hanging clothes and the third containing shelves.

From the living room area, you entered another room to the right containing a double bed and a single bed. A comfortable chair could be turned into a bed as well. As we ventured to the back of this room a door led to yet another bedroom, this one with a double bed, a desk, and shelves. Our roommate, whom we did not know yet, had already claimed that entire room for herself. The windows in the two back rooms looked out over the rue Poncelet.

Piling our luggage in the corner, we sank onto the sofa. Wide-eyed, Kristen, Ava and I kept wondering if we were ready for this, ready for Paris. That initial homesickness weighed heavy on each of us, that familiarity of home and the States now gone, far across the ocean. We felt fortunate to at least have each other.

Several hours later our roommate, Patricia, a model with the same agency, returned. She came from California and had been in Paris for two weeks. Although she seemed distant and suspicious, we proceeded to sop up any advice we could drag out of her about Paris. I could tell she wanted nothing to do with us. Finally, though, she softened a bit and agreed to go with us to the small grocery store across the street from the apartment. Perhaps she saw the wide-eyed fear in our eyes and heard the anxiousness in our voices, and a small part of her remembered what it had been like when she first arrived in the city.

With the few French francs I had exchanged at the airport, I managed to figure out how to buy milk (in a carton on the shelf, not the refrigerated section), Crousty miel cereal (with a picture on the front that resembled Cheerios), and instant coffee, totaling twenty-six francs, or about $2.60. We also learned to purchase bottled water and not to trust the tap water.

Near the grocery store sat a pharmacie, where I would later learn how to buy cold medicine and the like before our time in Paris ended. Also, nearby, a tabac sold cigarettes and postage stamps, two of my necessities. Other shops aligning the small street included a health food store, a bakery, and various small clothing stores. A laundromat conveniently sat right next door to our apartment building. Most days the street itself became an open market with sellers offering everything from fruits and vegetables to various meats, such as duck with the feathers still attached.

Back at the apartment, I unpacked my suitcases. I placed my stonewashed, pleated jeans and oversized sweaters in the closet and hung up the one dressy outfit I had brought with me, a beautiful black skirt with a red, white, and black striped camisole, and a short black jacket. The few pairs of shoes included lace-up boots I had purchased in New York along with a pair of cheap, low, black heels.

On Sunday, Kristen, Ava and I again stayed close to the apartment, only venturing out to use the pay phone around the corner. (This was before the days of cell phones or the internet.) We did have a phone in the apartment, but you could only receive calls, not make them. I guess calling the States was a costly expense, and the agency didn't want to be stuck with the bill. Yet we would soon learn from other models who had stayed in this same apartment that family could call collect, and we just had to accept the charges.

That evening, Ava and I wrote letters to family and friends back home while Kristen listened to her French language tapes.

We knew that the week ahead would be interesting and busy. But for tonight, we wanted to relax and prepare ourselves.

Monday rolled around quickly, and we put on a brave face before heading out together. Kristen and Ava had been awake until about 1:00 a.m. and I had tossed and turned for another hour before finally falling asleep. The time change was no joke.

We set out from the apartment around 9:00 a.m., with Patricia showing us how to buy tickets for the metro before leaving for her go-see. This quick introduction to the metro system in Paris included the realization that unlike the subways in New York which go either uptown or downtown, these went in directions. At the station closest to our apartment, Ternes, we boarded one heading in the direction of Port Dauphine, the end stop for that line. Disembarking at the Charles de Gaulle-Étoile stop, we then boarded the metro going in the direction Château de Vincennes to our final stop, Franklin D. Roosevelt. At first, it seems a little complicated, but with a map of the metro system, we quickly got the hang of it. The cars were much cleaner and brighter than the subway cars of New York City. We never had to wait long for the next one to arrive. We just had to be aware of which direction we were heading in at all times.

The metro turned out to be much easier to figure out than the street addresses in Paris. Once we exited the station, we walked in a complete circle until finally finding the agency over an hour later. It's a helpless sort of feeling when you realize you are lost and have no idea how to get anywhere. And on top of that, you don't speak the language, and it takes such great effort to ask a passerby for directions.

PARIS

First Agency, located at 55 rue Pierre Charron, sat just off the famous avenue Champs-Élysées, in the pricey eighth arrondissement, just south of our apartment. As we entered the agency front doors, a lady approached. I didn't catch her name, but she ushered us into a room to take our measurements. Mine were 87-60-88, and 1-78 in height. With everything in metrics, I gasped. *Am I too big?*

Shortly afterward, another lady led us into a room and provided a set of papers. Turns out it was a contract with their agency. Stunned, we all three looked at each other. Another contract? She also mentioned that we would need working papers and something about how they would be taking taxes out of our pay. Not fully comprehending any of it, we agreed that she would talk to Lawrine, our agent in New York, and then Lawrine would tell us what we should do.

Additional documents containing information about the agency and about Paris in general were given to us next. It was only then that we were allowed to enter the booking room, where the bookers sat around at desks in an open room, with phones ringing and photos of models lining the walls. The bookers, Étienne and Andy, greeted each of us, throwing their arms up and excitedly shouting "*Ça Va*" before shadow kissing us on each cheek, the standard greeting in France.

Kristen, Ava, and I sat down at a big table in the conference room just off of the booking room. Shortly, Étienne brought each of us a First book, a portfolio with the agency's logo on the front, to put our photos in to take on go-sees. Since we did not yet have composite cards (model business cards containing photos) to leave at go-sees, we quickly made a few xeroxed copies of our best photos and slapped a First Agency label on the bottom. We would hand these out at the go-sees.

Patricia had arrived at the agency by now, and the four of us headed out to an appointment located outside Paris city limits. Thankfully, Patricia took us in tow and showed us how to get around. We had a little time to spare, so we stopped off at a café for a hot chocolate. Then it was on to three different metros before arriving at our first go-see in Paris. Six models were already waiting when we arrived, so we joined them in line. Out of the three interviewers, only one spoke any English. As I handed them my portfolio, two wrapped sugar cubes that I had taken from the café fell out. My face reddened, but I did my best to laugh it off. One of the interviewers just smiled and handed them back to me.

Before returning to the apartment, Ava and I stopped off at the grocery store, getting there only moments before they were to close for the night. At the checkout, I pantomimed to the cashier to "S'il vous plait," *please*, write the total down on a piece of paper. She did so, and my total came to 133 francs or close to $15. We had lost Kristen in the rush to get to the store but found her back at the apartment. Surprisingly, we had made it through our first real day in Paris.

PARIS

You shall go home beneath triumphal arches.
--Napoléon Bonaparte, 1805--

Paris, I soon learned, is laid out differently than New York with its grid line and numbered streets. It is instead arranged in a circular pattern with districts, or arrondissements, rolling out from the center in a clockwise fashion.

Beginning in Paris, I learned to look at a city in relation to how it is laid out and to determine its pattern of streets and neighborhoods in order to find my way to the various appointments. The little red guidebook, *Plan de Paris*, quickly became my best friend and constant companion. It became my most prized possession. I learned to study it daily and write out my way to appointments: take this metro in this direction to this stop. After that go-see, walk down this street to this metro station, and go in this direction to the next go-see. I also noted which district, or arrondissement I would be in and which one I needed to go to next. That way I could visualize where I was and in what direction I was headed. You could say I spent more time planning my travel strategy than concentrating on the go-sees themselves.

Another practice I started in Paris was finding a famous landmark in which to show the way home. For me, that famous landmark became the Arc de Triomphe at the west end of the famous street, Avenue des Champs-Élysées. It rose stately and authoritatively above the rush of the city less than a half mile from our apartment, a short walk as long as you knew in which direction to be walking. The Arc sat in the eighth arrondissement but close enough to home in the seventeenth to cheer me on. On many long days, the sight of it became a sigh of relief.

From the start, Kristen, Ava and I knew that although we were in the City of Love, we were not tourists. We were there to work, to further our modeling career. I was so focused on finding my way to these go-sees and building my portfolio that I could have been anywhere, in any city.

Just four days after arriving in Paris, I was on my own, finding my way from go-sees to appointments. Trial by fire so to speak, and it wasn't easy. With my *Plan de Paris* in hand, I began. I boarded the metro, changed one time, then proceeded to get totally confused. I rode three extra stops just to figure out my mistake. I got off and boarded the metro going back in the other direction, getting off at Mirabeau and somehow actually walking in the right direction, to 9 rue Victorien Sardou in the sixteenth arrondissement. I found the elevator and rode up with another model. I smiled and she smiled, both knowing we couldn't communicate in any other way.

It was always hard to tell how the French models felt about you. No doubt they saw little competition in me. They all seemed so much more feminine, so much more self-assured. The client, Virgimie, spoke only in French and didn't appear too enthusiastic to see me. I shrugged my shoulders and headed out for my next appointment.

I studied my little red guidebook again then got on the metro, changed once, then got off at Madeleine and headed for 20 rue Royale where I found approximately ten models already waiting. When it was my turn, the two interviewers asked the other models if they could translate for us. Only one volunteered. They wanted to know about my hair, and if I would let them trim it on the sides. Apparently, this was for a hair job. I nodded yes, saying, "Oui." They wrote a few things on my xeroxed photo, I gave a smile and a *merci* to the model who had translated for us and found my way out to the street.

Taking the metro again, I got off at Étienne Marcel and once again felt lost. It wasn't the metro that got me—it was the streets and neighborhoods. Fortunately, a pleasant Frenchman asked if he could help and managed to point me in the right direction.

At 49 rue Étienne Marcel, I entered the first floor along with a new model from Sweden. We both dropped off a labeled xerox of our best photo then headed up to the next appointment which just so happened to be on the third floor of the same building. Two models were ahead of me, but soon were dismissed, being told in English, "Sorry, you are not the type she is looking for." When I approached, the lady accepted my book then asked me to walk across the room. I tried on a bathing suit, and then a blue dress for them before leaving. I thought they were interested in me and maybe, just maybe, I might get to work my first job in Paris very soon.

EUROPEAN DAZE

The day, overall, had been a success. I had to give myself credit for not giving up, even when I felt lost and hopeless. As if a reward, I turned around just in time to glimpse the most famous site in the city. You truly know you are in Paris when you see the Eiffel Tower for the first time, rising above you. Back in New York, I had been told not to look up while in a city for that will mark you as a tourist. But at that moment, I was a tourist, momentarily silenced by the iron tower before me, above me. All appointments, frustrations at finding my way, and such temporarily disappeared, and I was caught up in what I can only describe as awe. It was a different type of awe than when I saw the Arc de Triomphe, which made me stand a little taller, a little straighter at its sight. The Tower softened me, lessened the seriousness that had become a part of me starting in New York and carried now with me to Paris. I melted onto a park bench and finally allowed myself to slow down and breathe.

At the end of our first week of go-sees, my roommates and I experienced our first transportation strike in the city. Very few metros or buses were running, and we didn't know what to do. Calling the agency, Andy answered. These strikes were common, he said, and we would have to get used to them. Fortunately, there always seemed to be a way to get to our go-sees; it just required a little more time and effort.

Finding one of the metros running, Kristen, Ava and I rode it to Pont de Neuilly, then caught one of the few buses to rue L'Oasis. Although arriving on time, we were told to come back in thirty minutes, so we walked around the corner and found a tiny pizza restaurant. As soon as we sat down, the waiter brought each of us a small glass of red wine. We looked at each other, then grinned. Why not? It's the French way! As we took a sip, we continued pouring over the menu. We finally thought we had it figured out and ordered a pizza for the three of us to share. Turns out we ordered it with anchovies, the one thing I would not eat no matter what.

We returned to the studio for a few seconds, it seemed, then headed to our next go-see. At La Muette, we stepped off the metro and walked to the studio of British photographer Nick Anderson. He examined my shoulders and had me try on a T-shirt. The next go-see took us to the Concorde stop, then a short walk to 11 bis rue Boissy D-Anglas, to the office of *Marie Claire* magazine where a long line of models awaited their turn to dazzle the editors. Someone by the name of Maria Helen looked through my book, then stared at me, asking to see my left profile. As she did so, she wrote notes on the xeroxed photo I handed her; "great skin" being one of those comments.

By now I was already so tired at night I had to force myself to write in my journal. I knew that one day I would be glad I did. Before leaving me in New York back in September, my dad encouraged me to keep a journal and collect postcards of my travels, just like he had done during World War II. I knew he was right and I strived to add at least a few sentences in my journal each night. It soon became an outlet for my frustrations but also for recording my happiest moments. I did sense that my roommates were rather curious as to what I wrote. If they ever read my journals when I was away from the apartment, I never knew.

In another week our roommate, Patricia, packed up her belongings and moved out. She seemed bitter in some ways. Conceited in other ways. She always seemed so serious, and when the three of us were carrying-on and laughing, she would just stare at us and either head to her bedroom or leave the apartment altogether.

Before the door even shut behind her, the three of us scrambled to rearrange the furniture. We decided that I would sleep in the bedroom but then realized the room was too big for just one person. We moved Kristen's double bed into the room also, horizontally along the window. Ava slept on a single bed in the outer room. We were giddy with the new arrangement and our new-found freedom. It felt much more like home.

The air began to turn colder, and Ava and I knew it was time to buy a few warm clothes. We had not lugged bulky winter coats with us to Europe. Instead, while back in New York, other models had mentioned we could buy cheap warm coats at an air force store, much like the army-navy surplus stores in the States, once in Paris. We caught the metro to Place du Châtelet and found the store with little effort. Fashionable it wasn't, but we were only interested in keeping warm. What we wore underneath the coat, we compromised, would be more fashionable. Ava and I picked out similar long coats, each with a tweed-like pattern, and each costing only 249 francs or about $25.

My wardrobe selection was small, and I decided I needed to ramp it up a little. As we walked along the square, I entered a shop and found a long, black, knit skirt I had to have. I shelled out 379 francs, more than I paid for the coat, but I knew it was worth it. It would soon become one of my favorite go-to fashion items.

Unlike most models, I didn't have a keen sense of fashion. It wasn't something I grew up with or developed much of an interest in. I could wear shorts to high school in Florida, and casual seemed to be my natural style. Little did I know of the Hermès scarves or handbags, or the designs of the likes of Jean Paul Gaultier and Yves Saint Laurent. Even so, during our few shopping trips around the city, I did find a few items I liked. Besides the long, black, knit skirt, I found a black and white cardigan-type sweater which I paired with the skirt as one of my go-to outfits. I wore the sweater backward, letting the buttoned front hang down low on my back. Another find, a black sweater with fuchsia stars radiating out from the bottom to the top, also became a favorite.

Many of these finds were made at the various flea markets throughout Paris. Although it sounds almost like an oxymoron—a Paris flea market—the city is synonymous with this type of shopping. (In French, it is called *marché aux puces*, which, admittedly, is much more enticing sounding.) We most often visited Clignancourt, the largest one in Paris, where we found inexpensive trinkets, clothing, and almost anything else we wanted.

From back home in the States, I had brought a slate blue-grey men's jacket which I wore often, with its sleeves rolled up to show the shiny lining underneath. I would wear this with black tights and a turtleneck or V-neck sweater, or a T-shirt.

EUROPEAN DAZE

I began to experiment with the mixture of clothes I did have, making them uniquely mine, but not always succeeding at being fashionable. I would never be like a true *Parisienne*, and it didn't seem anyone would use the words *Haute couture* to describe me. Yet it was enough.

PARIS

During those first few weeks in Paris, I tested with several photographers. I found this confusing as I could have stayed in New York to do this. In one day alone, I saw four different photographers and then scheduled to test with three of them within the week. My understanding had been that I was in Paris to work and add tear sheets to my book—tear sheets being pages in a magazine torn out to add to my portfolio—not to do more test photo shoots.

Some of these young photographers seemed a little too eager. I became suspicious that this was more about putting money in their pockets than good photos in my portfolio. As the weeks went by, I could tell when a wannabe photographer needed money. I'm guessing the agency received a fee from the photographers, and the photographers charged the model. It all seemed so underhanded, taking advantage of naïve girls and guys blindly following their dreams. *Is the agency being a tad bit deceitful*, I wondered?

At the end of October, my roommates and I headed to the agency to talk with Capucine, another booker. She immediately sent Ava and me to a nearby hair salon to have our hair styled and to see if we might be a fit for a possible job. In other words, a go-see for a hair salon ad. The stylist at the John Paul David International salon sat waiting for us and ushered us to our seats. It soon became apparent that he wanted to cut our hair even shorter than it already was. We shook our heads no, but he kept saying that Capucine had told them they could cut our hair. Eventually, we gave in. Then he started cutting and cutting. When he started to cut my long bangs in the front, I reached up, stopping him. I shook my head adamantly, almost in tears.

We hurriedly changed back into our clothes, furious with Capucine. While Ava went back to the agency, I headed to the apartment to gather my things for a test photo shoot with an American photographer named Robert. I threw some clothes into a bag and took the metro to the agency. By this time, I was over an hour late, and Robert sat waiting.

As I entered the booking room, Capucine yelled nastily at me. "You're late!"

Now, normally I might apologize for being late, but the French didn't seem to think timing mattered as they, including Capucine, rarely were on time for anything.

I looked at her and said, "Yes, late and not very happy with you!"

She quieted, and her face softened. In her best innocent voice, she asked why. Incredulously, I pointed at my hair, telling her how I didn't appreciate being sent to a place that I am told is for a possible job, then having them tell me the agency told them to cut my hair even shorter. With this, I grabbed an apple out of my bag and took an exaggerated bite, chewing noisily as if to further show them what I really thought. They smiled, laughing. They all thought it rather cute, my little temper tantrum. This irritated me even more. Capucine attempted to exonerate herself by saying the salon was not supposed to cut our hair, but it did look good. She continued, saying they were to style it and see if they wanted to use a picture in their advertisements. Étienne chimed in, siding with Capucine as if that would conclude the discussion.

Meanwhile, Robert is sitting to the side watching the encounter. Kindly, he asked if I still wanted to shoot. He understood how upset I was. I said yes, let's do this. As we walked out of the building, he softly spoke.

"Do you think they are being on the level with you? Do you believe them?"

Before I could respond, he continued. "Some agencies I've seen do a pretty good job at covering up their intentions." He had seen it before. This wouldn't be the last time the agency would lie to me.

It wasn't just the overanxious photographers, or the suspected lying by the agency that began getting to me. Often the daily schedule would change with barely any notice. Appointments were grouped together in time slots impossible to meet. In early November, we had five go-sees within a two-hour time frame, all in different directions in the city. There was no humanly way possible to make it to all of them unless, of course, we had wings.

Often, we would get so lost and turned around, never finding the studio. Whenever this happened, the agents got mad and yelled at us, as if something were wrong with us, as if we were stupid. Other times, I would be sitting at the agency talking with the bookers, the accountant, or other models, and Capucine would come in and scream at me for not having my next appointment for the day. On one particular day, I had asked her three times if I had any more go-sees, and she had repeatedly said no. Now suddenly, a new one came up, and she was yelling at me for not already knowing about it.

Appointments were often at night, between say 5:00 p.m. and 7:00 p.m. I might be sitting down to eat dinner, or reading a book to relax, and the phone would ring, demanding that I immediately get to an appointment way across the city. And it was always in a *I should have known about the appointment already and been on my way* tone of voice. Obviously, I knew nothing about it or else I would have been. I soon became suspicious and mistrusted most everything they said.

To top all of this off, the majority of the photos from the test shoots were disappointing. The lighting would be terrible, the angle slanted too far to one side, or the background ugly or too busy and distracting. A model can move and take direction from the photographer if the photographer knows what he wants, what he is looking for. To many, it seemed more of a hobby than a career. In other photos, it was obvious that the shorter hair wasn't working for me, or at least not in my mind. I didn't feel pretty or special. I felt like someone half-naked in someone else's movie.

PARIS

Halloween rolled around, and Kristen, Ava and I made plans. Before Ava and I headed into the agency to meet up with a photographer for a test photo shoot, the three of us agreed to meet back at the apartment around 5:00 p.m. and get ready for a night out.

Once at the agency, the photographer, Hervé, arrived right on time and ushered us, along with a makeup artist, into his tiny car. As we zoomed around Paris, Ava and I leaned back and enjoyed a little sightseeing along the way. Hervé stopped in front of an eclectic clothes store, jumped out and motioned for us to follow. He had arranged to borrow clothes for us to test in, or at least he thought he had. Apparently, the shop owners changed their minds.

We climbed back in the car and headed to another bohemian style shop nearby and somehow, he managed to talk them into lending us two outfits for the afternoon. We rode around a while longer before pulling up and parking near the Eiffel Tower. Ava was up first, then me. I leaned against the spindly iron legs of the famous tower, at times hugging them like a lost lover. We laughed and joked all afternoon.

After returning the clothes to the shop, we made our way back to the agency. As I gathered my things and climbed out of the car, Andy came running outside, telling me I had another test photo shoot in a few hours, at 7:00 p.m. My happiness melted off of me like ice cream in a cone on a blazing hot day. Following him back into the agency, I walked up to Étienne, rudely asking him why I didn't know about this ahead of time. *Why can't these things be scheduled?* In the back of my mind, I kept thinking about our plans to go out and celebrate Halloween together. I had been looking forward to our first fun night out on the town. Finally, as always, I gave in and said I would go.

Taking four different metros, I finally landed at Bonne-Nouvelle. As I entered the streets, I quickly became lost. My map couldn't help me out of this one. Already dark, I walked in circles before going down a narrow street lined with hookers. I just kept walking, looking straight ahead, and searching for a phone booth. When I finally found one, I stood in line for a good ten minutes or more. Finally, it was my turn, and I dialed the photographer's studio. A man answered, saying he would come out and meet me at the Café de France, near where I was calling from. About twenty minutes later, we were in the studio. Seeing me in a tired and frustrated frame of mind, we decided to postpone the shoot. I felt relieved. When I returned to the apartment, Ava was home alone. Kristen had gone out with the same group she had been out with the night before. So much for our Halloween plans.

As it turned out, Ava and I were seeing less and less of Kristen as the weeks ticked by. While the two of us continued to spend most of our days together, with many of the same go-sees and test photo shoots, Kristen began to separate more and more from us. Not only did she have different appointments, but she started hanging out with a different crowd, including a Russian photographer named Sasha. She was often out at night, and we wouldn't see her again until early the next morning. I never asked her for details, and she never volunteered them. There was a silent understanding that as individuals, we were doing what we needed, or thought we needed, to do. There was never any judgment, at least from my way of thinking. I could sense that Kristen was somehow different. I couldn't put my finger on exactly how, but she just was.

Test photo shoot, after the agency-sanctioned hair shearing, at the Louve metro station, Paris 1984.

EUROPEAN DAZE

Test photo shoot at the Eiffel Tower, 1984

PARIS

Letter writing soon became a nearly daily pastime. Ava and I could sit for hours at night writing to family and friends. There was so much to share. Every day, we went into the agency to check for mail from home and were thrilled when we had one or more letters in our file. We couldn't wait to respond. For me, it connected me to home, to the real world.

I received sweet and encouraging letters from my Mom and informative and loving ones from my Dad. My sister, Trudy, wrote of her life still working on the world's most famous beach and how she planned to get out of Florida. I rarely received a letter from my brother Kurt, but in one, he encouraged me not to get too discouraged and to hang in there. He added, "Sometimes you just have to listen to some killer tunes," while mentioning the latest U2 album. In other words, I needed to find a way to chill—something I had never been that good at, especially when stressed. He also wrote that he had picked up a copy of *Vogue* magazine at the store, didn't see me in it, so put it back on the shelf. That made me laugh. My brother, the handsome beach lifeguard, was transforming into a college student with a focus, desiring to become an architect. I found it impressive that he actually had a goal. He was finding his direction. I was simply winging mine.

I also traded letters with friends back in Florida. Misty, attending Florida State University, was in the planning stages for her wedding and talked about looking for the perfect dress. Another friend, Mary, heartbreakingly dealt with her mother's cancer. Amy, a younger friend, wrote of becoming homecoming queen at our high school, and Billy, one of my closest high school friends, was currently living and working one country away from me, in Germany. All were planning their futures, settling into adulthood in one way or another.

Meanwhile, I was roaming all over Paris in a freaky and fabulous jolt of freedom, stressful in its own way however. Yet, I felt temporarily reprieved from having to grow up, get a degree, start a job I would be unhappy in for most of my life so I could pay a mortgage, car payment, and maybe start a family. I never was a planner and didn't even know what a five-year plan might look like for me. I lived in the moment, not worrying about the future.

Yet the longer I was in Europe, the less I heard from anyone but my parents. Everyone had their lives to live and were busy. I understood that. I was busy also. My experiences now were deviating far from my friends and siblings' experiences. It seemed as if I lived in a different world, and we were finding it harder and harder to relate to each other

I had written to Robbie Grey of the band Modern English while in New York, telling him of my new-found life as a model, and I received a letter back from him in mid-November. He started the letter with these words:

> Haven't you done well – one minute the Pagoda Hotel, the next the world at your feet. Isn't life exciting. Best of luck to you is what I say.

PARIS

Robbie went on to talk about Paris and its lack of nightclubs but its abundance of good food, and how, after leaving the States, he decided to move out of London, back near his parents. He still spent a lot of time there, but after four years of living in the city, he was fed up with it. As for the band:

> *The music is still the best bit at the moment. I have a lot of free time because we have left our record company to sign to another. It's all legal matters & bullshit really. But we can't put any records out till it's all sorted out.*

He mentioned he might just pop over to Paris to visit me around the holidays. I hoped I wouldn't be back in the States before he could.

PARIS

The test photo shoot I had postponed from Halloween night and rescheduled fell on a Friday evening. I still needed good photos for my portfolio which seemed painfully slow in coming together. It was close to 7:00 p.m. when I stepped off the metro at Bonne Nouvelle and eventually found my way to the studio at 40 rue L'Échiquier.

Fortunately for me, they had arranged for a makeup artist to join us. As I watched the transformation in the mirror, the artist began painting a word on my face. Either the word *TOM* or *HOT* on my right cheek. I couldn't tell in the mirror. For the next few hours, the photographers, Vivien and Ben, debated about what I should wear as I sat and waited, and waited some more. Finally, a basic tank top was chosen. By this time, the makeup artist had already given up and left.

It was almost 1:00 a.m. when we began the photos. Vivien shot the first roll, then Ben, then Vivien again. This back and forth continued for several hours until Vivien started to pack up her camera. Ben wanted to continue. After three or more hours, he still didn't seem finished. When Vivien left at 4:00 a.m., we were finishing up the last set. Thinking it a rap, I started over to the sink to wash the makeup off my face. Ben appeared beside me with a piece of silky lingerie in his hands.

"Put this on," he said, "and we will shoot another roll."

"Umm, it's after 4:00 in the morning, I've been here all night, and now you want me to put this on?" Maybe it was just me, but something didn't feel right about the situation.

"You know, I'm just too tired to shoot anymore right now."

He persisted. "Yes, but it is good for your career. Put it on. "

As I continued moving toward the sink to wash my face. I glanced back. "Not happening, Ben."

Changing back into my own clothes, he didn't say another word.

Arriving back at the apartment around 5:30 a.m., I tiptoed in, changing clothes in the living room so as not to wake anyone. I walked passed Ava sleeping soundly into the back bedroom. Kristen wasn't even home, so no need to worry about waking her. I crawled under the warm covers and instantly fell asleep.

Later that day, after slowly waking up around noon, I found the apartment quiet. It wasn't long until Ava came home and we sat together talking. I asked her about how her test shoot with Ben and Vivien, a few weeks earlier, had gone. Did Ben ask her to put on the lingerie after Vivien left? She said yes, but she had also refused. Was it a test? Or a missed opportunity to get more great photos for my book? Or maybe, was it what it felt like, a way to get me into the lingerie as a step to getting me out of the lingerie.

Late the next week, I stopped by the agency. Capucine excitedly looked up.

"Your pictures are so fucking great!"

Not sure which photos she referred to, I rushed over to her side. She pulled out the photos taken by Ben and Vivien during that night-long session. Clearly, the word on my cheek was HOT, and I had to admit, they knew what they were doing. I was finally starting to look like a real model in my photos.

In early November, Lawrine called from our agency in New York and seemed utterly surprised that none of us had worked yet. Not exactly thrilled ourselves, we told her about the agency and how unhappy we were with them. We complained about Capucine always yelling at us and giving us appointments at the last minute, making us a nervous wreck, and about how the agency had us meet with foreign agencies from Germany and Japan. This all seemed genuinely surprising to her.

I never got the impression that Lawrine was deceiving or manipulative. She had always been straight with me and I with her. She seemed just as confused by the Paris agency's actions as we were. I had no idea where this would lead, but I put my faith and trust with Legends, believing they would lead me in the right direction.

Although Kristen, Ava, and I spent time together on the weekends, we continued to lose Kristen while out on our shopping excursions. Or maybe she lost us. At first, I thought she was a bit of an airhead (but a very likable airhead) and just became easily distracted. But the more it happened in the coming weeks, I became a little suspicious that maybe she did it on purpose. With her desire to learn French and the friends she was making, it was as if she led two different lives—one with us and one elsewhere.

Yet as Kristen was finding her own way, I, too, ventured out and found my own people to hang out with. The biggest difference though, I believe, was that the people she found could help further her career, while the people I found simply were fun to spend time with.

Francois, a French photographer I had worked with on a test photo shoot, became my favorite photographer to hang out with. Only twenty-four years old, his blonde hair stood out among the French men I had encountered so far. Francois had a contagious comedic side to him, not all seriousness. His English was horrendous, so I made it my mission to help him with a few lessons. We occasionally met up at Tuileries before heading to a bar on the Place du Châtelet where they served a strange, red wine-beer concoction. His friends would show up, and we spent hours talking and laughing.

It felt good to be accepted by French people and to just have fun. I never invited Ava or Kristen to go with us and, now that I look back, I don't know why. I think we all knew that, although we had much in common, we were entirely different people, different personalities, with different interests and motivations.

We did, however, all like a group of fellow American models staying at a house on rue Faraday, just about three blocks away from our apartment. Kimmy, the only female model in the house, was seventeen and on her own for the first time, in Paris of all places. James, a male model with our agency, and Sam, a tall, blonde model who at first appeared arrogant and all Ivy League snobbish, also lived there.

PARIS

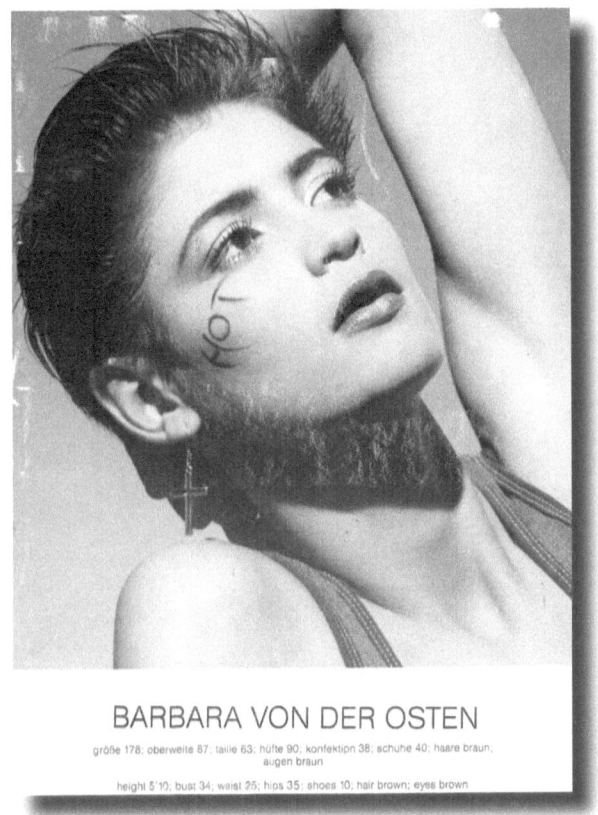

This is the front cover of my model composite card which I handed out at go-sees, castings, and auditions in several different countries. The photo is from the all night test photo shoot in Paris. This particular card shows my measurements in German and English.

PARIS

Suddenly snapping awake and glancing over at the clock, panic struck as I realized the alarm hadn't gone off. I jumped out of bed, waking Kristen as I scrambled out of the room. We were scheduled for a test photo shoot together, and the photographer, Boris, had told us not to be late.

Still half asleep, we rushed out the door, arriving at his apartment at 7:15 a.m. We knocked and knocked. Finally, a man came to the door in his underwear. It was the photographer, Boris. We had woken him up. And he told us not to be late! Kristen and I sat there while he and his two assistants slowly dragged themselves around the apartment. We were annoyed as we could have stayed in bed a little longer as well.

Two hours later we were at the beach. As I climbed out of the van, I looked out toward the ocean and thought it to be one of the most beautiful beaches I had ever seen, very different from those back in Florida. The wind whipped around the corner of the van, and the beach on this cold, damp November day, a Sunday, seemed deserted.

The hair and makeup artist, wearing a pair of white overalls and sporting long knotted hair, pulled out her enormous kit and began on Kristen first, then me. Boris left briefly, returning with sandwiches and wine. We sat together for a few hours, enjoying the lunch, before finally getting back to the reason we were there in the first place. By this time, it was already 2:00 p.m. and the light was the primary concern. We roamed around, looking for that perfect spot and perfect light.

I wore a bright pink, one-piece swimsuit with a loose black coverup dress as my first outfit, strolling along the beach, trying my best not to look like I was freezing. With the light moving away from us, we soon packed everything up and went in search of a better location. We walked and walked, finally ending up at a columned structure.

I changed into a pair of cropped, dark brown pants, a black T-shirt, and a black and brown checked wool jacket. The stylist flattened my hair and touched up my already natural looking makeup. I was to portray a French student who had traveled to Normandy to sketch the famous beaches of World War II. With a large portfolio by my side, I sat on the cold concrete and leaned against one of the white pillars of what I thought might actually be a monument. There were very few people around, and we had the place all to ourselves. It felt uncommonly serene.

As the sun dropped slowly in the sky, Kristen and I gathered up our belongings and climbed in the van for the drive back to Paris. The driver drove fast and reckless, much like my brother Kurt did back home. I gripped the armrest as Kristen gripped my arm. Once at the photographer's apartment, Kristen and I ran for the metro, anxious to get back to our own apartment.

When the phone rang that night, all three of us dove for it. It was my parents, and I couldn't wait to tell them about my day.

"We went to the beach about two hours away today to do a test photo shoot. It was incredible!"

"Oh?" my dad said with a tilt to his voice as if asking a question with just that word.

"It's nothing like the beaches in Florida, Dad. I don't know, there was just something so incredibly beautiful and peaceful about it."

I continued. "It was Normandy, Dad. Weren't you there in World War II?"

For a moment he fell silent. Then finally, "I was. My ship landed on the beach with army troops and equipment. We made several trips to those beaches back in June 1944, forty years ago."

I vaguely knew of my Dad's WWII experiences with the US Navy, serving in the amphibious force aboard the landing ship, USS *LST-388*. He had been a radioman and kept journals throughout the war. I made a mental note to be sure and read those one day when back in the States.

EUROPEAN DAZE

With my Dad in our living room in Ormond Beach, Florida (January 1984). He kept detailed journals during WWII and encouraged me to do the same while in Europe. During a test photo shoot I was able to visit Normandy, where my Dad's ship landed in June of 1944..

PARIS

By mid-November, I thought I might be falling in love with Paris, even though it was cold and rainy most days. More so, I believe, it was the lifestyle I was living that I fell in love with. Although still frustrated with the agency, worn out from traipsing all over the city each day with little result, it became my way of life, the good and the bad. With that acceptance, it seemed as if things were finally beginning to look up. Photos from the shoots at Normandy and the all-night shoot with *HOT* written on my face came out well, and the agency's excitement about them made me happy.

This new frame of mind really took hold with my first job as a working mannequin (model) in Paris. It was with a photographer by the name of Jean-Michel, whom I had interviewed with several times at his studio. The job would be for a German client, an ad for Wella hair products for their New Wave brand of gels, mousse, and hairspray.

Excitedly I made my way to the studio, arriving early. Another model, from Australia, had already arrived and sat in the makeup chair. I was up next. The makeup artist patted and slid her fingers across my face, careening down my nose like a ski slope. I could feel the weight of the foundation, then the powder, then the blush, the eye makeup. My skin undoubtedly shocked by so much covering. I was a minimalist, meaning

I wore very little makeup, preferring the au naturale, low maintenance look.

With a switch of chairs, the hairstylist went to work. He managed to make what little hair I did have stand tall, adding a few inches to my already five-foot-ten-inch statuesque height. Moving over to wardrobe, I momentarily stared at the selected clothes in disbelief before pouring myself into the pink and green plaid pants, bright pink tank top with its yellow trim, topped by a pink-flowered jacket and anchored by bright, lime green shoes. Ten minutes in front of the camera, mostly in profile shots, and we were done.

My second outfit wasn't much better than the first—a putrid green dress and sweater-vest. My hair, now flattened down, gave off more of an androgynous look but still somehow feminine. Added to this were dangling rhinestone earrings which reached the top of my shoulders. It only took another ten minutes in front of the camera, and my first job as a working model in Paris ended.

I changed back into my drab clothes and attempted to remove at least some of the blue eyeshadow as well as the stained orange-relish lipstick. I ran my fingers through my stiff gel-and-spray-drenched hair. Leaving the studio, I felt like I was walking on air. The weather turned rainy, overcast and bone-chillingly cold but I didn't care. Stopping at a pay phone, I called the agency to check in and found out I would be working again the following week for the same client, and the same photographer, Jean-Michel. Kristen would be working alongside me. I was giddy with excitement. Meanwhile, Ava had already worked one job and was jet-setting to Nice on the coast for another job. Things really were looking up for all of us!

PARIS

That night Kristen, Ava and I decided to celebrate by going out to a nightclub. Kimmy came over from her Faraday house, and the four of us shared a bottle of wine while getting ready. As the small cabs could only take two people at a time, Kimmy and Kristen took one, and Ava and I took another. Meeting up again, we walked to the nightclub, but not before passing through a section crowded with hookers, sex stores, and sex shows. The neighborhood, Pigalle, held the infamous Moulin Rouge, as well as all manner of businesses relating to sex.

Kristen and I laughingly held on to each other as we walked, with men and women from the various entertainment venues and shops trying to entice us. Kimmy and Ava hung on to each other right behind us, laughing just as hysterically at all the comments and scenes being played out before us. As we reached the door of the club, we mentioned we were with First Agency, and they let us in, no charge.

Kimmy had friends already at the club, and they had rented a table for the night. We joined them, drinking champagne together. An occasional joint made its way around the table, with many taking one inhale before passing it on. We were finally able to let loose and enjoy ourselves, if only for a night.

Later the next day, the three of us, moving ever so slowly, sat together talking about our night out. It turns out Ava, when she left the club at 2:00 a.m., couldn't find a cab and had to walk all the way home. Men constantly tried to pick her up. Kristen's legs were killing her from all the dancing. A painful ache radiated throughout both my ears accompanied by an incessant ringing. I couldn't even touch my ears they were so sore. *Had I damaged them*, I wondered?

My first print job in Paris, for the German client Wella

PARIS

I wish I could say I became an epicurean or relished French food during my time in Paris. But I have never been one to swain over a meal, or linger for hours over seven-course meals, savoring each one, dissecting the mystery dish by its varied flavors. If only I had read up on the works of M.F.K. Fisher I would have known how to experience food and to write about it. Or, even if I had glanced at Julia Child's cookbook to become familiar with what dishes to seek out and try while in France. Instead, I remained rather simple in my tastes.

What I did relish were the long lunches of wine and cheese and bread. When on a test photo shoot or a job, all action came to a halt come lunchtime, and we spread out a blanket, plopping down on it with a glass of wine. Never did we feel rushed to get back to work. Nor were we on a time clock, with someone breathing down our neck if late by a few minutes.

At restaurants, I would order something as simple as a tuna salad on French bread. Anything and everything tasted better on fresh, baked bread. Occasionally I treated myself to a *Salade Caprieshe* and a hot chocolate, a combination I found perfectly paired.

Fast-food restaurants had already found their way onto the sophisticated Paris streets, and Burger King became one of our quick jaunts late at night or in-between go-sees. It was a familiar place in a city of overwhelming choices. Many days I carried a pear or apple and a few slices of cheese with me to eat along the way.

Cheese soon became my true passion. Brie, Muenster, Roquefort, Camembert. A more pleasant eating experience didn't exist in my eyes. And to pair them with the incredible fresh breads, baguettes, and croissants, accompanied by a sip of wine made it even more enticing. It was times like this that I felt most French, most in the moment, most joyful. With over four hundred cheeses made in France, I would have been happy to try them all.

As for wines, I would never become a connoisseur, much less any type of sommelier. I let others choose the wine that best complemented what we were eating. My only find was the annual Beaujolais Nouveau, made from Gamay grapes harvested by hand in the Beaujolais region, just north of the French city of Lyon. Interestingly, this isn't a wine aged for years and years and then celebrated. Instead, Beaujolais Nouveau is fermented for approximately three weeks, then released during the third week of November every year. A red wine I very much fell in love with as much for the taste as for the hype, and ritual, surrounding it. I made a promise to myself to seek out a bottle every year going forward, even when back in the States.

There were many types of appointments, or go-sees, that we were sent on during our time in Paris. Go-sees for magazines, catalogs, advertisements, television commercials, all mixed into our daily schedules. Traveling outside of Paris to visit a client or photographer was also common. On one particular day, Ava and I headed to Salle Spectacle De Theatre at 4 rue Chezy. We didn't know what it was for, but it had to either be a television commercial or a small part in a movie. When it was my turn, I had to walk, sit, twist my head, smile, and laugh in front of a camera. Then I had to put a swim cap over my hair. The client smiled, saying repeatedly, "*Très bon.*"

Late one day I made my way to 9 rue Belidor to the studio of Valérie Marku. After showing my book, I entered a back room where six people sat at a table. One of them, an English bloke, motioned for me to stand in front of the camera. I twirled, ran my figures through my short hair, and smiled with my eyes. I felt comfortable and continued to joke with them and laugh. They told me it was a great audition. What it was for I didn't know. I would return there one more time before leaving Paris, for an audition for a coffee commercial, in French.

The locations of go-sees could be anywhere in and around the city, even on a boat. In mid-November on a cold, rainy day, Kristen and I headed to Place de la Concorde. As we exited onto the streets, we saw the Seine River in front of us and walked toward it. We were looking for a boat named *Zephyre*. Our frustration grew as we walked up and down every dock, becoming more drenched by the second. Finally, an hour later we found it and climbed aboard. We knocked on the cabin door, but there was no answer. No one was on that bloody boat! We were sopping wet, and a little more than mad. We stomped all the way back to the apartment.

PARIS

I awoke on Thanksgiving morning with the beginnings of a head cold. This was the first time I had been away from family for the holiday. Since my mom and her twin sister celebrated their birthday in late November, with it every few years falling on the Thursday of Thanksgiving, our two families always spent this time together. It was our holiday to share. Now I would just hear about the celebration back home as I spent it in this foreign city, a city that didn't even celebrate the same holiday.

Working again with Jean-Michel, I thankfully didn't have to be at the studio until almost noon. When I arrived, I found some good coffee and changed into a broad-striped outfit. The makeup was all-natural colors, normal instead of outlandish. I had two hairstylists working on my hair at the same time, naturally important since this was yet another job for hair. Ironically, my biggest let-down in Paris—the agency sanctioned hair shearing—had now become my bread-and-butter.

As I stepped out of the hairstylist's chair, and before I could even get in front of the camera, the crew broke for lunch. All work and all talk of work stopped. We entered the adjoining room where food lay spread out over the table, and all ten of us sat down together. Wine poured from three bottles into our glasses. Fresh bread, sumptuous cheeses, and more had us sharing stories and laughing. Maybe not the Thanksgiving meal I was used to, but the comradery and laughter were well worthy of my thanks.

When our two-hour lunch ended, I was heralded back into the makeup artist chair for a touch-up, then a hairstylist checked my hair. Now it was my time with the photographer. Jean-Michel, a well-known photographer in Paris, knew what he was doing and how to coax a look out of his model. Polite, respectful, he gave little direction, and I naturally followed, adding my own look here and there. Jean-Michel kept calling me his "Florida girl" as I moved around him. There were just some photographers I felt more comfortable with, and Jean-Michel was one of them in Paris.

Afterward, as I changed back into my street clothes, the German client, Rita, came over to me with the model release. Based in Hamburg, Germany, she said she hoped to work with me again. I hoped so too. Not only was the money good with the German clients, but they were respectful and fun to work with. Thanksgiving had been a success, and I was happy.

I waited for Kristen to finish her shoot and change back into her own clothes. We then went into the agency, mostly to pick up our mail and talk to them about the black-tie party that Paul, the head of the agency, was giving later that evening. Knowing I didn't have much to choose from in my scant wardrobe, we spent a few hours shopping close by. I bought a black silk skirt with a loose layer of lace over the top of it, acceptable looking earrings, a white shirt, and black heels. Back at the apartment, we assembled our look for the evening.

We were the first ones to arrive at L'Observator, a brand-new nightclub where the party was being held. Drinks started flowing. Free champagne all night. I danced most of the night with Sam, the model living at Faraday with Kimmy and James. I also ran into several photographers I had worked with as well as other models and stylists I had met during my time in Paris.

Afterward, Sam and I walked the streets of Paris for a while, talking about our lives back in the States. He didn't reveal too much about himself, but I had heard rumors that he was married, and his wife remained back home. As we approached my apartment building on rue Poncelet. I invited Sam upstairs, and we sat in the living room talking until early morning while Kristen and Ava slept in the next room. Although I enjoyed his company, his arrogance and married status kept me at arm's distance. When he left at 4:00 a.m., I crawled into bed, exhausted.

We all three woke with a champagne hangover of epic proportions. The agency thankfully hadn't scheduled any appointments for us until 3:30 p.m. After a quick meeting with a client at the agency, I headed over to Media Print and picked up a few of my photos the agency had ordered for my portfolio. They were from our day at the beach at Normandy. In one, I truly did look like a French student.

The day continued to darken. Dreary, rainy, and oh so windy, Ava and I stopped off at the nearby Burger King for a quick bite. The wind blew stronger as we left and Ava couldn't keep her umbrella from blowing upwards. We laughed at our situation, rushing along the avenue. Everyone seemed to be laughing along with us, or maybe at us. We found our way to Bastille, locating our last go-see of the day before 7:00 p.m. Patrick Vandor's studio was on the third floor, so we begrudgingly climbed the stairs to his door. We tried to straighten out our hair and wipe the water from our faces. Fortunately, we could remove our wet winter coats, and at least part of what was underneath remained dry.

Once inside, I showed my book, which now consisted of several more photos, to the client. They had me lie horizontally, supporting each end of myself on two opposing chairs. The job was for an ad where a guy is holding up his girl like this. Vandor took a photo of my strained face and tense body across the chairs, the best balancing act I could muster. After a few portrait shots of my face, we were done. The exhaustion from the night before and the rainy cold of the day hit me as I exited the studio. All I could think about was a hot shower and bed.

A windy Wednesday arrived, and I traipsed all over the city again. After stopping at the agency to see my slides from a test photo shoot with a photographer named Nadia, I headed to an appointment with photographer Jean-Loup Sauvertac. He wanted to "present" me to a magazine client, and I had heard it might be for the cover. When I arrived at his studio, mass confusion surrounded me. Several models were there working, throwing clothes on and off. Stylists hurriedly adjusted clothing on models who lay on the floor while the photographer stood on a ladder above them.

Shortly, the German client pulled herself away from the shoot and motioned for me to join her in the next room. I showed her my portfolio, and we talked, a friendly, easy banter of sorts. Fortunately, the German clients spoke English almost as well as I did. She decided she wanted to shoot me right then. If you've ever been around enough Germans, you know they say what they mean, very straightforward. We called the agency, and the decision was made to return the next day for the shoot instead. I don't know why this happened. I felt ready to work, but maybe the agency needed to assert some kind of control over their model and make it sound like I had something more important to do that afternoon. (I didn't.) Upon leaving, I skipped all the way back to the metro.

Back at the apartment, Ava had already heard from the agency about my cover try and seemed excited for me. She herself had to catch a plane the next morning to Germany for a job. It seemed the Germans loved us while we were in Paris, but what about the French? Why weren't we being sent to French clients and magazines for consideration? That's where the good tear sheets for our books would come from. Maybe we were, and they just didn't like us.

We had already met editors and stylists for *Cosmopolitan*, *Marie Claire*, and *100 Idees* magazines. But our more recent go-sees, and eventual jobs, all seemed to be for hair advertisements, or fashion shows or commercials. Don't get me wrong. I was thrilled to be working for the German clients, for advertisements, magazine editorials, and now, for a cover. In retrospect, maybe we were interviewing for those type of jobs with those type of clients for financial reasons. We all needed money to live on, and the agency, of course, depended upon us making money for them as well. What we really desired, however, was balance—a balance between well-paying jobs and good opportunities to build our portfolios.

Awake early, I excitedly made my way back to Jean-Loup de Sauverzac's studio to shoot the cover for *Petra*, a popular German magazine. Realistically, it was a cover-try photo shoot. Nothing is ever guaranteed. After the makeup artist added light makeup to my face, and the hairstylist went to work on my hair, I put on a plain blouse, then two different scarves were wrapped around my neck. The photographer made it all seem so easy. We changed my hairstyle at one point, then continued shooting. The crew brought in an abundance of cheese, bread, and wine for us all to enjoy together. Afterward, I signed the model release and again skipped back to the metro.

After a quick stop at the apartment for a warm cup of coffee, I headed out to more go-sees. Arriving at the first one, a studio called Clapboard, I found myself in a room full of male models. Was I in the right place? Did the agency mess up yet again in giving me my appointments? With that surprised, lost look on my face that I often wore in moments such as this, I finally connected with a man standing in the front of the room. He took down my name, age, height, and which agency I was with. Then I waited. Shortly, about fifteen of us were escorted into another room to show our books to an older gentleman sitting alone at a table. Each male model passed through, then made his way out the side door. When it was my turn, the older gentleman asked me to wait a few minutes until he had seen everyone's book. I returned to the lobby, and again I waited.

Once all the male models had departed, I was called back in to be videotaped with a little acting required. I had to argue with the cameraman. He offers me a cigarette, and I politely say, "No thank you." He keeps insisting until I get mad. An odd audition to say the least. As I walked out of the building, I suddenly realized I had chewing gum in my mouth the entire time.

PARIS

First agency's accounting office sat just off the main booking room. With the weekend only a few hours away, I made my way in to review my account and withdraw enough francs to shop for Christmas presents. This is when the accountant sat me down and provided my first painstaking lesson in the business of modeling.

My list of debts—almost $1,000—included charges for test photo shoots, printouts of photos, copies of photos, my very first advance when I arrived in Paris for 1000 francs, and rent on the apartment. It's not that I didn't know I had a few debts, but I didn't expect them to be so much. I had planned to take out about 500 francs but now settled for an advance of a smaller amount. Payment from my last job with the German client had not yet reached the agency and would, fortunately, clear out the debt. Then I would be on the plus side, at least temporarily.

This is how it all worked. The agency would advance money to me, and when I worked, the money that came in would go to pay off whatever I owed them. In a way, this was good, as they had even more incentive to send me out on go-sees and promote me. But it was also bad, as I seemed to be in debt to them more often than not. These debts were in addition to the twenty percent off the top of any earnings required by contract to be paid to my agency in New York. The Paris agency then took their cut, and the rest went first to paying off my debts. Anything left over, if any, was mine.

After leaving the agency, Ava and I headed to Les Halles to look around for Christmas presents to take home to the States. However, I just wasn't in the mood to spend money. Reality had brought me back to reality. I now began thinking of the go-sees as job interviews. Jobs I must "win" in order to support myself, just like jobs my friends had back in the States.

This was my first real lesson in business management, you could say. Always be aware of your expenses and your debts. Control what you can and accept what you must. It was obvious to me that what I had suspected from the start about all the test photo shoots the agency pushed on us was indeed true. Everyone was in the business to make money, one way or another. I would have to be smarter going forward.

December rolled in quietly. The new agency headsheet came out, and Kristen, Ava and I were on it. This is a poster of the models the agency represents, sent out to all clients and photographers. The photo they chose for me was one of the HOT photos, one where I am looking directly at the camera. One thing that became apparent early on in my modeling career is that my best angles are profile angles, not frontal shots. Confused by their headsheet choice, I again wondered if they were doing anything in my best interest.

It was obvious to everyone that I wasn't satisfied with First Agency. Ava didn't seem to be either, and although Kristen said she also wasn't pleased with them, I didn't really believe her. The agency seemed excited about her and pushed her hard.

She appeared frantic at times, but her nervous energy kept her going.

Lawrine and Kay called from New York one night when we were all three at the apartment. Talking with me first, they excitedly told me of an agency in Milan, Italy, who had expressed interest. Lorenzo, with Fashion Model Agency, saw my pictures while in New York and took a few back to Milan with him. He showed them to several clients, and they all wanted to work with me.

Meanwhile, there in Paris, Jean Luc with Carin Models Agency, a competing agency to First, also saw my pictures and said I should be working every day. Kay went on to say that Jean Luc would be in touch with us later in the week. I was eager to hear from him and switch to his agency. And I was excited to hear more about Milan.

The next morning, I called into the agency to confirm the day's schedule. Andy answered. Lawrine had already called and told him about my going to Milan soon. He was still trying to get in touch with Étienne to discuss this new development. It seemed a drama was unfolding.

Later that afternoon after my go-sees, I stopped by the agency, and Andy immediately pulled me into a side office. He talked negatively about Milan, telling me what a horrible market it was. Paul, the agency manager, entered a few minutes later and also bashed Milan. Confused, I called Legends in New York and managed to reach Louis, one of the bookers. I needed a little reassurance, a little encouragement. He made me laugh, then told me my photo was hanging on the wall at Legends. My New York agency hadn't forgotten me.

EUROPEAN DAZE

In the days ahead, Kristen, Ava and I kept expecting to hear from Jean Luc, with Carin Models Agency, but we never did. I suspected that First Agency had talked to Lawrine and Kay and dissuaded the move somehow. Or, perhaps, the competing agencies pulled power moves to prevent the move from happening. I turned my focus instead to the agency in Milan, excited that they were excited about me.

PARIS

Kristen and I hopped in a taxi to the Musée d'Art Moderne de la Ville de Paris, the city's Museum of Modern Art, located in the Palais de Tokyo at 11 avenue du Président Wilson. We had been chosen for a fashion show being held in the museum which displayed works by Picasso and Matisse, as well as various other artists.

Upon arrival, we quickly joined the mass of people, and the ensuing chaos unfolding. Eventually, we found our way to our section, and I was whisked into the makeup chair. Sporting green eyebrows and other questionable colors in interesting places, the hairstylist grabbed my arm and led me to his chair. He squeezed gobs of gel into both hands and saturated my hair, from the roots to the ends, standing it straight up all over my head. Then he sprayed it with different colors, no doubt a work of art in its own right.

As if on an assembly line, the wardrobe group snatched me up next and handed me a loose, Japanese style pantsuit to put on. Not gorgeous by any stretch of the imagination, but it was silk and felt soft against my skin. Shoes were next. Instead of heels, I was given what reminded me of the shoes Herman Munster wore. Blocky. With all my disappointment in my own outfit, I glanced over at Kristen just in time to see her slipping into a long, colorful peasant dress, with a matching scarf tied around her head. I wasn't sure which of us got the better deal.

Nervous, we peeked out at the audience. Approximately 4,000 people filled the hall, waiting for us. They included photographers, magazine reps; you name it, they were there. Finally, it was my turn to hit the catwalk. My nervousness disappeared as soon as I stepped out, feeling the energy of the crowd, I clomped down the runway in my blocky shoes, then back up. For the finale, we all filed out, one by one, down the catwalk so the audience could get one last look.

Backstage we celebrated with champagne. But the night wasn't over yet. We had to give a second show, same as the first. It all went the same, no trips, no wardrobe mishaps. Afterward, I decided to leave my hair the way it was, but I wiped a little of the artsy makeup off my face and changed into my normal clothes. Kristen and I met Ava in the lobby and walked around for a while. When we had had enough, we decided to walk down the Champs-Élysées instead of just heading back to the apartment. The excitement of the evening fueled us on, and we felt like we were on cloud nine.

Working again the next day, I arrived at 83 Ave. Marceau and rushed up to the fifth floor just in time to be whisked into the makeup artist's chair first. The other model for the day, Tiffany, showed up shortly afterward. I had worked with her before with Jean-Michel.

It turned out to be a long day for the both of us, shooting five different outfits each. This was an editorial job instead of an advertisement or catalog shoot. These types of photos show action, and personality, whereas catalog shots are simpler, with all importance on showing the clothes. With editorials, you can experiment, focusing mostly on the photographer and his direction and excitement at anything you are doing. It didn't pay as well as catalog shoots, but well worth it for the possibility of getting good tear sheets for my portfolio. The photos in my book so far were somewhat static, with the same looks on my face. I needed to show more personality, more variety. Editorial jobs could help with that.

We spent the following weekend shopping, finding the Porte de Clignancourt flea market much larger than we initially thought. I bought a carry-all tote bag, which I desperately needed, a pair of bright green gloves, a scarf, socks, and a set of black fingerless gloves which would become one of my wardrobe staples and signature items. I also purchased two sweatshirts with "Universität De Paris" on the front. To my way of thinking, you could never have too many sweatshirts.

In the days ahead, tensions increased in our tiny, cozy abode. Ava left early for her job one day and took my hairdryer and Kristin's converter. Kristin was furious, and when Ava returned home that evening, she screamed at her. I had never seen her so angry. Kristen had this nervous kind of energy, and her emotions came out through every part of her body, like a wave. Ava, more subtle in showing her anger, nevertheless had her days of being on edge. As for me, I often wore my emotions on my sleeve with the agency and with everyone else. We obviously weren't all best friends. But the one thing we had in common, and it was a big thing, was the fact that we were beginners, new models learning how to be in the business of modeling. And that was enough to keep us together.

PARIS

I spent most of a cold, windy Wednesday once again racing all over the city, visiting photographers and clients, many I had already seen at least once before. I felt worn out by the time I returned to the apartment. The day wasn't over yet though. Of course not.

The three of us combed through our small wardrobe selection in search of something different to wear for the evening event. I finally decided upon a creation of my own sort. I put on the black silk skirt with its top layer of lace, pulling the lace part up to my chest, making it like a slightly see-through halter dress. Kristen and Ava helped me tie it in the back, and we found a belt to wear around my upper waist, to also keep it from falling down. I topped it off with the short jacket from my only other dressy outfit in the closet and added stockings and black heels.

My hair had grown out slightly by now, and I styled it much like it had been done at one of the photo shoots. Not funky or wild, but more full and sophisticated. I also added a little more makeup, giving up my au naturel look for the night. I was rather pleased with my creative and somewhat daring look. Who said I couldn't learn to be fashionable?

We poured ourselves into a taxi and headed to the Blvd. de La Tour Maubourg, on the Left Bank of Paris, just off the famous Quai' d'Orsay. Arriving just past 9:00 p.m., we made our way up to the extravagant third-floor apartment which was home to Paul, our agency manager. A butler met us at the door, taking our coats before handing each of us a tall glass of champagne. We had no idea what to expect or who else would be there. We had just been told to dress nicely and show up promptly.

As Kristen, Ava and I sat in the living room, talking with Paul and the other few models who had been invited, the butler announced that the guest of honor had arrived. We turned toward the front door, and in walked Prince Albert of Monaco, accompanied by two men in matching suits and ties. Were they his friends or his bodyguards? I thought it best not to ask, especially at that moment.

Everyone immediately stood and began forming a line. I finally figured out it was some sort of receiving line, and what you do when you meet royalty. Fortunately, I knew how to watch and learn. I could fake sophistication as well as anyone.

Prince Albert graciously made his way down the line, shaking everyone's hand. There were about twenty of us there by now. Afterward, we returned to our seats, and everyone began talking again, just like before he had arrived. It never failed, every time my glass neared empty, the server showed up with his never-ending supply of champagne to fill it again.

I found myself moving over to one corner of the room to talk with James, a male model living at Faraday with Kimmy and Sam. As we laughed, I felt someone by my side. Prince Albert had joined us. He asked how we were enjoying Paris. My face burned, from the inside out, no doubt turning all shades of embarrassing red. Relief overwhelmed me when we were finally called to dinner.

As we entered the large dining room, two round tables occupied the room. Each elegantly set, I searched for the place card with my name. When I found it, I looked up just in time to see the Prince approaching the chair directly across from mine. Instantly, I became nervous. I mean, how can you eat in front of someone who lives such a sophisticated life all the time? This was not at all what I was used to. The night was becoming more challenging by the minute.

Two women I didn't know also sat at our table, although one was referred to simply as the "baroness." Paul, the agency manager, two male models, my roommate Kristen, and another model named Alex rounded out my table.

The first serving, oddly enough, appeared to be square pieces of pizza. The waiters served the women first. It was all too old-time Hollywood for me, and I felt incredibly uncomfortable. I was even beginning to wish they had sat me at the other table with Ava, the agency bookers, and the bodyguard-friends. They were all laughing and having fun. No stuffy routine there.

But the show must go on, and I knew it would all be over eventually. I berated myself internally for not studying up on table etiquette. Where was Emily Post when you needed her? The main course arrived; it was a delicious serving of some type of meat and various vegetables, beautifully arranged on the plate. (I wouldn't know until later that it had been lamb.) The salads came next, which is customary in Europe. Salads often came after the main course.

EUROPEAN DAZE

To complete the meal, the waiters placed a small soufflé in front of each of us. Once again, I had no clue what it was. I watched the others discreetly, observing what utensil they used, then took mine up. Taking my first bite, I must have made a face as it was such a different taste. Prince Albert noticed, and, calling me by name, described what it was and asked whether I liked it. *Great, now he's watching me eat. Will this night ever end?* I thought in a sudden panic.

Never have I been so glad that a meal was over. The food indeed was delicious, but who in the world can enjoy such fare when a prince is at your table?

Fortunately, Paul's apartment was huge, and I could find a place far, far away from the Prince after dinner. I sat talking with Ava when the bodyguards or friends (no one ever told us), Eric and Oliver, came over. What a relief to find them so funny. Hysterical is more like it. Meanwhile, Kristen stayed close to Prince Albert, talking, and laughing rather loudly. I thought she might even be flirting. I had to give it to her—she felt comfortable in her own skin and didn't hesitate to talk with anyone, anywhere, anytime.

As the night wound down, and after many bottles of champagne, several of us decided to kick it up a notch and go dancing. We headed over to Atmosphere Night Club. Somehow, Kristen, Ava and I wound up riding to the club with the Prince and his two sidekicks. Fortunately, I enjoyed their company, and Kristen enjoyed the Prince's. Details of the car and the drive over elude me as I became caught up in a banter more like between friends who had known each other a long time.

PARIS

It's hard to describe the feeling of walking into a nightclub with the Prince of Monaco. It was both thrilling and embarrassing at the same time. I didn't like being stared at, being the center of attention. (And yet, I was a model. Go figure!). I did my best to act as if this was the most normal thing in the world for me. I doubt I pulled it off, however.

We checked our coats, then the six of us hit the dance floor. The Prince, only seven years older than me, easily moved to the music without hesitation. After a few songs, we walked over to an area that had been cleared out just for our group. Bottles of champagne magically appeared and once again my glass was filled. At one point, the Prince's younger sister, Princess Stephanie, showed up at the club. This would have been weird for me if it hadn't been for the superb champagne. Besides, I had already experienced dinner with the Prince, so what did one more royal matter?

During our hours at the club, I noticed how social Prince Albert was, talking to everyone around him. A very unpretentious guy it seemed. The kind of guy both men and women like. I watched but didn't dare talk to him. It was obvious that Kristen wanted a little more of his attention, so she stayed close. At moments, it seemed as if she were upset. Was he ignoring her somewhat, or was he just being the social royal that his title calls for? Still, I felt bad for Kristen at those moments. I saw something akin to despair racing across her face and consuming her lithesome body.

A few hours later, the DJ slowed the music, putting on the song "Drive" by the Cars. As I talked and laughed with the others near the table, the Prince walked up beside me. Taking my hand, without saying a word, just a stare into my eyes, we headed to the dance floor. As he placed one hand around my waist to my lower back, he pulled me in close, astonishingly close. We were alone on the dance floor, surrounded by onlookers but it seemed as if we were the only two people in the room. As the song ended, he held on as another one started. This time, George Michael serenaded us with his hit song "Careless Whisper." When the second song ended, we smiled at each other, and the Prince walked me back over to the table. Those were the only two slow songs played all night, and I felt dazed, wondering why he chose to dance them with me. Kristen would have been the more likely choice.

It was after 3:00 a.m. before we finally began to close out the night. I was now amazed at how down to earth the Prince, Eric, and Oliver were. Yet, Ava and I decided to catch a ride home with another model, a French model we knew who had her own car. Maybe it was Ava that swayed me that way, or maybe I just knew it was the right thing for me. We said our formal goodnights, with a kiss on each cheek and also said goodnight to Kristen, as she was going with them.

Once back at the apartment, I didn't second guess myself but instead knew of the wonderful memories I had just created. It wasn't until much later that they brought Kristen home. We didn't talk about where they went and what happened. Kristen seemed upset, or distracted, her mind racing as always. I can say this. Kristen may have acted a little ditzy at times, but she *always* knew what she was doing, or at least it seemed that way. You could get irritated with Kristen, but you just couldn't dislike her.

A few days later I reread some of my journal notes from that night. One reminded me that, in the future, one mustn't blush when meeting a Prince, and should not try every maneuver she can think of to avoid him like the plague. Yet, my shyness, often covered up by my forced socializing, was such that not even a modeling career could cure it. Prince or not.

It had been a fairytale of a night.

PARIS

At the agency, Paul, Capucine, Andy, and Étienne were all exceptionally nice to us during our remaining days in Paris. Relations between them and Legends in New York, however, turned less than friendly those last few weeks. After First had shown us yet again to German and Japanese agents, Kay Mitchell sent Paul a hot telex. Apparently, only the base agency is to show its models to other agencies in other countries. There is also some type of commission system in place, possibly a finder's fee of sorts. I didn't get caught up in all the particulars. The modeling business it seems is full of secrets and deceits, much like any other type of business.

After receiving Kay's telex, the bookers at First began to complain to me, asking me why I would tell them everything in the first place. Why they thought I was the only one complaining to the home agency, I didn't know. Maybe I had been too vocal. Maybe it was because I showed too much independence. Étienne and I did not get along in the slightest. I said what I needed to say to him and he said what he needed to say to me. We never held back.

Later, when I had time to reflect about my overall Paris experience, I honestly believed that my coming to Paris had hurt my career, not helped it. My New York experience had been accelerating, and I felt it was going somewhere. Here in Paris, mistrust of the agency interfered with my advancement. Trust needed to go both ways for me.

Another thought that crossed my mind was that maybe I should have gone to Japan first, to earn enough money to allow me not to worry so much about expenses once in Europe, or back in New York. My parents helped me as much as they could, but I knew their resources were limited. I had to find my own way. I had to find a way to pay my own way.

If the chance to switch to the other Paris agency, Carin Models, had indeed materialized, I might have had a stronger experience in Paris and been more successful. I wasn't sure what was happening back in New York, but there seemed to be strained relationships and Legends descended into some type of turmoil. Charlie, the booker who had taken those first good photos of me at Art on the Beach, quit the agency and joined a different one.

Speaking with Lawrine one night before returning to the States, I again told her about my inability to get along with First Agency. I didn't think they were doing anything in my best interests. The relationship just didn't click. She assured me that in January I would not be returning to Paris but instead would be going straight to Milan, Italy to work with Fashion Model agency. They had already lined up jobs for me, starting in the new year.

As for the trio—Kristen, Ava, and me—our paths seemed to be diverging, paths that just eight weeks before had converged in New York and led us to a tiny apartment on rue Poncelet in Paris, France. It seemed we had reached an intersection, and while Kristen and Ava would stay the course ahead of them, I might well be taking a turn, in a new direction.

Ava flew home on December 14. Little did we know at that moment that we would not see each other in January nor would we ever see each other again.

Kristen and I spent our last day in Paris together, reminiscing about our time in France. It seemed almost unbelievable that two months had already passed. Later that evening, she went to First Agency to say goodbye to everyone. I just couldn't make myself go. I didn't feel it necessary. Étienne called, and we talked for a bit and cleared the air between us. I thanked him for the good things that did happen and wished him well. Capucine and Andy kindly said farewell.

I cleaned every plate and pan in the apartment and put them away neatly. I wanted to leave the apartment nice for Kristen and Ava when they returned in January. Sam came by, and we walked back to Faraday for dinner and a bottle of Beaujolais Nouveau. Afterward, he walked me back to the apartment, and we said our goodbye. We kissed, but in the end, we decided to leave it at that. I had one last night in the apartment on rue Poncelet, and I would spend it alone.

The next day, the driver navigated the taxi onto the Avenue des Ternes, heading toward Orly Airport. Just eight weeks before we had taken this same drive, but in reverse. Three anxious gals in a foreign city for the first time. Now, I felt different, I was different. A stronger, more confident me began to emerge.

My time in Paris had been incredible. I worked enough jobs to pay all my debts, and still buy Christmas presents and have money in my pocket to take back to Florida. Most of my jobs in Paris had been for German clients such as *Petra* and *Freudian* magazines, which paid well and introduced me to what would become one of my best markets. I had learned my way around a foreign city and even learned a little French. I spent time with French men and women and shopped at the famous flea markets of Paris. What more, really, could a gal ask for?

Before entering the airport terminal, I took one last look out and around, barely noticing the cold. Although I felt it in my gut, I didn't truly realize that this would be my last time in Paris. How could I have known I wouldn't be back in the City of Love, at least not as a *mannequin*, ever again. That Kristen, Ava and I would never again spend so much time together. Like in the 1942 movie, *Casablanca*, I could soon say, "We'll always have Paris."

MILAN

JANUARY 9 - MAY 25, 1985

As the TWA Flight began its descent, fog shrouded any hint of a city below. I leaned back in my seat, staring out into the blankness. After two full weeks in Florida with family and friends, I now found myself on this plane cutting through the fog that consumed most of the European continent. My new agency, Fashion Models Agency, had pre-paid for my plane ticket, and I departed New York's Kennedy Airport the evening before, bound for Milan in northern Italy.

Waiting for the cue to land, a renewed sense of energy and excitement welled up inside me for the days ahead. I also felt a profound sense of relief that I wasn't returning to Paris or the confusion and chaos of my agency there. Yet, I was now going into a foreign country all alone. Kristen and Ava were on their way back to familiar Paris, to the familiar apartment on rue Poncelet, not an unknown Milan. Excitement tainted with anxiety gushed through me. I was on my own.

As I entered the baggage claim, the driver from the agency recognized me immediately. In his broken English, he welcomed me to Italy, smiling as if I were a long-lost relative. Already this was starting out better than Paris.

As we drove away from the airport, my first views of Milan were of the fog induced variety, seeing one building at a time with the last one fading away as the next one appeared. Pulling up in front of one, my driver raised both hands, moving them up and down to signal me to stay put. He pulled my luggage out of the back and took it inside the double doors. Shortly he returned, telling me this would be where I was to stay, at an agency apartment in the building. He had left my luggage with the concierge. Intrigued, I found myself smiling at the thought of living in a building with my own concierge. With no time to waste, we continued on in the fog to my first go-see in Milan. I would have to wait until later in the day to see my apartment and settle in.

As my driver waited outside, I entered Studio Carrard. It seemed similar to many of the studios I had visited while in Paris. Both the client and the photographer stopped what they were doing and came over to greet me. Smiling big smiles, it seemed they instantly liked me. Wanting me to work immediately, they called my agency only to be told they must wait until the following day. Apparently, I needed to take care of a few things at the office since I had only just arrived in the country. Feeling somewhat relieved and thankful, I climbed back in the car, and we headed to the agency. The fatigue began to hit me head-on, but I did my best not to show it.

Fashion Models Agency sat at Via Francesco Petrarca 6. At this early point in my adventure, I had no idea about the layout of the city and how to best get around. I knew I would figure it out eventually so put it out of my mind for the time being. Within minutes of walking through the agency door, I felt comfortable. I liked it there, and more importantly, I instantly liked Lorenzo, one of the owners. After taking my measurements, a task it seems every new agency must do, we sat down at a large table. One of the bookers, Sophie, handed me a Fashion ledger, a voucher book, and an address book containing all the studios in Milan. *How organized, and different from Paris they seem*, I began to think. *I am really going to like it here.*

With all the paperwork done, all the measurements taken, and the initial getting to know each other completed, I could now finally return to my new apartment and see where I would be staying during my time in Milan.

Casalbergo Garden Residenca (the Garden Residency), located on via Fratelli Salvioni, a tiny street slanting off of Corso Sempione, one of the main throughways of Milan, was to be my home base for the months ahead. As I entered the small lobby, the concierge smiled and beckoned me over. I had to sign in at the desk and receive my keys—one to the outside door which would be locked at nighttime, and the other to the apartment itself. Riding the two-person elevator up to the second floor alone, it all started to hit me. Incredulously, the words, *I am in Italy* kept repeating in my head. When the elevator stopped, I stepped out onto the small landing, seeing only two doors. Slightly to the left I saw IID on one of them and inserted the key.

My new abode, although tiny, felt instantly cozy and homey. The combined living room and dining room held a sofa, chair, and a small table. The bathroom had a full-size bathtub, sink, toilet, and a bidet. The only bedroom contained two twin-sized beds with closets and a chest rounding out the room. At first, I thought no kitchen existed, then I slid open what appeared to be a closet door in the living room. Lo and behold, there it was. Along the wall sat a refrigerator, stove, and sink. My closet kitchen.

Concierge and maid services were included in the rent, and I could lease a television and other amenities as well. The phone in the apartment could be used to call out, to anywhere, and could also receive calls from anywhere. The only exception was that to call overseas, I would have to go through the concierge downstairs. The phone bill would come straight from the concierge, and we paid him directly for it.

As I unpacked my bags, the nonstop activities of the last two days drained the last ounce of energy from my body. Before crawling into one of the beds, I called my parents and spoke with them briefly, letting them know I had arrived and how my day had gone. I awoke a short while later to the ringing of the phone. On the other end of the line, Sophie provided the details for my two jobs the next day—a morning job and an afternoon one. What luck! I took down the information, thanked her, then dozed back off, but not before setting my alarm clock. I had to be sure I would wake up on time. I couldn't be late for my first job in Milan.

MILAN

My second day in Milan, a Friday, arrived quickly and the concierge in my building called a cab for me. A heavy fog still shrouded the city, so I sat back and prepared myself for the day ahead. Shortly, we arrived at Studio Carrard, the same studio I had visited upon arrival in Milan the day before. For three long hours, I posed in one outfit, grateful to be working and at the same time dreaming of sleeping in on the weekend. As soon as we completed the set, I changed and climbed into another taxi to my second job of the day, at a place called Super Studio. Upon arriving, I met Barbara, a makeup artist from Canada. We immediately hit it off, and she went to work transforming me for the style of photo ahead. The photographer soon joined us, introducing himself as Alessandro Jilani.

For the one photo, I dressed in a silky green tank top, long hiking shorts and a jacket. My props were a walking stick and a backpack. This photo would appear in an upcoming issue of *Amica*, a monthly women's fashion magazine. All seemed to go well, but I felt a bit reserved. The client apparently didn't want much personality in the shot, and I didn't disappoint.

I changed back into my regular clothes and began packing up the few things I had brought with me. Alessandro joined me, and we sat talking, my telling him how I had only arrived in

Milan and knew nothing about the city yet. As any good Italian would do, he asked me out to dinner. I thought to myself, *Why not? I don't' know anyone here yet, and this is an opportunity to get out and make connections.*

Later that evening, I met Alessandro and another couple in the lobby of my building. The four of us dined at a small, quaint restaurant where white wine flowed along with several different fish dishes. The three of them conversed mostly in Italian, but I didn't mind. I took it all in and felt comfortable in this Italian city, already more comfortable than I had in Paris, even after eight weeks of living there.

After dinner, Alessandro and I took a cab to his new studio, which was still under construction. He showed me one of his many portfolios, and I looked around, marveling at his vast experience. At one point, he moved closer to me and began whispering. Surprised by his actions, I stepped back.

"This is a fast business, Barbara," he cooed in my ear.

Looking at him, my jaw dropped. "I think you should take me back to my residency now."

He continued, "I can do great favors for you, like talk with Jean-Luc with Carin Models in Paris."

I smiled, not wanting to be too dismissive of his offers to help. "I need to go, Alessandro."

Obligingly, he agreed without a further word. Climbing out of the car in the front of my residency, I thanked him again for dinner, then quickly walked to the door, not looking back.

Fortunately for me, the weekend arrived, and I had two full days to rest and acclimate to my new city. I slept in on Saturday, then ventured out in search of a grocery store, finding one about four blocks away. Proud of myself for managing to decipher the packaging of items, I lugged two full bags back to the apartment. The rest of the day I spent straightening up, putting all my clothes and books away and out of sight. My new roommate would be arriving soon. I had no information about her whatsoever, and I only hoped she spoke English.

Emily, tall with short dark hair similar to mine, arrived around noon the next day. She had flown in from New York, represented by the renowned Ford Modeling Agency there. We talked as she unpacked her belongings then went out in search of a restaurant open on a Sunday afternoon. She didn't seem nervous at all about being in a new country. As we walked back to the apartment, a light snow began to fall.

After knowing each other only a few hours, I could tell that Emily didn't seem the model type, and I couldn't quite understand why she came to Milan. Obviously much smarter than most of us, she also seemed much more sure of herself. That is, except as herself as a model. She didn't seem excited about the role. As we talked that evening, eventually she revealed that her father owned a new company called J. Crew which I vaguely knew of as a clothing catalog company. She didn't say much more about it, and I didn't pry. I was happy to have a decent, English-speaking roommate to experience the city with.

When Emily and I awoke the next morning, the entire city lay blanketed in snow. I looked out toward Corso Sempione, to the stillness. Milan seemed to have been ground to a halt overnight. Once downstairs, the concierge called me over and handed me a small package. I raced back upstairs to open it.

EUROPEAN DAZE

A hand-sewn cloth doll with a satchel full of candy fell out of the wrapping. The card read, *With love, from Alessandro*. This surprised me as I thought I might never hear from him again after I dismissed his advances two nights earlier.

Back downstairs, the cab had arrived. I poured myself into it and headed to the studios for *Amica* magazine. They had chosen to work with me again, and I couldn't have been happier about it. The snow, although beautiful, caused delays everywhere and when I arrived at the studio, only the hairstylist had managed to make it there on time. We waited for the others as they slowly straggled in.

Three additional models showed up at various times. The photographer, Nadir, and his assistant Alexandra, readied the lighting while the client from the magazine, Bruno, organized the clothes. Even with the dreary winter sky outside, the light and fun surrounded us all day in the studio. I posed wearing several pairs of earrings and various other pieces of jewelry.

Finding the shirt and jacket for the last photo too small for me, we decided to ditch them, and I wore nothing on the top half of my body. I'm not sure what compelled me to agree to this. I felt so comfortable with this group that it suddenly didn't seem like a big deal. Clasping my hands in front of me, I planted my elbows in front of my breasts. Bracelets and belts were wrapped around my black-gloved wrists, sporting a look of bondage. Yet it was all about showing the accessories—the gloves, the bracelets, and the belts—and we found a rather creative way to do just that.

The snow continued to fall on the city the following day. I had to wait over an hour for my taxi due to the snow blocking the roadways. Once back in the *Amica* studio, the makeup artist went to work. Another model, Linda, with short blond hair and blue eyes, showed up shortly afterward. The two of us would be doing all the photos for the day.

The first photo combined parts of each of us. Linda wore red socks and a pair of tan, flat, closed-toe Divarese sandals and lay stomach down on the studio floor with her knees bent and feet sticking up in the air. Wearing a red cashmere sweater to match Linda's socks, I sat beside her, leaning back in a makeshift backbend, placing the back of my head on the soles of her sandals, like some contortionist twisting and bending her body in abnormal ways, creating an illusion that caught people's eyes as they flipped through the magazine.

For another photo, a pair of shoes was to be the subject, but Nadir wanted to include my face in it somehow. Slipping into a regal, low-cut green silk blouse, the stylist slicked my hair back except for the bangs which she gelled straight up, then saturated my lips with the reddest lipstick in her kit. I held the shoes up in front of my eyes, elbows out, for over an hour so Nadir could get that perfect shot.

With all the photos complete, I rushed to change clothes and gather up my belongings. Everyone wanted to get home before more snow fell and clogged up the streets even further. Linda and I raced out together in search of a cab to share. We couldn't find one anywhere. We walked to the closest bus stop, and, fortunately, Linda already knew how to get around in Milan. Even so, we soon learned that the bus we were waiting for sat stuck about three miles down the road. We decided to wait in a small café nearby, sipping on cappuccinos for almost an hour. We now began to feel stranded and could either laugh or cry about it, so we decided to laugh. With this, we ordered a shot of whiskey each. Not much of a whiskey drinker myself, I drank it down, warming up my insides as much as my outsides.

Linda and I finished downing the shot just in time to see the bus nearing the stop. We raced outside. Climbing aboard with a sigh of relief, we sat back and relaxed. A few minutes later the bus halted, and we were all told to get off. Stunned, we did as we were told and, luckily, another bus sat waiting for us. Finally, we thought we were on our way. Yet it wasn't long until it too came to a sudden halt. Apparently, a tram was stuck across the roadway a short way up from us, and we would have to wait until it could be freed in order for the bus to continue.

Fortunately for us, a small Chinese restaurant flashed its open sign, and we hastily ran inside. A table by the heater waited for us, and a bottle of wine beckoned. We would try to make the best of it, we decided. I filled my belly with a chicken and cashew dish while sipping on the wine Linda knew how to order. The entire time we laughed, not so much from anything funny but maybe from a delirium of sorts. We were both upset by the turn of events. We just wanted to get back to our warm apartments for the night.

After paying our bill, Linda and I slowly made our way back out into the cold. Darkness began its slow descent to end the day. We were still too far north and had no idea how we could get home. So, we just started walking, even though my clothes and boots were completely inadequate for such cold temperatures and deep snow. Our strategy, we thought, would be to reach one of the monuments in the middle of the city, and from there we would have to part ways as we lived in different directions. I didn't have a map with me and berated myself mercilessly for this. I would make sure to always take it with me, every day from now on, no matter what. I hadn't been in Milan long enough to know the slightest way around, much less how to find my way home, on foot, in the dark.

A lone car moved slowly through the snow-laden street, approaching us. Out of its windows, the heads of three Italian guys popped out. Linda could speak a little Italian and told them of our plight. I'm sure her blond hair didn't hurt either. They immediately offered us a ride and, with very few other options available at that moment, we quickly took them up on it. At this point, I had no way to tell them exactly where I lived, so we rode in circles, finally lucking upon my residency. I said a profound and heartfelt *Grazie* to them all and told Linda to call me when she got home so I would know she hadn't been abducted. Already it seemed that the models I met in Milan were of a different sort. We looked out for each other.

Exhausted, I made my way into the building and up to my apartment. By now it was almost 1:00 a.m. It had taken over six hours to get home. Frustrated and tired, I began having negative thoughts about the city, about the business of modeling. This always happened when I had a stressful day. Learning to chill wasn't a skill I had yet attained.

This snowfall turned out to be the worst winter storm to hit Milan in forty years. Word had even reached my hometown in Florida and in a letter I received from my parents they included a news article entitled "Bitter Cold Weather Hits Much of Europe" from the *Daytona Beach News-Journal*. The first paragraph began, "Parts of northern Italy were in a state of emergency Thursday after the heaviest snowfalls in 40 years...." Later, it reported, "Schools and factories were closed in several cities in northern Italy, including Milan, where traffic was brought to a near standstill despite efforts by workmen and soldiers to clear 2 feet of snow...." Yet I didn't have to read about it, I lived right there in the middle of the worst snowstorm in forty years.

The next day brought even heavier snow. I couldn't believe so much snow could fall on one city. No chance of catching any cabs, trams, or buses this day. Emily and I decided to try our luck and walk to the agency. Cold, wet, and tired, we finally arrived.

With my appointments for the day, I headed out alone as Emily had a different schedule. It was time to learn the metro system. I found the station, purchased two tickets at 500 Lire each, and surprisingly found my way to the go-sees easily. By late afternoon, I returned to the agency, proud of my accomplishments of the day. Lorenzo quickly pulled me into a conference room, so no one else might hear, to tell me I had to go on one more appointment—to see the editor-in-chief of *Vogue Italia* (*Italian Vogue*) magazine.

I raced out of the agency and easily found the office not far away, meeting with the editor. She glanced at my book then said thank you. No enthusiasm, no disgust. Just a nod and a *Grazie*. What did that even mean? I would prefer some type of emotion instead of none. I slowly made my way back to the agency, shoulders slumped and head down.

MILAN

Lorenzo tapped me on the shoulder, and I looked up. "She loved you," he said with a sweet, sinister grin.

That night Alessandro picked me up for dinner. If you wonder why I would go out with him again, I honestly cannot tell you. My irritation with him seemed to take a second chair to his beguiling charm. As we ate, we talked about anything and everything, from photography to modeling to politics. I enjoyed the conversation for a change, that is, up until he said something to the effect that he didn't like feeling this way about someone, especially after just meeting. Ever skeptical, I just rolled my eyes.

After dinner, Alessandro and I had plans to do a test photo shoot so he could show my photos to a client of his. Shortly after arriving at his new studio, we discovered that the lighting system wasn't working yet. He shrugged off this new dilemma, but I knew I had been had once again. I asked him to take me back to my apartment, and he obliged, no doubt unsure why his charms weren't working on me. Once back at the residency, he walked me to the door, now locked and requiring my key. As I searched for it in my bag, he leaned in, whispering in my ear, "I love you." I inserted the key in the door, said goodnight, then quickly shut the door behind me.

MILAN

Italy is not for beginners.

--Tim Parks--

For all the poetic language found in books that meander through the wonders and culture of Tuscany, Rome, or Venice, you would be hard-pressed to find one focusing on the beauty or simplicity of Milan. Sitting in the rich industrial north, it stood counter to the romantic notions of an Italy of love, wine, and good food. It instead reminded me of New York City, with its dark greys and browns, and its frantic hustle and bustle pace.

With so much to do during my first week in Milan and the surprise snowstorm, I didn't get a chance to learn my way around the city. I relied mostly on taxis and walking when necessary. Now, however, I needed to know more. I couldn't let myself feel so stranded and lost again as I had during that snowstorm.

As with New York, then Paris, I began to examine the layout of the city more closely, particularly in how it related to me. Milan consists of nine administrative zones, all laid out in a concentric circle with the first administrative zone as the common connector, the center. Each of the other zones angles off the center zone, like petals of a flower, connected but separated. Yet these zones didn't tell as much about the city as the arrondissements in Paris had. Milan seemed bigger, wider, and I struggled to find the logic in its layout and how best to move within it. I needed a landmark.

Sempione Park (Parco Sempione), located in the center of Milan, angles up and out towards the northwest. You enter this ninety-five-acre park at the grand Castello Sforzesco, the Castle that once housed the rulers of Milan as well as where Leonardo da Vinci supposedly lived while working on *The Last Supper*.

From the castle, moving in a northwesterly direction, through the park, you eventually come to its end, at the Arco della Pace, or Arch of Peace. As with the Arc de Triomphe in Paris, this arch was constructed during the time of Napoléon Bonaparte, designed initially as a triumphal arch for his victories. For me, this Arch of Peace would become my own sort of victory, my way home, a landmark signaling that I was near, and in what direction I needed to go in order to arrive at my door. I could orient myself according to the Arch and find my way home. I just had to get to that Arch from wherever I was in the city.

Crafted out of marble, the Arch mesmerized me. Even in passing, one of the carvings or sculptures would ultimately catch my eye and cause me to pause. Three sculptures sit atop the Arch – in the middle, a six-horse-drawn chariot called the Chariot of Peace, and on each side of the Arch, a rider sitting atop a horse. These are referred to as Victories on Horseback. I found the Arch of Peace more beautiful even than the Arc de Triomphe in Paris, although that may be because of its location by a park as opposed to it being in the middle of a busy street.

MILAN

On the other side of the park, just beyond the Arch of Peace, the Corso Sempione, a main thoroughfare, begins and continues in a northwest direction up to the Piazza Firenze, a massive roundabout with avenues branching off to the north, south, east, and west. My street, the via Fratelli Salvioni, or via Salvioni for short, began as a slant off the Corso Sempione, between the Parc Sempione to the southeast and Piazza Firenze to the northwest. Less than a block in on via Salvioni sat my residency. Now, as long as I could find the park, and find the Arch of Peace, I could find Corso Sempione, and then my street, and finally my apartment. This knowledge grounded me in the city and made me feel more secure about my movements within it. It's how I built a foundation for my days ahead.

The closest mode of transportation to my apartment turned out to be a tram stop. The Milan tramway system overall proved to be more efficient in getting around the city than many of the buses or metros. The tram tracks radiated outward from the center of the city, heading in all directions, and I found this to be my favorite way to get around.

Another option was a bus line, which would take me to a metro or close enough to my intended destination. I became familiar with the route of the #61 bus and planned my trips around it whenever possible.

The Milan Metro consisted of only two completed lines at the time—the red (M1) and the green (M2), with two more soon under construction (yellow (M3) and lilac (M4)). As such, the metro would not become my main mode of transportation in the city.

EUROPEAN DAZE

I did my best to write out my routes for the days ahead. Usually, it started with a tram ride to a metro or a bus, or the address itself. I didn't mind the trams at all although they were always crowded and I had to watch closely for my stop and yank on the wire. Many times, I ended up way past my stop and would have to backtrack, usually by walking.

I began to feel confident in my abilities to find my way around the city. And each day I found something of beauty within its heavily business-oriented streets. Perhaps the most spectacular, awe-inspiring scene in all of Milan is the Duomo in the heart of the city. A Gothic behemoth rises above you as you near the piazza; its bristling spires seem to reach towards the heavens. Its light coloring, like the imperfect whites of perfect pearls, stood out against the browns and greys of the city surrounding it. Often, as I stared at it, I realized that the Italian Catholics went to extravagant lengths to be noticed. Growing up Lutheran, then Methodist, with a touch of Primitive Baptist on my mother's side of the family, this showiness seemed rather odd for a religion. Yet I didn't associate it with religion at all. Instead, I saw it fully in terms of historical art and architecture, and its grandness in scale to the world around it.

MILAN

In the days and weeks ahead, I worked consistently and became immersed in the model world of Milan. On a particular day early on, I was once more working for *Amica*. When I arrived at the studio, it bustled with models, makeup artists and hairstylists. The job was for beauty. This meant close-ups, showing makeup or hairstyles. But this would be a little out of the ordinary, somewhat off the scale of real beauty. Each model would be made up to represent different types of animals – fish, zebra, bird, snake, and lynx. My assigned animal would be the chameleon, one of those lizard creatures that can change its skin color to match its surroundings so as not to be seen.

I sat in the makeup chair for over three hours as the artist painted on the makeup, at one point laying a wire grid over part of my face to simulate a lizard's skin. She then painted red under the whites of my eyes. Next, the hairstylist spent about thirty minutes designing a hairstyle to somehow match the makeup. The photographer, Frank Huc, approached. After several seconds, he sat down. He just couldn't relate to the look and tried desperately to wrap his head around it, and how to shoot it. Finally, after staring at me for the longest time, he decided on the lighting and posing required to capture the best look. I thought the shoot would never begin or end once it did start.

With all the consternation and apprehension, when the photo appeared in the magazine a few months later, it looked rather artful and had even been strongly considered for the cover. It seemed a good photographer could sometimes work what equated to a miracle. The creativity and vision of the makeup artist, and the hairstylist to a lesser degree, had also helped turn this challenge into a success. I realized then that we all had important parts to play, and together, sometimes the outcomes could be remarkable.

Another Sunday arrived, and my plans were, once again, with Alessandro. He had been persistent that I have lunch and a serious talk with him, so I gave in. He had a type of charm that felt less threatening and more honest.

Alessandro picked me up at my residency, and, strangely, brought along an American friend. This led me to thinking about my conversation with Emily recently about the white slavery racket we had heard about. Rumors of girls, including Americans, being abducted, and smuggled out of the country to unknown places, rumbled throughout the fashion world. Nervousness shot through me as Alessandro steered the car out onto the Corso Sempione. A short while later, we approached a set of iron gates.

Santa Barbara Military Barracks felt cold and an odd place for a romantic lunch and serious talk. The three of us exited the car and walked through a large door. Soon we found ourselves escorted to a large room to await our host. The commanding officer entered, and we stood. His English wasn't very good, but I felt sure I wasn't meant to understand most of the conversation anyway. After informing me that he and former Secretary of State Henry Kissinger were good friends, we followed him into a smaller room where a table had been set for four. The room felt cold and drafty, reminding me of a cave. I don't even recall what we had for lunch as I felt too distracted by the cold, the white slavery fear, and the lack of conversation in English.

Fortunately, after finishing our lunch, we were heralded down to the Officers Club and sat by a raging fire, sipping on a warm caffè. I continued to smile politely but inside felt extremely annoyed. Alessandro and I hardly even talked at all. Why had I even been invited?

Abruptly, the three men finished their intense conversation, and the commander led us outside for a stroll around the base, passing several tanks and platoons of soldiers along the way. We ventured into the stables to see the horses, a surprise to see on a military base, to say the least. He said I could return anytime to ride them, and I politely thanked him, knowing full well I wouldn't take him up on that offer.

I had no idea what this day was about. I felt like some type of spy, or maybe just a prop for the other man who may have been an actual spy. *Am I supposed to be impressed*, I wondered, *visiting a military base that just so happened to share my name?*

After dropping off the other American, Alessandro and I talked as he drove me back to my apartment. He told me he had a daughter by a model who now lived in Paris. He had been with this model for the past three years and just didn't love her anymore. Now, though, he thought he might be in love with me and wanted to know if I was ready to have children with him. I fell silent, wondering if Italians were always so confusing and surprising and overly dramatic. He decided that I should think about it, and we would talk at a later time.

I immediately relayed all this to Emily back at the apartment. She advised me adamantly to tell him I didn't want to see him anymore. Emily became my confidant, and a voice of reason in the madcap world we found ourselves in. So much more level-headed than anyone else I knew, I decided she was right. For a split second, however, I considered what it might do to my career. Could Alessandro really talk to others and convince them not to work with me? Would I be jeopardizing my career and guaranteeing myself no more work in Milan, or even in Paris? I had to be willing to take that chance.

A short time later, I would have a similar encounter with another photographer, Federico Li Fonti, after working with him on a job for Modasport, a sportswear company. Federico fell into a habit of asking me out to dinner and calling me at odd times of the day or night. Again, my concern that this would affect my career bothered me, but I did my best to smooth over any hiccups, without giving myself away.

A few weeks later, while at a dinner party talking with other models, someone brought up Federico's name. Apparently, they all had had similar experiences working with him. Lorenzo, overhearing our conversation, told us we no longer had to work with this photographer. This, of course, would mean that certain jobs would now be totally off limits for us. We weren't sure if this would turn out to be a good thing or not.

MILAN

A few nights later Federico called again, saying he wanted to take photos of me in a swimsuit to show to a client for an upcoming trip. I decided to be straightforward and honest with him and proceeded to tell him about the rumors and his bad reputation among models. He seemed surprised, either by this news or maybe because of my willingness to tell him about it. For over an hour we talked. As I hung up the phone, I knew it would be the last time I would hear from him, or work with him. And it was.

MILAN

My agency couldn't hide the excitement as I walked into the booking room late one morning. I had been confirmed for four days in Rome, by *Italian Vogue*, for publicity for the Collections. Their contagious excitement shot through me, and I was thrilled, even though I had no idea what the Collections were, and why they were so important.

Trying not to appear too naïve and simple, I asked a few questions, mentioned a few things in conversations with the other models out in the lobby. The Collections, it turned out, were the famous designers' new styles for the autumn/winter season. This publicity event in Rome would showcase those designs in upcoming issues of the magazine.

I was to fly to Rome on a Sunday. Snow fell all night, and I dreaded the thought of my taxi not showing up as arranged. Fortunately, there was no need to worry as the taxi showed up promptly at 8:00 a.m. With no delay, I arrived at Milan's Linate Airport, early. That's when the slide began.

The plane for my flight to Rome had been delayed in London, so I sat at the gate and waited. When the plane still hadn't arrived an hour later, I approached the desk agent, only to be told the flight had been delayed once more. It wouldn't be until a few hours later that the announcement came that my flight to Rome had been canceled completely. The damn snow wreaked havoc all over Europe, and all flights coming and going. It didn't look like anyone was leaving Milan by plane anytime soon.

Just short of panicking, I found a phone to call the agency. Graziana, one of the bookers, thankfully answered, even though it was a Sunday. She told me to get to Milano Stazione Centrale, Milan's main train station, immediately and take the first train I could find to Rome. Without giving much thought to the fact that I didn't know where the train station was, or how to buy a ticket, I grabbed up my bags and hightailed it out to the taxi stand. Fortunately, there were several waiting, and I jumped in the first one in line.

As we drove through the city, I could barely hold back tears. The disappointment and anxiety weighed on me. Once at the station, I climbed out of the taxi in a panic and began looking for a ticket counter. An old man pulling a cart started towards me, offering to help with my bags. As far as I was concerned, he was an angel, sent to help me find the ticket counter and find a train that would take me to Rome.

After purchasing a first-class ticket for 52,200 Lire, the porter led me to an old elevator, which we took down to the trains. He helped me locate the train going to Rome and found a car that had several seats available. I climbed aboard, stored my luggage up top, and snuggled into a seat, hoping for a little time to relax and gather my senses. Before the train even left the station, I must have dozed off. I awoke a short time later with a man standing in front of me. I finally realized he must be the ticket man and handed him my ticket to punch.

MILAN

I sat back and looked around the car and out the windows. It felt surreal to be on a train, barreling south in Italy. Still, I felt on edge. I took out my new book, *The Mosquito Coast* by Paul Theroux, and settled back into my seat. Alternating between reading and listening to tapes on my Walkman, I began to relax. I had handled the transportation situation back in Milan, and now on my way to Rome. I felt proud of myself.

Then, the train stopped. Twenty minutes later I heard someone say, in English, that the engine had broken down and a new one was on its way. In what seemed like an hour but in reality was only fifteen minutes, the new engine arrived, and we were again on our way.

A short time later, the train stopped again, and several people got off. I couldn't read any of the signs and, once again, panic began to creep in. I pantomimed to a guy sitting across from me, and he answered in broken English that we were in Venice. I asked him how much longer to Rome. When he said three hours or more, I almost burst into tears. That meant I would be arriving in Rome around 9:00 p.m., missing the dinner and any chance of relaxing before the busy day on Monday. I suddenly became angry, berating the Italians in my mind. *Why didn't that plane take off? Couldn't Europeans fly in fog and snow?* I began to miss the efficiency of the States.

As I would later learn, I had indeed purchased a ticket for the next train to Rome, but not the most direct route to Rome, or the fastest train. In looking at a map, anyone can see that Venice is out of the way, taking you east before heading south to Rome.

So, there I sat, on a southbound train. I had brought only a few snacks with me since I believed I would be taking a short flight. Taking an inventory, I found I only had two lifesavers left. I had no idea if I could get any food on the train and had no idea where the bathroom might be. It had been an absolutely miserable day with no redemption in sight. I sank further into my seat and sulked.

When the train finally pulled into the Roma Termini train station around 8:30 p.m. I felt exhausted, both physically and emotionally. As soon as I exited the station, a man approached, saying, "Taxi?" Without thinking, I said yes and handed him my bags. The taxi turned out to be an old white car, and the driver charged 25,000 Lire for the trip to the hotel. It was then I realized my mistake. I should have gone outside to the official taxi stand. We had been warned by the agency and by other models not to accept rides with anyone other than the taxi companies. This guy just wanted to make money, and he succeeded. I'm just lucky he didn't sell me into white slavery, or worse, kill me.

Embarrassed, I climbed out of the clunker of a car in front of the impressive Savoy Hotel on the Via Ludovisi. A wave of relief poured over me as I entered its doors. At the check-in desk, I learned I would be rooming with Karolina, a red-headed German model who lived in the same residency back in Milan. Leaving my passport at the hotel desk, as required by Italian law, I took my bags up to the room and freshened up the best I could. As I returned to the desk to pick up my passport, I ran into Lorenzo, from my Milan agency. He was on his way out to dinner with five other models, so we spoke for only a few minutes. I returned to my room for a nice shower and room service. It had been a long, challenging day and I, in all honesty, had never felt so alone.

Around 3:00 a.m. there came a slight knock on the door, loud enough to wake me. My roommate Karolina apparently didn't have a key. I let her in, and we talked for a few minutes. She had gone out to dinner with Lorenzo, and they had dined with the Fords (Eileen Ford and her son Billy, from Ford Modeling Agency in New York), and with John Casablanca (of Elite Modeling Agency also based in New York). After that, she went out with actor Matt Dillon who had also been at dinner.

Although I felt a quick pang of envy that I didn't get to meet Matt Dillon, it quickly passed. I had never been in awe of celebrities, with the exception of a major crush on Leif Garrett back in my pre-teen days. They are just like any of us. This is what I realized back during that spring break when I met the bands playing in Daytona Beach. They are people, not gods to be put up on pedestals. Still, it would have been fun to see what Matt Dillon was really like in person.

The next day arrived before I felt ready. I had to talk myself into being confident for the day and not crawl back in bed and hide. I forced myself to go downstairs with Karolina for breakfast instead of ordering room service. The lobby and restaurant were full of models, agents, and all others involved in the fashion industry. The place buzzed with excited energy. Eventually, I met up with three other models, and we walked to the Hotel De La Ville, about five minutes away from the Savoy. Checking in there, I learned I would be working with *Italian Vogue* photographer Gordon Monroe. I raced outside to catch a cab to his studio. When I arrived, two other models were already there, getting their hair and makeup done. Two more models showed up shortly after I did, for a total of five for the shoot. I sipped cappuccinos while awaiting my turn in the makeup chair, and enjoyed a conversation with Bonnie, a model from Canada, and Sylvia, a model from Belgium. I knew nothing about Belgium. I even wondered if I could find it on a map.

As Bonnie and I continued to talk, we both noticed that the magazine editor at the shoot kept staring at us. We felt like she didn't like us for some reason. We attempted to avoid her eyes and just go on with our conversation, but her stare unnerved us.

Shortly after having my hair and makeup completed, all activities stopped for lunch. As I finished eating and downing my last drop of wine, the magazine editor pulled me aside and informed me that the photographer had decided to use all blondes. She had already called Lorenzo with my agency to let him know. So, after spending six hours there, I had nothing to show for it. One other model had dark hair, and they sent her away as well. They had to re-shoot the one shot she had been in prior to lunch. I felt dejected at first but determined to make the best of my time in Rome, no matter what. It's as if you know you have to pick yourself up, out of disappointment, and keep moving forward.

I returned to my hotel room and ordered a lite meal before taking a long, hot bath. I did manage to pick up a USA Today downstairs and enjoyed catching up on what was going on in the world beyond fashion. Lorenzo called and invited me to join a group going out to a restaurant around 9:15 p.m. I decided it to be in my best interests to go and be seen, so I quickly got ready and headed downstairs. Like I said, just keep moving forward.

Lorenzo and I walked a few blocks away to a nice restaurant, where we joined Danielle and Billy Ford from New York, Sasha from an agency in London, Giorgio, part-owner of Fashion Agency in Milan, and five other models. We sat at two tables. I managed to order a meal with rice and mushrooms, followed by veal with spinach. The food didn't seem all that good as many at the two tables kept sending theirs back. Yet they did so in a highly snobbish manner. I preferred the nicer approach. Afterward, we topped dinner off with a delicious gelato containing chocolate and nuts. No one sent this back.

It became a late night for all of us. I stayed and did my best to be energetic and fit in, but I had felt uncomfortable with this group from the start, and that didn't change all night. The Fords didn't even look my way, much less talk with me. They seemed uptight, snobbish, too self-important. With that being said, however, you couldn't help but appreciate the role Billy's mom, Eileen Ford, played in the lives of the models she represented. I had heard that she acted rather motherly, mentoring her models, and keeping them away from the seedy side of modeling. She seemed the complete opposite of Kay Mitchell, head of my agency, Legends.

Although Kay didn't force any of us to do anything, she also didn't advise us or mentor us in any way. Either we had it or not. Either we chose to have sex with photographers and playboys or not. Our lifestyles did not seem to concern her. Or at least, mine didn't. As it was, I felt like I had to wing it on my own, with no advice, no guidance. Just a moral compass, wavering at times, to a simplicity of thought which didn't always serve me well.

Day two of my Rome adventure wouldn't start until mid-afternoon, in a shoot with a photographer named Capra. There were three of us models: Meredith, Vicky, and myself. Five sets of easy, casual photos. A much better day than the day before. No glitches, no staring from the magazine editor, no wasted hours. Relieved, by the time I left the studio, I felt confident and happy again. As I walked the streets back near the hotel, I made a quick detour to sneak in a few sightseeing moments, making my way to the famed Trevi Fountain. Times like these required you to step off the treadmill, and out of your head, and see something of beauty.

The Trevi Fountain gleamed in the little sunlight that found its way through the clouds. With the sea reef made from travertine (a type of limestone) and the sculptures made of marble, I found it breathtaking. The center of the fountain held the sculpture of Neptune, his chariot being pulled by two sea horses, which in turn were being led by two Tritons. The ornate detail of every inch of the fountain captivated, and I could easily have sat there for hours.

Back at the hotel, I found Karolina wouldn't return until well after 9:00 p.m. We had agreed to wait for each other for dinner. With it being so late, we decided to stay in and order room service, going all out this time. I ordered the chicken salad, followed by fettuccine and beef stroganoff, with an Aqua Minerale to wash it all down. Karolina, appearing exhausted, confessed she might be pregnant and had stopped at the drugstore to buy a pregnancy test on her way back to the hotel. We sat and talked, just being friends, and temporarily forgetting the world of an International Fashion Model. Two young women talking about normal things.

Day three in Rome would descend into chaos rather quickly. Arriving at the *Vogue* studio around 9:00 a.m., I plopped into the makeup chair first. After a few shots, the editor told one of the models she could leave as they weren't going to use her after all. Admittedly, this made me feel a little better about my first day here, being sent away by a different editor. Before we could continue with the shoot, however, they decided they wanted our makeup and hair changed. The makeup artist had left temporarily to work on a cover shoot at another studio, so we had to wait.

Once the makeup artist returned, I quickly washed my face so she could begin again. It didn't take her long, and I stood up, ready to shoot the next photo. Suddenly, everyone stopped. Again, this was how most of our days went. When it was time for lunch, everyone and everything halted—and not always at the best of times. To my way of thinking, we could at least have finished the set, then had lunch. Silly me.

While we settled in to enjoy the food spread across the table, it seemed all hell suddenly broke loose. With hands gesticulating rapidly, and voice inflections all over the place, we could tell something had happened. We munched on our paninis and drank our wine as we watched the drama unfold. Finally, we were told that the fashion designer didn't like the photographer's style, especially the floor of the studio. All photos taken in the last two days were for nothing. All would be tossed out.

I changed back into my own clothes and prepared to leave, realizing that after three days in Rome, I would not have even one photo in *Italian Vogue* to show for it. Before we could get to the door, however, the magazine editor stopped us, saying we had to stay because another client was coming. So, we settled back in to wait some more, all of us chain smoking until every pack was empty. I had started smoking a few cigarettes a day after graduating from high school. I just thought it looked cool and wanted to give it a try. Once in Europe however, surrounded by smokers, it felt normal. Then the waiting and waiting for photo shoots had led to a chain-smoking habit as a way to combat the boredom.

As we continued to wait, I felt perturbed because I had plans to go sightseeing around Rome with a friend, another model named Vicky who I had worked with the day before. So much for having any fun while in Rome. Finally, a different hairstylist arrived and immediately went to work on us, changing our look dramatically, from stylish nymph to aristocratic grown-up. When the clothes finally arrived, we poured ourselves into them lackadaisically and didn't even try to act interested. It was more of a let's-get-this-over-with type of shoot, for all of us including the photographer.

The clothes had been designed by Clara Centinaro, referred to as one of the pioneers of Italian fashion. Her designs were more sophisticated and noble looking as compared to the quirky haute couture of the previous designer's masterpieces for the new season. Both photos would include two of us models, wearing dresses and dress ensembles which complemented each other. Up until this point, my look had been one of a young girl. Now I appeared as a mature wife, perhaps, of a foreign dignitary.

For all the disappointments on this trip, I could now at least say that I might have two photos in *Italian Vogue* to show for this fiasco of a few days. Trudging back to the hotel, I made my way to my room and shut the door solidly behind me. I ordered room service again and went to bed early, feeling as if this had been a wasted trip. I had learned a lot about the model world and the fashion industry itself, and I can't say I liked any of it.

I awoke on the final day, relieved to be leaving Rome, or rather, leaving the famous magazine and all its chaos. Doggedly determined to see something of the city, with only a few hours free before my flight, I hurriedly got ready and raced out into the gloomy overcast morning. I would at least get to see one of the most incredible sites in the Ancient Center of Rome before leaving.

As it came into sight, I leaned forward in my seat. The Colosseum loomed large, a massive site leaving me speechless. Absentmindedly I paid the cab fare and stepped out. As I walked towards the entrance, I managed to catch a tour, which was just beginning and followed the guide inside. As we entered the arena, I somehow felt the excitement of the spectators, the strength of the gladiators, the chill of death, and the relief of victory all at once.

The tour guide led us through the underground passageways now missing their ceilings, which had been the wooden floor of the Colosseum, covered in sand to soak up the blood of the fighting. The guide, regaling scenes of past lives, showed us where animals most likely were held before being let loose in the arena to take on a gladiator. These may have included bears, lions, tigers, rhinos, elephants, crocodiles, and even giraffes. A surprised guffaw escaped my lips as I thought of a giraffe and a gladiator, fighting to the death. And to think, some fashion designer worried about the floor of a photographer's studio.

Racing back to the hotel, I grabbed my bags from the room and jumped in the taxi waiting outside, all the while praying that my flight back to Milan would be on time and would actually get off the ground. The weather in southern Italy remained calm, although overcast and wintery. Fortunately, there were no delays, and I climbed aboard my scheduled flight at the scheduled time. Once off the ground, I felt relieved. I would put this whole trip behind me and move forward as soon as I landed back in Milan.

Arriving at my apartment, I lugged my bags to the elevator. As I reached the door to the apartment, it jerked open. Emily raced out, saying a quick hello and goodbye before disappearing into the elevator. She was on her way to an overnight catalog shoot in Venice.

Spending the rest of the day in reflection, I realized I should have paid more attention to the travel plans to Rome, asking questions beforehand. I seemed to have this bad habit of just showing up and trusting that all would work out. I also failed to follow my own advice, my own practice of looking at a map to see where I am going and how it is to get there. My attempts at planning were scattered at most. I needed to be more consistent.

I also thought about the networking opportunities presented in Rome, and how I had dreaded most of them. I needed to find a way to enjoy these more. Not necessarily to kiss ass but to enjoy meeting people, and, in reality, selling myself. And above all, believing in myself regardless of what others thought.

Finally, feeling a bit rundown, I began to understand the importance of taking care of myself by eating well, exercising and, most of all, relaxing. I had to find ways to deal with the stress if I wanted to continue this lifestyle.

MILAN

February arrived, and work continued to come my way. For my first job of the new month, I found myself working for *Anna*, formerly known as *Anna Bella* magazine. As the makeup artist worked on my transformation, the editor-in-chief of the magazine walked up and asked me to try on a two-piece bathing suit. She wanted to see if I would be a good fit for a big shoot coming up, a ten-day trip to an island off the coast of South Africa. I happily obliged, changing into the swimsuit and modeling it for her. She nodded as she walked around me. Yes, she said, I would go to the island of Mauritius for ten days. Never mind that I had no clue where in the world Mauritius was.

The next day, a Saturday, I again worked for *Anna*. I made my way to Showroom Pelligrini for another full day of photos. At midday we took a lunch break and walked to a quaint restaurant nearby, each devouring our own pizza. I felt stuffed by the time we returned to the studio to finish up. I enjoyed these days and enjoyed working with the editors of this magazine.

A few days later I worked for *Anna* yet again. Taking the tram to the Conciliazione metro stop, I then took the #1 (Red) line one stop to Cadorna, then the #2 (Green) line, heading northeast for about thirteen stops, to Cascina Gobba. From there I walked to the studio on Via Rizzoli. I finally knew how to effortlessly get around in Milan.

Once at the studio I learned that two photo shoots were happening simultaneously—one for beauty and one for fashion. I joined the fashion group, and the photographer turned out to be Mario Nadori, the same photographer I would be going to the island of Mauritius with. Working with him before the trip would help me get to know him and his style and personality, making it easier once I was on the island.

Fortunately, I would work with the magazine again the following day, and many of my days while in Milan. We—*Anna* magazine and I—as it turned out, were a good fit for each other.

Yet magazines weren't my only clients while in Milan. Waking extra early one Monday morning, I already knew it would be a long day. Before 7:00 a.m. I left the apartment and walked around the corner to the Safety Apartments to meet Cissy, a long blond-haired model also from the States. We were both working in Brescia, a town due east of Milan, for the day. We jumped on the tram to Cadorna, hopping off to catch the metro to Milan Centrale. Once at the train station, we quickly located the train to Brescia and climbed aboard. The trip took about one and a half hours, so we dozed off, almost missing our stop. We probably would have ended up in Verona, or worse, Venice, if we hadn't awakened in time.

The town of Brescia sat at the foot of the Alps between Milan and Verona. From what little I was able to see of the town, it seemed more quaint and sunny in personality than Milan. The photographer and the client waited patiently at the train station for all of us to arrive. The male model for the shoot, a Brit named Jon Pierson, arrived shortly after us, along with another model and the makeup artist for the day. Jon and I climbed in the photographer's car, at his suggestion, and the others took a taxi. On the ride, we were told not to talk about how much we were getting paid for the job. Apparently, I was making 900,000 Lire and Jon 1,000,000 Lire. The rest were making only 500,000 Lire for the day.

Instead of a studio, we pulled up in front of a large hair salon. The job would be for an advertisement for the salon itself. After having my makeup done, the client asked if I would let them put highlights in my hair. Why not, I thought, all the while thinking it would be blond highlights spliced into my dark brown hair. It turns out the highlights were candy-apple red instead.

After completing several doubles, triples, and a few photos combining all four of us, we made our way to the client's house for dinner, an unusual treat which never happened in Milan. Steaks and sausages were cooked over a fire in the fireplace and complemented with fried potatoes. We followed this up by gathering in an upstairs room to watch a video. During the day, we had been videotaped, showing us at our best, and possibly at our worst. We laughed and joked as we watched, titling it "The Day in the Life of a Model."

It soon became a race to make the midnight train back to Milan. As we entered the station, a tall, pudgy police officer pulled Jon aside and began interrogating him. What was he doing in Brescia? Where was his passport? Eventually, three more cops showed up. They searched his bag and attempted to look threatening. I couldn't figure out what the problem might be and stood back. None of us had our model portfolios with us, so we didn't have to worry about being asked for work permits or anything of that nature. We had heard of similar instances happening whenever a foreign man traveled with several women in Italy. It seemed they got a cheap thrill out of it. Finally, they let him go, and we climbed aboard the train, settling in for the ride back to Milan.

The next morning, panicking about the candy-apple red highlights, I washed my hair three times. Still, the red remained. I headed into the agency, expecting to be scolded like a disobedient schoolgirl. Surprisingly, they liked it as well yet we all agreed that I should have it dyed back to my natural color for my trip to Mauritius. We didn't want to upset the client, *Anna* magazine, in any way. Gratzianna called ahead to the Bataguia Salon, and I made my way there. Once in the chair, however, I asked them to leave in a few of the highlights. This was the first decision, albeit small, I had been brave enough to make for myself since arriving in Europe, including back in Paris.

Speaking of Paris, I tried calling Kristen and Ava a few times at the apartment on rue Poncelet but never could reach them. In mid-February, I ran into a model by the name of Sarah at a go-see for *Gioga* magazine. I introduced myself, and she stopped short, asking if I was the Barbara that had lived with Kristen and Ava in Paris. I excitedly said yes. Sarah had lived with them also, at rue Poncelet for a short time and they had mentioned me often. She said they were doing well. I missed them. Kristen and I would eventually talk a few weeks later when she was in Milan working. There wasn't time to get together, but we did talk for over two hours on the phone late one night. I hoped we would all run into each other again someday.

While in Fashion Agency on another day, I met yet again with Jean-Luc from Carin's Model Agency in Paris. He is the one who told my New York agency, Legends, that I should be working every day in Paris. Per Kay and Lawrine, he was to call me while still there but never did. Now here in Milan, he said he looked forward to working with me back in Paris as soon as Lorenzo gave the okay. I didn't understand that statement, nor the relationship. Was I now the property of Lorenzo, and Fashion Agency? Was Legends in New York no longer calling the shots as far as I was concerned?

These thoughts were quickly put to rest with the arrival of the owner of Legends, Kay Mitchell, in Milan. After a long, full day of go-sees, Lorenzo picked me up in the evening and shuttled me to the Principia & Savio Hotel to have dinner with Kay. The following evening, I returned to Kay's hotel with Tresse, another Legends Model who lived around the corner from me on Corso Sempione. Cissy, who I worked with in Brescia, was also there. Kay, Cissy, Tresse and I talked for a long time. I liked Kay but we never connected the same way as Lawrine and I did. Truthfully, I don't believe Kay and I ever really hit it off back in New York. A hard one to read, she seemed to keep me at arm's length. After Milan, she headed over to Paris to see Ava and Kristen. I asked her to tell them hi for me.

As it turns out, a few days later I would find out that Kay referred to me as "being off in my own little world." That didn't settle with me too well. I wondered if it had anything to do with my statement back in New York, after my first photo shoot. When asked how I could move so well in front of the camera, I had responded that I just put myself somewhere else in my mind. Was that now translated into putting myself in "my own little world?" Was it a negative comment, or just an off-the-hand remark? Eventually, I shrugged it off, feeling distant from my New York agency and drawing closer to my Milan agency.

Photo shoot in Brescia with models Jon and Cissy. Cissy and I would work together, or run into each other, in every country going forward, including Tunisia.

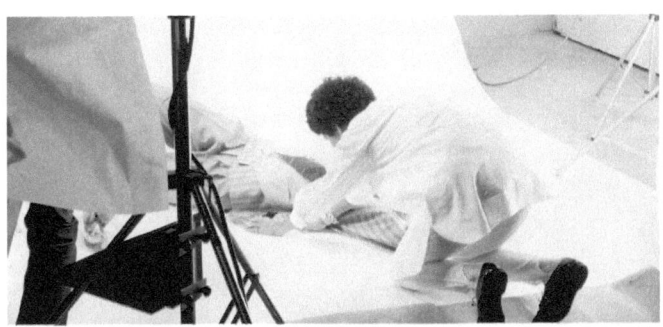

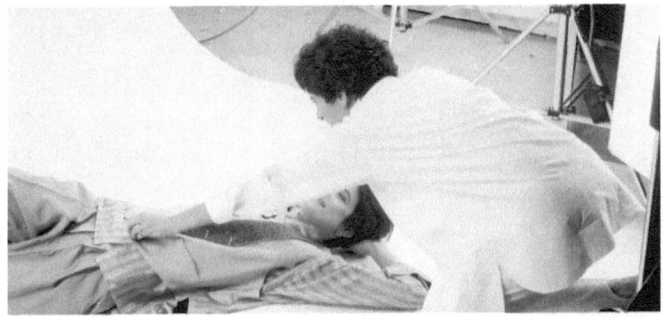

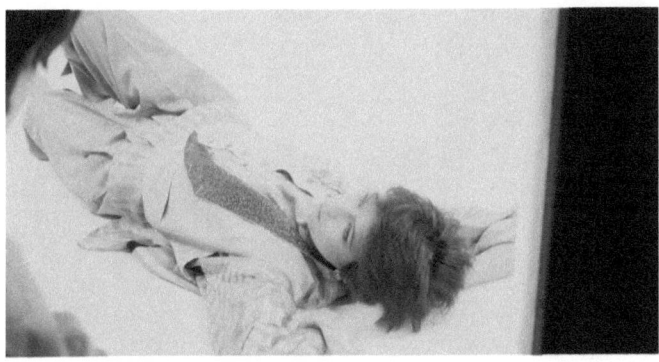

Photo shoot for *Anna* magazine. The editor adjusting the clothing is Cristina Milanesi, who also hired me for a shoot on location in Mauritius, an island off the coast of South Africa.

MILAN

As I entered the lobby at Linate Airport, I instantly recognized Franco, the hairstylist traveling with us to Mauritius. With a *ciao bella*—hello beautiful—and a kiss on each cheek, we plopped down into the café seats, ordering up cappuccinos while waiting to meet the others. The photographer, Mario Nadori and his assistant Bruno arrived first, followed by Cristina Milanesi, the editor for *Anna* magazine. The other model, a sandy-blond, with hair sitting at the top of her shoulders, bounced up to the group. Allison wasn't new to this crew. It seemed they had all worked together before. She also came from Florida and, only eighteen years old, had spent her senior year of high school on the road with an occasional tutor, foregoing the high school experience to begin her modeling career.

By mid-afternoon we were ensconced on an Air Alitalia flight, flying to Frankfurt, Germany, and by midnight, we had boarded a Lufthansa flight on its way to Africa. The next thing I remember the flight attendants clanged down the aisle serving breakfast. We had been flying all night.

After a quick refueling stop in Saudi Arabia, we were off again, making one last stop, in Africa somewhere, to change the crew. For over an hour we sat on the tarmac, sweating, waiting for our new pilot and co-pilot, and cabin crew, for the final leg of the journey.

Four more hours of flying time, and we approached our final destination. Thick fog and clouds shielded the island from view. As the pilots circled the island, we were told to brace ourselves, with our heads down on the pillows on our laps. The plane bumped hard against the ground, bouncing up again before settling into its run and eventual stop. I had never been so glad to get off an airplane in all my life.

It took time to collect all our luggage and the photographer's cameras and accessories, as well as the trunks of clothes we would be modeling. By the time we reached our hotel, the Resort Trou-aux-Biches, we were all beat. Allison and I headed straight to our villa, skipping dinner. As the rain beat down during the dark night, it felt like we were out in the middle of nowhere.

The next morning, we all slept in. Spending the day recovering from the over fifteen-hour travel time had been built into our schedule. The lagoon with its sandy beach sat in the back of the resort and upon seeing it for the first time I felt underwhelmed, finding it rather unimpressive. Maybe because of the cloudy day, or because I had spent the last several years living just a few blocks from the beautiful beach in Florida.

With overcast skies looming overhead, Allison and I spread our towels on the sand. Soon Franco and Cristina joined us. Both Allison and Christina whipped off their bathing suit tops and lay out topless. I had never done this before and struggled momentarily whether to act like it was a normal thing for me. Reluctantly, to fit in and not seem like a prude, I removed my top as well. Besides, I reasoned, I couldn't have tan lines because this job required me to model several different types of bathing suits. Cristina, being Italian, had no qualms about this whatsoever as she freely walked up and down the beach, still topless. I drew the line at that. No topless walking down the beach or anywhere else.

Rain began to fall, and we returned to the resort, joining Franco in the verandah restaurant, overlooking the ocean, for lunch. As it rained most of the day, we all did our own thing. I stayed in and read my book. I had recently discovered the author Robert Ludlum and his book *The Bourne Identity*. When the sun finally came out later in the day, I wandered around the resort, stunned by its actual beauty. It consisted of several small villas spread throughout a lush tropical garden. You could easily get lost trying to find your own villa as most looked alike.

In the evening, as the photographer whisked us off to dinner at a seafood restaurant outside the resort, I marveled at their tales of previous trips to Mauritius. The thought of the expense of such trips, dozens of times a year, dazed me. Traveling all the way to Mauritius, an island nation in the Indian Ocean, for a photo shoot? Wasn't that a bit extravagant?

The rain continued to fall the following day delaying the photo shoot. We all met for dinner then headed to the outdoor theater for a show. Little did we know we were to be the show. The Miss Trou-aux-Biches Playmate Contest pitted four contestants, including Allison and myself, against each other for the coveted title. There were five events to be judged: bathing suit, sarong, questions/answers, talent (reading a poem), and, finally, a ballet to be performed by each contestant. It proved incredibly embarrassing for me, but I shouldered through, winning runner-up to Allison, losing out on the coveted crown by one point.

On the third day on the island, the weather cleared, and we began working. Franco didn't like the way we did our own makeup, so he became not only the hairstylist on the trip but also the makeup artist. I definitely didn't mind. My first shot put me in a yellow one-piece bathing suit. After several attempts, the light still wasn't right. At 4:00 p.m. we headed down to the public beach to shoot a set of blue and green clothes instead.

By the end of the day, Allison and I realized our mistake. We hadn't worn enough sunscreen protection from the sun on this side of the equator. Two days' worth of sunburn put two Florida gals to shame. The pain became too much, and we headed straight to the infirmary after the shoot. With a medicated gel to soothe our shoulders, we finally felt relief, although it would be a challenge to wear clothes for the photos in the days ahead.

A routine schedule began to develop. It seemed the light on the island was perfect early in the morning and again late in the afternoon, so that is when we did most of our photos. In between, I sat out by the pool, reading or writing out postcards, then swimming and sitting at the pool bar. I also took long walks on the beach with one of the others or by myself. After shooting in the mid to late afternoon, we met up for dinner, followed by a few of us attending the resort show or just going our separate ways.

On one particular day of shooting, Allison and I spent several hours running up and down the beach, leaping into the air in our bathing suits for action photos for the magazine. I wore a one-piece tropical flora swimsuit while trailing a sheer sarong above my head as I leaped across the sand, over and over again. With each leap the swimsuit slipped lower and lower down my long torso, barely covering my breasts. My long legs, spread wide, in an attempt to appear like a ballerina, accomplished not quite the look of a split in mid-air but close enough. After the sixth leap, I gasped, my face contorting, my mouth locking down into a stern determined look, instead of that casual look of leaping joy. I only hoped that I didn't look constipated in at least one of the photos.

For another photo, this time wearing a green and yellow floral one-piece swimsuit, I made vertical jumps, straight up in the air, with a white sarong waving behind me like a pair of wings. I did this until I thought either my arms or legs would fall off, or my lungs would explode.

A location we found perfect for photos in the afternoons turned out to be a small house on the coast. Various sized rocks poked out of the water near the shore, and we waded out, standing on them while the photographer snapped away. I felt the smaller rocks slice into my bare feet each time I returned to shore. Although I always walked barefoot in Florida, the skin on my feet was baby soft, and apparently paper thin.

In the first photo one afternoon, I waded out to the biggest rock, which would be covered at high tide, and climbed on top. I wore a black, one-piece swimsuit with fringes hanging off in layers. With my hair spiked up all over my head, sunglasses on, the reddest lipstick on my lips, and a red flower tucked in the top at the last minute, I attempted to get my footing just right.

EUROPEAN DAZE

Once steady, the photographer's assistant, Bruno, waded out to hand me a lit cigarette to use as a prop.

For the next photo, I wore only a black bathing suit bottom, the full type that cuts up on each side. Adding a costume jewelry bracelet and earrings, I returned to my rock, trying my best not to flash everyone there, although I had laid out on the beach topless around most of them already. Once on the rock, I crossed my arms over my breasts, in a loose self-hug. I turned and raised my face slightly toward the sun, then closed my eyes.

Stumbling my way back across the rocks while trying to cover my half-naked self, I made my way to the house. The tide began to come in, and soon our rock would disappear beneath the salty water. I quickly changed into a one-piece swimsuit with a comic design of an old-fashioned pose of a man leaning in to kiss a woman. For fun, the photographer snapped a Polaroid of the owner of the house and placed it in the lowcut front of the swimsuit. Back out on my rock, I placed my hands on my thighs, leaned forward, closed my eyes, and puckered my red lips, as if reaching out, and waiting expectantly, for my own lover's kiss.

Rising not too early, showering, and throwing on a pair of shorts and a tank top to head to a delicious breakfast became my way of starting each of the following days. No makeup, no hairstyle, just me in all my naturalness. It felt wonderful. Sometimes after breakfast, I might have to do one or two photos, including a cover-try, but then I had several hours off to do as I pleased. In the afternoon, usually around 3:00 p.m., we would head out to a destination to shoot.

MILAN

One of these shoots took us into the nearby town where we shot photos for a spread containing only madras clothing. The garments, made of lightweight cotton, with a plaid design, contained an easy island flow to them. I posed in a long orange skirt and two blouses in front of a white iron bed in one of the small houses nearby. In another photo, I sat on a bench, fanning myself while two children from town sat by me, looking at the camera. Still, in another, an elderly woman sat beside me, spectacles sitting on her nose as well as on mine.

A few afternoons were reserved for beauty, for shots for the cover of the magazine. This required different makeup and hair and special lighting. Allison and I both shot with the same outfits, including a green striped tank top with a sweater, and another with a one-piece red swimsuit. Hopefully one of us would make the cover.

Toward the end of the trip, several of us decided to attend the show at the resort after dinner one night. Allison and I had had quite a few drinks and felt pretty high. I excused myself to go to the restroom and once in there, the door to my stall became stuck. Feeling trapped, I pulled and pulled, but it wouldn't open. Finally, I leaned down to look at the lock, and as I did, I yanked with all my might. It opened alright, and smacked me hard, right above my left eye. I shrugged it off and returned to the gathering at the bar which now included a large group of men from South Africa who were in Mauritius on a fishing vacation.

With ravenous mosquitos blanketing the island. I awoke in the middle of the night feeling as if I were being eaten alive. That's when I knew something was wrong with my eye. I reached up, slightly touching it. Swollen and sore, I gasped. *What have I done to myself now?* Apparently, the restroom stall door had hit me harder than I thought. And it didn't just hit my forehead but my eye as well. Mortified, I made my way to breakfast a few hours later, asking the kitchen staff for an ice pack to place on it. The photographer and editor arrived, looked at it but shrugged it off. Maybe it didn't look as bad as I thought. They said I could just wear sunglasses for the day's shoot, or we would just shoot from the other side for a profile shot. I guess cover shots were out of the question now.

Our group climbed in a hired van for the day and headed up to the top of a mountain. When we arrived, we found ourselves surrounded by curvy mounds of what looked like clay that seemed to change color in the scant sunlight. The location sat in the southwestern part of the island, referred to as the Chamarel plain, or Seven Colored Earths. The clay dunes, the photographer revealed, show up in at least seven different colors, including red, brown, violet, green, blue, purple, and yellow.

Muddy in spots, with the vampire mosquitos out in full force, we set up for the shoot. The swelling of my eye had fortunately begun to decrease after applying a cream provided by Franco. As I had now learned, not only does a model have to be in shape to run around and leap for the camera, she also has to be careful and not do anything stupid, like forcing a jammed door open near her face. I was learning a lot on this trip.

As if to match the surrounding clay-like dunes, we dressed in bright orange and yellow clothes—stretchy leggings, loose flowing dresses, and knit shorts and tank tops. The heat and humidity were almost unbearable, and with sweat pouring down, the mosquito squads attacked. I did my best to hold the poses as long as needed, but all I wanted to do was run away, screaming, before diving into the van and covering myself with a blanket.

On what was to be our last full day on the island, I sat reminiscing about the previous nine days. My thoughts floated from those first few hours when I timidly sheltered myself in my villa, not wanting to venture out to explore, to the full days of sun, fun, and exploration around the island. This last day had been reserved for any needed reshoots. We only had four.

In the evening, we celebrated with a nice group dinner and drinks at the resort, followed by attending the resort show, a Mr. Trou-aux-Biches Playboy Contest. Allison and I served as two of the judges. Afterward, champagne once again flowed. I took a long walk on the beach before turning in. I had truly enjoyed myself on this job, with this group, on this island. It would be a trip to remember.

Morning arrived and, after packing up my things, I ventured out to the resort store to buy a few T-shirts and gifts for my family. Our local travel agent raced up to me. Our flight out of Mauritius had been delayed. The plane, an Air France flight, remained stuck in Lyon, France. It had been hijacked.

With an unexpected extra day on the island, I lay out on the beach, wrote more postcards, swam, went on the glass bottom boat ride, and relaxed. Although enjoying myself, I began to think about how nice it would be to have someone to share the experience with. Someone special. I never needed a boyfriend before, but now it seemed my feelings were shifting.

EUROPEAN DAZE

The next morning, we flew first to Madagascar, then boarded an Air France flight to Nairobi, Kenya, then on to Paris, where we spent the night. Once back in Milan, I headed to my little apartment on Via Salvioni. On the dining table, along with a box of chocolates, I found a note. My roommate Emily had gone back to New York. She had been too bored with the model lifestyle to stay any longer. I would definitely miss her and her intelligent voice of reason. It wasn't totally unexpected though. I could always tell she was meant for more.

The photos taken while in Mauritius would not appear in just one issue of *Anna* magazine. Instead, different sets would be spread across three issues. That had been the reason for the different types of clothes and swimsuits, and the various locations on the island. I would have to wait two months or more to see which photos made it into the magazine.

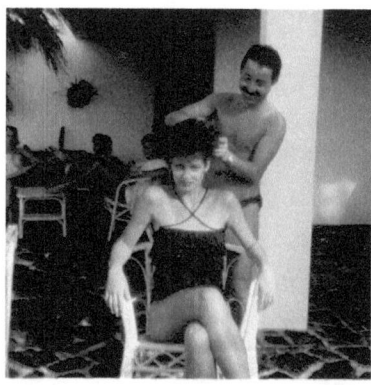

Franco, the hair and makeup artist for our photo shoot in Mauritius, styles my hair for a bathing suit shot.

MILAN

It was now early March, and I had been in Europe for two months straight. In the days ahead, I remained busy, working for *Anna* and *Donna Piu* magazines. My new roommate, Hetty, arrived, hailing from Austria, and carrying a dual United States-Austrian citizenship due to her parents' differing nationalities. Hetty had recently returned to Europe from Japan where she earned a large sum of money to carry her for a while. Before we had a chance to get to know each other, and only a week after returning from my trip to Mauritius, I found myself again heading to Rome for a job, this time for only one night.

I arrived early at Linate Airport and sipped on a cappuccino while reading my book. As I minded my own business, an airport guard came by with his dog who stopped at my bag momentarily and sniffed. I didn't worry as I had observed this several times that morning.

As the time for my flight grew closer, I headed to the gate. From out of nowhere, the same guard from earlier, now without his canine companion, stepped in front of me. He spoke rapidly in Italian, and when he discovered I only spoke English, he ordered me to hand over my passport. I pulled it from my side pocket and handed it to him. Without even glancing at it, he turned and walked away. Initially stunned,

I raced after him, hurriedly catching up. He escorted me into a small room off the baggage claim where I waited until an English-speaking guard arrived.

"Do you smoke?' he asked accusingly.

"Yes," I responded while pulling out my pack of cigarettes from my purse.

"No," he shook his head vehemently. "You know what I mean!"

Finally, it dawned on me that he was talking about something other than tobacco. I shook my head and pointed to the cigarettes. He said something in Italian and then grabbed my carry-on bag and started going through it. All he found were cookies.

I looked up at the guard, grinning. "Your dog must be hungry if that's what he sniffed." The guard didn't reply.

Another woman sat in a room across the hall with the door open. I heard a man talking to her but couldn't see him. Suddenly, she stood up, whisking off her long, white fur coat. As she did so, I caught a whiff. No doubt about it, this mysterious woman had smoked more than a cigarette. Maybe I had been standing near her and the scent drifted across to my clothes or bags.

The woman began yelling louder and louder, then suddenly started removing her clothes. All of them. At this point, the guard handed back my passport and motioned toward the door. I gladly raced out.

My flight arrived in Rome on time, and I took a taxi to the Savoy Hotel, the same hotel I had stayed at back in January. With it being late, I stayed in and ordered room service. The

MILAN

next morning, I made my way to Alberta Tiburzi's studio. Tiburzi had been a model herself back in the 1960s and had transitioned into a fashion photographer in the 1970s. I looked forward to working with her. Most of the photographers I knew and had worked with up until this point had been men.

The shoot turned out to be for elegant wedding gowns and would appear in *Italian Vogue*. The makeup artist and the hairstylist took turns working on me, both focused intently on my transformation. Tiburzi wanted everything to be perfect, the lighting in particular.

I modeled three extravagant wedding gowns, full of fluff and layers. For one I held a violin in front; for another I stretched out on a wooden chaise, my shoulder painfully pressed firmly against the wooden slat. I stayed like this for over an hour, pain radiating throughout my body while I did my best to maintain a relaxed composure. Even so, this had been by far one of the best experiences as a model I had had up to this point. Sophisticated, respectful, and ever so professional. I actually felt like a true model, not an imposter. This shoot convinced me that I could be a model worthy of big photo shoots, and for the more prominent magazines. As it turned out, these pictures for *Italian Vogue* would be a few of my best and most favorite photos of my entire modeling career.

Before flying to Rome for this shoot, however, I caught a nasty cold, and as I left the studio, it began to sink in more heavily. Once at the airport, I attempted to check in but was told I would have to go on standby. Something about a delay in flights. Maybe a strike of the transportation workers, I guessed. I didn't know what to do, but I found a group of businessmen also going to Milan. They helped me get my name on the flight standby list.

The cold built up further in my head and sinuses and, by the time I found the waiting area, I felt like a wet sponge, slapped repeatedly against a concrete wall. I was doing my best to hold it together, at least until I got back to Milan.

I sat and waited from 6:00 p.m. until the last flight to Milan departed at 11:30 p.m. My name had not been called for any of the flights. I knew I didn't have the money on me to take a taxi back to the Savoy Hotel for the night. Nor did I have the money to pay for another night at the hotel. I did not own a credit card and relied only on what cash I made and had on me at any given time.

An older gentleman with whom I had been talking off and on with during the night asked me what I was going to do. He offered me money, but I couldn't accept it. I felt uncomfortable taking money from a stranger. I didn't trust anyone's honorable intentions, if they were indeed honorable.

Shortly, a younger Italian man approached. I had seen him earlier in the night watching me. In his broken English, he introduced himself as Emilio, saying that he was at the airport with his mother, whom he pointed to as he spoke. She had to fly to Milan for surgery and would now also have to wait until the next day for a flight. Emilio continued, saying his mother would like me to come home with them for the night and return to the airport the following morning. His sick mother was offering me, a stranger, a place to stay for the night, free of charge! At first, I felt I couldn't possibly accept as it would be too much trouble for her. I never thought for a minute someone

Photo shoot in Rome with Alberta Tiburzi.

would be so kind. Finally, the fatigue bore down on me, and my cold seemed to whisk the last ounce of independence out of me. I gave in and graciously accepted their generous offer.

I climbed in the car and Emilio drove us to their small, cozy home. Upon arriving, his mother said goodnight and retired to her room. All I wanted to do was crawl into bed and sleep also. But Emilio and his cousin, both about my age or a little older, excitedly talked about going out to a quaint restaurant not far away. Surely, I was hungry they said. My conscience got the better of me, forsaking my health, as I felt it only fair to spend time with this kind family. At the local place, we sipped on beer and talked in our broken way. Although feeling horrible, their positive, good humor kept me going. It would be 3:30 a.m. before we silently returned to the house. The bedroom held twin beds situated in different corners of the room. Emilio and I would share this room for the night, while his mother slept just down the hall. She obviously trusted him, and so did I.

A few hours later we were on our way back to Rome's airport. The three of us, Emilio, his mom, and I, waited. I sat dazed, tired, and perhaps the sickest I had been in years. When they finally called my name for a flight, I almost didn't hear it. Emilio poked at me and pointed to the agent. Relieved, I said my goodbyes and made my way to the plane. Finally, I was going home, or at least back to my own bed where I could stay for a few days.

Landing in Milan after the fifty-minute flight, I dragged my disheveled self off the plane. I felt miserable and didn't try to hide it. I wore it like a glove, sniffling and moping about as

I made my way to the door and outside to the taxi stand. I felt eyes on me, from all around me. At one point, I looked back, shouting something rudely, incoherently. I had to get back to the apartment. I couldn't die right here in the middle of all these annoying Milanese Italians. Delirium had taken over.

Pouring myself into a cab, I prayed I had enough Lire to get to the apartment. So much traffic jammed the roadways. *For the love of God*, I kept chanting to myself. When the taxi finally pulled up outside the residency, I handed the driver what Lire I had and hurriedly made my way up to the second floor, opening the door after several tries, then firmly shutting it—shutting Italy—behind me. After a few minutes, I calmed down and called the agency to let them know about the trip and my sickness. Thankfully, Lorenzo answered, and I sniffled my way through the conversation, telling him that I had to go home with someone to have a place to sleep when I couldn't get on a plane to return to Milan.

"Barbara! No, Barbara," he wailed.

Then I explained that a nice family had offered me a place to stay for a few hours and how thankful I felt. Even he seemed surprised. I booked myself out for the rest of the day and went straight to bed. Hetty, my new roommate, returned later in the day and cooked dinner for us. All this kindness and we hadn't gotten to know each other at all yet.

I spent the weekend in bed, going out only to the pharmacy nearby for cold medicine. The pharmacist there told me that the best way to treat a cold or flu, and the way most Italians do it, is by using suppositories. I decided to stick with the tablets. When Monday arrived, I still could barely function, but I had already been booked for a big job for the day and needed to suck it up. I made my way to the Modit, a location known for holding fashion trade shows. Three other models arrived around the same time. The job was to model coats and jackets for *Gap* magazine. Somehow, I managed to hide as much of the cold as I could and posed all day for the photographer and client.

MILAN

In mid-March, my twentieth birthday arrived, and I happily left my teens behind. Hetty and I decided to head down to the city center, the Duomo, for a quick birthday lunch. As we entered the lobby, the concierge called me over and handed me a small package. Emilio, whose family I had stayed with that one night in Rome, had dropped it off while in Milan recently. It contained an adorable teddy bear and a sweet note. His Mom had had her surgery and was now back in Rome recuperating nicely. A warmness entered my heart.

After lunch, I quickly packed a bag to take with me on my three-day job outside of the city. Arriving at Piazza Castello, at the far end of Sempione Park, I purchased a ticket for the Autostradale bus which would take me to Bergamo, about twenty-five miles northeast of Milan. While waiting to board, I spotted a tall blonde man with striking good looks standing in a crowd of Italians and knew instantly he had to be an American model. I approached, smiling, and asking if he were perhaps going to Bergamo. He smiled back and nodded yes.

The bus ride to Bergamo took about an hour and once there, Mike and I sat at a tiny bar, waiting for the client. A tall, dark-haired guy approached, and we recognized that model look. Models often gravitated toward each other in public spaces, as if we all contained some type of homing beacon. He introduced himself as Jeffrey and sat down to wait with us. A short time later, a man walked up and said he would take us to the client. We climbed into a van already full of people, including two stylists, a photographer's assistant, and one other model, an eleven-year-old boy named Alan. Mike, Jeffrey, and I introduced ourselves and squeezed in where we could. As it turned out, we wouldn't be staying in Bergamo after all, but instead, the driver took us due east, stopping two hours later for paninis and wine.

After another hour of driving, we pulled up in front of the Viktoria Palace Hotel. The photographer had already arrived and greeted us at the door. We were in Chioggia, part of the metropolitan area known as Venice. The town sat on a small island at the southern entrance to the Lagoon of Venice and lay situated about sixteen miles from the historic center. Just beyond our hotel, water taxis ferried tourists to the famous St. Mark's Square and to the gondolas and canals of postcard Venice. We would not see any of this part of Venice, however, not only because we were working but because the weather turned nasty, requiring the photographer to create lighting for the shoots and look for windows of clear weather.

That evening, the group sat down to dinner together, and I ordered a salad. I was trying to watch my eating as I felt I had gained a few unfriendly pounds since arriving in Italy. The client went around the table asking everyone their age. When she got to me, I said, "I'm turning twenty, today!" Happy birthdays went up, and toasts were made. *There are worst ways to spend a birthday*, I thought to myself.

MILAN

The job entailed several shots for a catalog, which paid rather well. I had to do my own hair and makeup which is just not something I ever became very good at. Fortunately, for these types of shoots, it didn't seem to matter.

Early on the first morning, we met downstairs for breakfast before heading out into the freezing cold day. We shot on a walkway bridge over the water, first doing solos, then one with Jeffrey and me. We moved to a dock and Mike and I posed together, followed by a walk to the beach to shoot a few photos with Alan, who I now called the Wonder Kid. I found him rather adorable and did my best to teach him a few sentences in English, while he did the same for me in Italian.

Once back at the hotel, I decided to get out and take a walk into Chioggia. Although cold and rainy, I didn't want to miss a chance to see at least a little of the area. On my walk back to the hotel, a car stopped and the driver jumped out. He introduced himself as Zebra and said he had been in a store and saw me pass by. We talked a bit, and he offered me a ride, but I politely refused. Maybe I was naïve, but I just couldn't determine if these Italian men were trying to be helpful and gentlemanly, or just trying to pick me up. It all seemed so confusing.

Calling it an early night, I crawled into bed. Then came a knock at the door. Mike wanted to know if I would go out for another walk. He seemed restless, with something weighing on his mind. I said yes and threw a few layers of clothes back on. We walked among the boats and docks and talked about anything and everything. Mike had been a gym teacher at a junior high school in New York. He still seemed somewhat unsure of his new role as an International Fashion Model and his place in the fashion industry. I had no wise insight for him, but I listened, even when he became silent.

Mike had extremely good looks, almost too good. I had a tendency to be attracted to men with less perfect, more rugged looks. What I did find attractive about him, however, was his thoughtfulness and intelligence. You could see these in his eyes and in his mannerisms. I almost felt sorry for him and his inner identity struggle of sorts. To me, being a male model seemed a bit emasculating at best.

We spent the next morning on the beach shooting various photos wearing jeans—first with Mike, then with Jeffrey, then with Alan, the Wonder Kid. I painted on another pair of jeans and did two solo shots. After a few photos back on the docks, we stopped at a store to buy paninis and other treats to take back to the beach for a picnic lunch. The sun had finally decided to show up, even if just for a few hours. We did two more cover tries after lunch, one with Mike, Alan and me, and another with Jeffrey, Alan, and me.

The weather on our final day turned even uglier, if that were possible. The rain poured down, and the temperature seemed to drop several more degrees. We all met downstairs, with our luggage packed up and stored in a room off the reception area. Changing into my first outfit, I made my way across the street to the beach for a double with Jeffrey, each of us doing our best to stall our shivering. We then climbed in the van with the others and headed back to the walkway bridge over the canal. I changed into yet another outfit and walked over to the bridge. I did my best not to look cold, but I shook uncontrollably. Water splashed over the walkway, soaking me as I continued

MILAN

to smile and look at the camera. The others watched, cuddled in the warm, dry interfolds of the van.

After a few more solo shots at the docks, we found a new location in town on Main Street. I slipped off my socks and replaced them with open-toed sandals and walked into the flooded street, drenching my feet in the cold water. The photographer and his assistant struggled to find enough light for the photos, using a makeshift reflector made out of cardboard covered with aluminum foil. Finally, after several clicks of his camera, the photographer shouted "Finito." I hurriedly waded back to the van.

On the Sunday following my return from Chioggia, Lorenzo treated a group of us to a surprise day out in the country. As we left the city streets of Milan, greenery returned, and small houses dotted the countryside. I sat quietly, gazing out over the hills as they rolled past. After a half hour, we arrived in Venegono Superiore, a tiny village town northwest of Milan. Passing through a gate, we wound our way further into the green, until an enormous house came into view. This was Count Umberto Caproni di Taliedo's country estate.

The Count himself came out to greet us. He quickly informed us that the estate covered forty acres and the mansion itself contained some fifty bedrooms. Taking us on a walking tour of the grounds, we stopped at what had been an old monastery but now served as a museum which housed World War I airplanes invented by his famous father, Giovanni (Gianni) Battista Caproni.

Gianni Caproni, an aeronautical engineer, founded the Caproni aircraft manufacturing company back in 1908. A pioneer in Italian aviation, designing the country's first successful aircraft, he also designed bombers during World War I and World War II. As if to further impress the Americans among us, Umberto mentioned that a tribute to his father could be found in the Air and Space Museum in Washington, DC and, at one time and maybe still, his portrait hung next to the Wright Brothers in the White House.

A few small planes remained in the old monastery, but the majority of Caproni planes were now housed in a larger museum at the nearby airport. As I continued asking questions, the others in the group snickered, either surprised that I liked history or because they knew nothing about history. *If they want to remain bubble-brains for the rest of their lives, then so be it,* I irritatingly thought to myself. It would be a few hours later that two of the models approached me, mentioning how much they enjoyed learning a little World War I history. They just had been too embarrassed to mention it in front of the group.

The sun finally began to warm up the day. We lounged outside for a while, watching as deer ran across the vast estate. A black swan, obtained from Australia, coasted across the lake. We had our choice between archery and badminton, as well as tennis. We sipped wine as we watched several of the men play tennis then returned to a wing of the house for lunch.

By now we were all calling the Count by his first name, Umberto. After lunch on the patio, I asked him if he would take me back to the museum so I could take a few photos of the Caproni planes. He kindly obliged. Umberto seemed to be rather normal for a Count, very gentlemanly, soft-spoken, refined yet down-to-earth and friendly. Yet for the life of me I couldn't figure out what it was he did to maintain the estate and its associated lifestyle. Did he just live off his father's ingenuity and fame?

The last day of March arrived, and once again I returned to Umberto's estate. This time, Umberto himself, along with an American male model named Daniel, and Alexa, a photographer from Australia, picked me up outside my apartment. Once we arrived at the estate, Umberto gave us a tour of the house which showcased an incredible array of antique furniture, as if we had stepped back in time. Yet the overall interior of the house seemed dark, and empty of emotion or energy, even sad. Surely back in the day, it had glowed with family and guests but, apparently, those days were no more.

Umberto's hobby of falconry became the next topic of conversation, and he honored us by showing us his falcons. Then, just when I thought there couldn't be any more to see, he ushered us down to his wine-making cellar.

For the rest of the day, I lay outside in the sun near the tennis courts. I attempted to take it all in, to comprehend such splendor, such history, such a way of life. We headed back to the house, or rather, to a wing of the house for a late lunch. The salad ingredients had been pulled fresh from the garden just outside. There was nothing simple about a salad under these circumstances.

More people soon showed up, including models from different agencies. With everyone wandering off on their own to the sauna, to take a nap, or drink more wine, I decided to walk around the estate and take pictures. I wanted to share this with my family back home.

Throughout the grounds are caves, or rather small rooms set back in the earth, where a stream runs through, keeping the temperature pleasantly cool. I entered one and sat down on the stone bench, thinking what a good place to rest from the heat outside or to sit and read as enough light streamed in from the entrance. I secretly hoped I would be able to visit again in the summertime just so I could take advantage of one of these cooling spaces.

Next to the monastery, which now held the few Caproni airplanes, sat a small chapel, with a lily pond just outside its front doors. Umberto had mentioned that all family weddings and funerals took place there. No doubt in springtime it became a beautiful setting for a wedding and a peaceful setting for a family funeral any time of year. A 1930s' swimming pool sat empty along with the remains of a once well-designed and maintained maze. The tennis courts nearby, while functional, seemed in need of resurfacing.

A little further away I passed a small cabin, built at the edge of a pond. The small balcony allowed you to look out over the water and to the trees beyond. Inside, you find a quaint room, complete with its own fireplace. Umberto's grandfather, it is rumored, built this cabin for a rendezvous with a peasant girl from the nearby village. She would slip through a small opening, which had been created just for her, in the large wall surrounding the estate.

As I continued roaming around, I noticed how brown and unkempt the grounds were. The harsh winter and all the snow had damaged the lush plants and trees surrounding the estate. Overall, it had the look of a place that had long been neglected and rejected.

Wing of Count Umberto Caproni's country estate where we spent most of our time. The estate itself spread across 40 acres and the house consisted of 50 bedrooms we were told..

MILAN

April arrived, and a few days later I was again off on another trip for work, this time to the Italian seaside, on the west coast of Italy. As usual, the agency didn't give me the name of the shooting location, but only instructions on where to meet the group. At the meeting site, everyone introduced themselves before piling into a van. Two hours later we stopped for a panini, then two more hours of driving brought us to our hotel, high up on a rocky cliff with breathtaking panoramic views of the sea below. We were in an area known as Cinque Terre on the Italian Riviera. A string of old towns dots the rugged coastline in this part of Italy with houses of various colors clinging to the terraces which slope down toward the sea.

The other model, Madlyn, and I shared a room that looked out over the cliff. Although a year older, Madlyn acted much younger. Her constant talking and hilarious entertaining kept the moments lively. At least, this is how she acted in front of the client and photographer. Once back in our room, however, she calmed considerably, as if it all had been an act for the client's sake. She seemed almost relieved to be away from the spotlight. I found this real Madlyn more to my liking. Yet, the minute the client or photographer appeared, she flipped the switch and became what she thought they wanted her to be,

Marvelous Madlyn. I quickly grew tired of this. I related much more to Linda, our makeup artist and hairstylist. More mature and soft-spoken, Linda and I clicked and enjoyed talking and laughing at the ludicrous industry we found ourselves in.

We were at the seaside to shoot a spread which included several different outfits for the magazine *Benissimo*. With an early start the next morning, a long day stretched out ahead of us. Madlyn and I each had six outfits to model, mostly solo. When the sun came out, we made quick work of the first five, beginning at the beach, then moving to the nearby docks. For the first time since arriving in Italy, the editor and photographer decided to delay lunch in order to complete all the photos. We returned to the beach for the sixth and final shot, a pink skirt and white sweater for me. Afterward, we all joked around, taking goofy group pictures and laughing. It had turned out to be a good day.

Returning to the hotel, I hurriedly packed up my things before we all headed to the enormous flea market to shop. Linda and I walked around together and did our best to talk the prices down, using our terrible Italian. I ended up buying a jean jacket, socks, a few magazines, and candy. With no time left, I said *ciao* to everyone and raced to the train station. I couldn't stay the night because I had to work with a different client the following day back in Milan.

The next morning, I reported again to one of my best clients, *Anna* magazine. As I had worked for this magazine numerous times before, I assumed the clothes would be similar to those in the past. After having my hair and makeup done, I sat and waited. And waited some more.

Finally the editor walked over and handed me my first outfit, a silky full body slip. The job, it turns out, would be for underwear. I didn't mind modeling bikinis but felt rather uncomfortable modeling underwear or lingerie. I had even told my agency that I would not do this type of photo shoot. So why had they accepted this job for me? Too late to back out now, I reasoned with myself. I changed into the slip, feeling awkward and unsure of myself. I pretended all was fine and did my best for the photographer. I did the same for the next shot, a bra and panty combo.

Once back at the apartment, I made a cup of peppermint tea and began leafing through the magazines I had purchased while still at the seaside. Opening *Grazia* to the first page, I stared at the advertisement for a hair salon. Looking closer at the guy in the photo, I swore I knew him. Then I saw Brescia beside the salon name, and it hit me. I looked over at the gal leaning back against him and smiled. There I was, full hair and all! The ad was the result of the shoot we did over a month ago in Brescia before my trip to Mauritius.

This is how I usually came across my tear sheets. Rarely did the agency notify me when my photos were in a recent issue, nor did the client inform me when photos would appear. It soon became a habit to stop by the magazine stand and look through all the ones I had worked for each week or month, to see if I was in them. Each and every time I found my picture, I felt the same giddiness and excitement, even for the ones that were not that good and where I looked as if to have a double chin, an odd look on my face, or a crinkle in my skin. Finally, all my work began to pay off, adding needed tear sheets to my portfolio. Milan, as it turned out, had been good for me so far.

There were plenty of Italian designers in the city of Milan. I didn't understand how it all worked but would hear this and that about how a model's career could be made by just one designer liking her a little more than all the others.

Several times I visited the Giorgio Armani offices, meeting with assistants who looked at my book, had me walk across the room and back, then stashed away copies of my best photos in their files. Other times I showed my book to clients to see if they thought I might be too tall, or too long-waisted, to do an Armani casting. One of Armani's assistants seemed to really like me yet never hired me.

As it turned out, it wouldn't be Armani that I would work for, but Gianfranco Ferré. On one of my go-sees, I visited his offices on Via Della Spiga. The interviewers liked me and the next day I reported back there for a spread in *Women's Wear Daily*, a fashion trade journal out of New York. The day turned out to be a long one with the photos alternating between outdoor locations and the studio.

I also worked for *Anna* magazine on a spread showcasing the designs of Gucci. The year was 1985 and the designer's grandson, Maurizio Gucci, ran the company after his father passed away in 1983. He had only just begun his reign over the company, and the *Anna* article showcased several of the newest Gucci designs. Over ten photos accompanied the article, from a business look complete with black skirt, long belted jacket,

MILAN

and heels, to a more casual look including a pair of graphic shorts, short jacket and a thin flowing coat that stopped mid-calf. I found it to be one of the most professional shoots I had experienced to date. There was no goofing-off and laughing as was often the case on other photo shoots. The serious and sophisticated side of me came out, just as it did during that shoot in Rome for wedding dresses with Alberta Tiburzi. I liked this side of me.

MILAN

Another Friday night arrived, and my roommate Hetty and I decided to go out dancing. Amnesia nightclub had become my favorite club in Milan, and I often danced to the wee hours of the morning. Entering its doors, I walked up to my favorite bar and ordered my usual, a Tanqueray and tonic. Out of the corner of my eye, I caught a glimpse of a man with long, thick, dark hair staring directly at me, with no pretense of trying to hide it. I glanced across him as if scanning the room, not wanting to hold his stare even for a second. But even with such a quick glance in his direction, I could see his eyes, the meanest expression radiating out from them. The intensity of his stare startled me, and it felt as if, with it, he could bore a hole right through me.

The bartender returned, plopping a lime wedge in my glass and handing it to me. Without glancing back, I joined the models on the other side of the club. Pulling Hetty aside, I told her about the staring man. She glanced over to see who I was talking about, then grabbed my arm, speaking low and deep into my ear.

"Barbara, do not talk to him! Or even look at him! He is bad news." She didn't elaborate and I, somewhat shocked by her reaction, didn't ask any further questions.

Obviously, the man was some sort of bad news. I could tell that. Yet feeling his stare on me unnerved me in a way no one ever had. All night, I did my best to avoid him and those piercing eyes. I knew there was a dark side to Milan, where models occasionally drifted for the money and drugs, but until this night I had been able to stay far away from it.

A few weeks later, Hetty and I stopped in a new restaurant just down the street from our apartment. With no separate table for two available, they sat us at a table filled with what I clearly could see were Italian playboys. As soon as we finished eating, one of them, a man with long flowing reddish-blonde hair, started talking to me in English. He introduced himself as Luca, and I found him to be a complete gentleman, not a bewilderingly charming Italian of my experience. We mentioned we were going to Amnesia nightclub, and they said they might meet us there.

The staring man stood in the same corner of the club, and the minute I walked in he saw me. I didn't look his way, and I definitely didn't look into his eyes. After getting our drinks, we headed over to the area diagonal to where he stood, where people we knew were already partying. Shortly afterward, Luca and his friends arrived from the restaurant. I walked over and began talking with him, mentioning the dark-haired guy on the other side of the bar. Luca glanced over, then grew silent. He seemed to stiffen where he stood with his jovial facial expression disappearing instantly. Finally, he spoke, telling me the man's name, Paolo, and nothing more. I didn't prod, and his silence made it clear to me that any conversation on the matter was clearly over. I knew well enough to leave it alone.

Paolo's staring soon became too unnerving, and I began to wonder if I would have to stop going to the club at all. Finally, I had had enough. With several gin and tonics in me, I decided he wouldn't run me off. Turning, I looked at him briefly, into his eyes, and smiled. Instantly his eyes changed from one extreme to another—from harsh to friendly. I took my drink over to my friends and continued with my night. Somehow, I felt, I had disarmed him.

As the night grew closer to an end, Hetty and I hit the dance floor one last time. I spotted a guy in the back corner and, liking the way he moved, made my way closer. Tall, with dark hair, he wore a black beret and suspenders. Unshaven and appearing a bit rugged, I drew even closer. We held each other's eyes for a few seconds and continued dancing. He came closer, leaning into my ear.

"Do you speak English?" he asked in an unmistakable British accent.

I smiled and nodded, "Of course."

After a few more dances he leaned in again, "Will you marry me?"

I laughed and spun around, grooving with my best dance moves. Sean, it turns out, was also a model, living the dream in Milan.

As the lights came up, signaling the club was about to close, I walked off the dance floor to say goodbye to several people. Sean walked up and asked for my phone number. Playing a little hard to get, I told him I couldn't remember my number but that I lived at the Garden Residency on Via Salvioni. I figured if he truly wanted to find me, he would.

With Sean disappearing out the front door, I slowly made my way over to leave also. As I did so, Paolo suddenly appeared in front of me. He still had the softened eyes that I had seen earlier.

In a slow, deep voice, he spoke. "You deserve much better," referring to the guys I had been talking with all night, including Sean. "I can give you so much more."

Stunned by his hypnotizing voice, I managed a slight smile. About that time, Hetty grabbed my arm, pulling me out the door.

Later the following week, rumors reached me that Paolo was part of the Mafia, high up, and he had beaten up his old girlfriend, another American model. I recalled how Luca's voice and face changed when I asked him about the man, picking up on his apprehension. Those two had some kind of connection. I never saw them talk, or even stand near each other. All clues to what I already suspected and knew: I had to stay far away from both of them.

The day after playing hard to get and not giving Sean my phone number, I felt miserable. Why had I been so coy? Why didn't I just give him my number? I continued to beat myself up about it until the phone rang.

Hetty answered, then handed it to me, whispering, "It's Sean!"

MILAN

Thrilled, I grabbed the phone, talking for a few minutes before accepting his invitation to dinner the next night. I felt like a schoolgirl going out on her first date ever.

I met Sean downstairs, and we strolled to a restaurant called Austriette. We talked and talked, yet neither of us felt like we had to keep the conversation going in order to avoid silence. It felt good to be together. Afterward, he walked me back to my place, and we kissed goodnight in the lobby.

My nights soon became less about dancing at Amnesia and more about spending time with Sean. We would often go to the Angelica Theatre (English theater) and see movies such as *Ghostbusters* and *Once Upon a Time in America*. Following the movie, we might stop at the Quik restaurant nearby for a hamburger and french fries. I could feel the loneliness resonating from the both of us. Everyone at some time feels lonely in this business, and Milan can often feel like a very lonely place.

Sean and I also spent a lot of time roaming around the English bookstore. I made sure to read every book by Robert Ludlum, from the Bourne trilogy to *The Parsifal Mosaic* to *Chancellor Manuscript*. Someone recommended reading books by Wilbur Smith, and there were several of them to be found in the bookshop. Smith, a South African, wrote novels immersed in his home country, and all of Africa. I found his descriptions of scenes and locations mesmerizing and could spend most of a day just reading. I also read classics such as *A Tree Grows in Brooklyn* and *A Farewell to Arms*. It turned out I had found my way of chilling, recuperating from stressful days and situations – a good book, a good movie, and Sean.

EUROPEAN DAZE

Music too became a tonic. During the mid-1980s, the music felt new and exciting, and particularly so in Europe. My favorites included "Black Cars" and the slower "It Hurts to Be in Love" by Gino Vannelli, as well as "The Riddle" and "Wouldn't It Be Good" by Nik Kershaw. I also liked an occasional sappy love song, including "Cherish" by Kool & the Gang. It seemed listening to my cassette tapes on my Walkman while sitting on the sill of the open living room window, day or night, relaxed me. Now I had discovered another way to detach and just be in the moment, ensconced in my own little world.

Shopping had never been my thing, and that didn't change even in the high fashion world of Milan. Even if I had had much more money, it's doubtful I would have spent my time shopping or concerning myself with my daily wear. I did find one store in Milan that thrilled me, however. Fiorucci, a funky, eclectic designer, had a shop completely out of the ordinary showcasing tight jeans, T-shirts, and thongs. As if by coincidence, my very first modeling experience, back in Florida on the Burdines Teen Board, had been a showcase of Fiorucci fashions. And now, here I was, shopping for the designer's clothes right in his hometown of Milan.

My roommate, Hetty, never seemed to be without ideas to entertain us. Bored one night, she decided to seek out her friend, Tatiana, who had been murdered by a boyfriend two-years earlier. With a makeshift Ouija board, made from letters spelled out on paper then torn into pieces and spread out on the table, Hetty began. I placed my hand lightly over a small glass as she started talking to her friend, asking her to come to us. I felt the glass move ever so slightly across the table before stopping in front of the letter "I." At that moment, I freaked out, quickly picking up the glass, then scooping up the paper letters and throwing them in the trash. We never tried that again.

Hetty and I soon got to know Sean's friends, Tabor, an American, and Ian, another Brit, and the five of us were always together. For dinner, we usually ended up at a restaurant we called Rhiskios, where we all ordered an inexpensive dish of spaghetti with pepperoni and a load of garlic. As soon as the waiter brought it out, everybody in the restaurant turned to look at our table. The garlic aroma wafted out the kitchen door, saturating the air. One man joked with me about my breath after eating such a meal. Fortunately, we all ate the same thing so wouldn't notice.

The foods of Italy, *la cucina italiana*, soon became, by far, my favorite type of meal. Growing up, my family never ate spaghetti or any other Italian dish that often but when we did, it was memorable. One of those dishes was my mom's incredible eggplant parmigiana. Not like what I see at restaurants today with a large, single slice of breaded eggplant topped by a red tomato sauce and cheese. No, my mom layered the eggplant, the sauce, and the cheese, not once but twice. There's no better way to get a kid or a teenager to eat eggplant than to cleverly disguise it in red sauce and cheese.

Now in Italy, a simple plate of spaghetti with a tasty tomato sauce and cheese became my comfort food. Pizzas were, of course, not new to me, but somehow, they just tasted better in Italy. Surprisingly, after my first taste of it, fried veal, or Veal Milanese, (or *Cotoletta alla Milanese*), became one of my favorites as well. Dishes specific to the area always ended with alla Milanese, a style rich in butter. Risotto alla Milanese, a saffron rice with onion, white wine, and Parmesan cheese became a staple, as did a wild mushroom risotto.

We often met up at a small café, The White Bear, between my agency, Fashion, and Sean's agency, Beatrice Models International. Here my go-to lunch consisted of mozzarella e pomodoro, alternating slices of perfectly ripe tomatoes and mozzarella cheese, with fresh basil, drizzles of olive oil, and a little salt. I could eat this every day. I soon began buying balls of mozzarella and shopping for the freshest tomatoes at the market so I could have them at the apartment anytime, day or night.

Dessert in Italy became an event not to be missed. From the second I tasted my very first tiramisù, I was hooked. With its ladyfingers doused in coffee then topped with an egg, sugar, and mascarpone cheese mixture, it felt as if heaven melted in my mouth, stopping time. Tartufo, a ball of ice cream with a chocolate shell on the outside, and a creamy surprise in the middle, also became one of my favorite desserts. And of course, there was always gelato in many different flavors.

As for alcohol, I never learned enough about wines to speak about them intelligently. The ones I did consume at formal dinner parties and informal lunches at photo shoots were incredible and perfectly paired with the meal. Europeans are gifted with the ability to choose just the right wine for the occasion. Besides my Tanqueray and tonics at the clubs, I occasionally joined the guys, knocking back a Guinness dark

MILAN

ale or rounds of Wührer beer, a pale lager founded in nearby Brescia back in 1829.

I grew fond of Sean and always wanted to be with him. Yet, in the back of my mind, I kept asking myself if this was wise. It seemed that to be successful in modeling, you needed to stay unconnected and devoted, some say married, to the profession in order to be taken seriously and get ahead. A relationship with Sean could instead become a distraction.

Sean and I walking off the elevator at my apartment in the Garden Residency in Milan. We spent nearly every minute together when not working.

MILAN

By the end of April, Milan was overcrowded with models. They were everywhere. We jokingly referred to it as the meat market. Yet it was hardly a joke as we were sent out on fewer go-sees, and the jobs began to slow down. At the agency one day, Graziani, a booker, pulled me aside. She told me she continued pushing me because I offered so much more than all the new models in town. I wanted to believe her. I trusted Fashion Agency much more than I ever had my agency in Paris. We all struggled with what to do next.

Meanwhile, my home agency, Legends, had been rather quiet the last few months. Rumors continued to circulate that some type of turmoil consumed the modeling world in New York and that changes were on the horizon.

Sean's London agency called and wanted him to come back for a few days to work there in the city. He knew he needed the work, the money, and the opportunity to get good tear sheets for his book. I told him he should definitely go. We had to take advantage of every opportunity that came our way.

While Sean shuttled back to London, I decided to join a few friends for an overnight stay at Umberto's estate in the country. As a beautiful spring day arrived, hinting at what summer might be like in the months ahead, I made my way to the Cadorna train station at Milan's center to meet up with fellow models Pat, Mira, Emma, and Sharon. Taking the train to the countryside near Umberto's estate, we got off and chose to walk the rest of the way to the main house, arriving just in time for lunch. We were looking forward to a fun, relaxing weekend away from the city.

Umberto and his sidekick, Daniel, the male model from Louisiana, waited for us on the patio. I would be sharing a room with Mira, a model from Sweden whom I first met back in New York. Umberto escorted us to our room in the main house, to what everyone called the Blue Room because all its walls were painted blue. It also had another title, the infamous *haunted* blue room. No one ever elaborated as to why they thought it to be haunted. It didn't bother us, and we laughed it off. It was, however, located on the second floor of the main house, far away from the wing where we spent most of our time, and far away from where everyone else would be staying.

After a dinner full of fresh ingredients from the gardens on the estate, the party began. Daniel told ghost stories as we sipped our wine. Naturally, drinking games followed – Concentration and Captain Timmili – both of which I can no longer remember how to play. Eventually, I grew tired of the wine and switched to my gin and tonics. A short while later I found myself cornered in the kitchen by one of the male models who had come with us on the train. "Not going to happen," I told him and pushed his arm away as I walked out.

Finally calling it a night, Mira and I started toward our haunted room in the main house. Daniel followed, as his room, the Yellow Room, sat next door to ours. (Yes, you guessed it, because all the walls were painted yellow.) It was well known that Daniel, so afraid of ghosts, would never stay in the main house by himself. So, when he announced he was too scared to sleep alone in the Yellow Room and crawled in our bed, I wasn't all that surprised. I lay down on my side of the bed, and Mira lay down on the other, with Daniel smack in the middle. It wasn't long before I felt one hand on my leg and heard him move the covers to place his other hand on Mira's leg. At that exact moment all the wine, and all the gin and tonics, along with my loathing of his nerve, got to me. I suddenly sprang up in bed, yanked off the covers, and stood up. Before a word could be said, I started walking toward the door. It creaked as I slowly opened it, then headed out into the hallway in the pitch darkness.

Daniel, convinced I was sleepwalking and that ghosts were at play, yelled out for the evil spirits to leave me alone. I halted in the hallway, suddenly turning toward a door in the wall which led to an old elevator. What I didn't know at the time was that this elevator had always terrified Daniel. Racing out after me, he attempted to pull me back, but I wouldn't budge. I remained as stiff as a board. Finally, he picked me up and carried me back to the Blue Room, yelling for Mira to wake up. They began arguing, and I attempted to get up and go back to the elevator. He held me down. I clawed at his hands. Sometimes I wonder if maybe I wasn't possessed by something after all.

Frantic, Daniel decided he needed to throw me in the shower to wake me up. I lay back calm, as if asleep, as Daniel went in to turn on the cold shower. I nudged Mira, whispering to let her know it was all a practical joke. Mira played her role well, telling him he couldn't just throw me in the cold water. It was then that Daniel really seemed to panic. Maybe it was all the alcohol in his system, but he began to lose it. He wanted to go and wake up Umberto. I decided to end the charade and pretended to slowly wake up, yelling at them as I did so for being so loud. I then rolled over and fell asleep.

Awakening in the morning, Daniel immediately began telling me about my sleepwalking episode. Of course, I "didn't remember" anything about it, and more importantly, didn't believe him. As we got dressed for the day, he headed to breakfast ahead of us. When Mira and I arrived, everyone remained quiet, staring at me as if I were still possessed. Hesitantly, they began asking us questions. It wouldn't be until a little later in the day that I confessed to our host, Umberto, that it had all been a hoax. Still, he from that day on regarded me warily. And, of course, he told his wingman Daniel that he had been had. Who knows, maybe I should have gone into acting instead of modeling.

MILAN

In early May, we found new neighbors had moved in next door to us in the Residency. Hetty and I stood outside our door talking with Peter, an American model, when his roommate stepped out into the hallway. As he did so, we stared at each other, not saying a word. Sam, from Paris, stood there in front of me. Four months had passed since we kissed goodbye back at the door to my apartment on rue Poncelet. Much had happened since then for both of us.

As the night wore on, Sam and I slid down the wall to the floor outside our apartments, sitting there talking until 5:00 a.m. He told me his wife flew over to Paris, and they had arranged the divorce papers, yet he confessed he had not yet signed them. I knew Sam felt conflicted and needed time to sort out his feelings. He also told me he hadn't gone out with anyone else since I left Paris. True or not, it didn't matter to me. We had kept each other company while in Paris, with only kissing and spending time in conversation. We had no ties or commitment to each other. I believed it all boiled down to being in the same place at the same time, nothing more, nothing less. Now, we were in a different place, and things were no longer the same. I told him about my work in Milan and about Sean.

EUROPEAN DAZE

The following weekend my friends and I all gathered at Amnesia, and I danced a few songs with Sam. Although Sean and I were there together, we had had a bit of a tiff at dinner beforehand. Sean often spouted on and on about politics, revealing his seemingly deep hatred for Americans and their ways. I did not find this side of him endearing in the slightest. His arrogance and condescension annoyed me.

Work remained slow, and my patience began to grow thin. Anxious and irritated, I felt stagnate in Milan. As if to appease me, or torture me, I'm not sure which, the agency agreed to a job for me modeling at a light demonstration show. I wouldn't get any tear sheets from it, but it did pay well.

The audience for the show turned out to be a room full of photographers. My first pose, a headshot, required me to lean my neck back over a chair. As the instructor positioned different lighting directed at my face, I held the position, for over an hour. They discussed, in Italian, methods of lighting your subject, and everyone practiced, snapping away with their own cameras. Finally, the lesson concluded, and I attempted to raise my head. My neck felt stuck in the backward position, and pain shot through when I attempted to bring it back up into a normal position. I signaled the assistant with my hands, and he came over and helped me up. I massaged it repeatedly to loosen up the locked muscles and finally straighten my head.

For the second demonstration, I pulled on a one-piece swimsuit. The instructor wanted me to sit in front of a mirror which lay on the ground. In the creative lighting, this mirror would appear to be water. Receiving instruction to sit with my legs spread wide, on either side of the mirror, I scoffed, refusing. After arguing, we finally compromised. I would sit on my bent legs and lean backward. Again, like the first pose, I sat frozen in the position for over an hour. When finished, it took two of them to help me stand up.

To wrap up the day, the other model, Henrietta, and I posed together on a Vespa, dressed to the hilt in black and red leather. After sitting astride the scooter for over an hour, the demonstrations finally reached a close for the day. I dashed out into the pouring rain and raced home. The rainy spring weather only added to my darkening mood.

I returned to the show the next day for the second session. Again, poised astride the Vespa, switching off from doubles with Henrietta, to solos, we filled the entire day. When it finally ended, I breathed a sigh of relief and made a note to myself to stay away from such jobs in the future. Desperation for work didn't bode well for me, and I would find another way.

MILAN

In contrast to the quiet despair of my friends, my bad moods continued to increase, and I wasn't afraid to lash out at anyone, anywhere. I kept asking myself over and over if I should stay in Italy any longer. Should I go back to Paris, and give the other agency a try? Maybe I should go to Germany and make some money? Work continued to slow considerably in Milan, not just for me but for everyone I knew. This feeling of worry and anxiety gnawed at me constantly.

The agency itself seemed to switch from warm to cold, cold to warm. One minute they liked you, the next they pushed you aside. It began to dawn on me that I had overstayed my welcome in Milan, and with no guidance from my New York agency, I had to become my own best fan.

Meanwhile, Sean and I tried to boost each other up. At times I felt like I loved him, at other times he irritated the living shit out of me. We needed an escape, if only for a day. Early on a Sunday morning, Hetty, Sean, Taber, Ian, and I walked across the street from my apartment to the train station, purchasing round-trip tickets to Lake Como. Set against the foothills of the Alps, Lake Como had the reputation of being an upscale area but also provided incredible scenery, ancient villas, and explorable towns along the waterfront. It sounded perfect.

We joked and laughed as the train made its way north, relaxing more and more by the minute. Arriving at the Como San Giovanni train station an hour or more later, we emerged as if completely different people. We settled into a small café nearby to enjoy a cappuccino. Sean and Ian ate paninis, and Sean refreshed himself with a beer. With no idea where to go, we wandered down to the water's edge. A water taxi approached a landing, and we scrambled to meet it. Studying the map and the rates, we determined we could afford to go three stops and climbed aboard.

The light breeze blew steadily as we gazed out over the land as the boat made its way along the shoreline. I took in the fresh, clean air, exhaling out all the stale Milan air. At the third stop, we stepped off, not knowing anything more about that area than we did the last. The unknowns thrilled us. Glancing inland, I caught sight of a track straight up a mountainside, then glimpsed a cable car descending from the top.

"Let's see where that goes," I ventured. I had no idea what sat at the top, but I imagined the views of the lake had to be spectacular.

The funicular, a type of cable train on the mountainside, slowly proceeded up the mountain to the small village of Brunate. Quaint, quiet, and beautiful, we hopped off the cable car, walking along the streets and taking in the beauty surrounding us, smiling, and laughing as we went. Finding a small country bar, we entered and treated ourselves to paninis and beer, a perfect meal on a perfect day. The spectacular view of the lake caught our eye on the way out, and we began to search for a way to get a little closer to that view. Walking down the side of the mountain a short distance, we found a beautiful lookout point, seemingly deserted. As we gazed out over the lake to the snow-capped mountains in the distance, everyone suddenly grew quiet. For me, the constant chatter in my mind ceased, and all thoughts of Milan or fashion or modeling faded entirely from my thoughts. I felt at ease, a sensation I hadn't felt in a very long time.

Pooling our remaining money, we found we had enough for ice cream. Once again laughing and carrying on, we walked through the village, until we chanced upon a makeshift soccer field with golden grass waving in a slight breeze. We lay down in the middle of it, staring at the blue sky, the mountains in the distance, and soaking in the sun, dozing off and on for hours.

With late afternoon beckoning, we scrambled back down the mountainside to the landing, catching the water taxi back to our starting point. On the train back to Milan, we sat quietly, leaning our heads against our seats. It had been the best day ever.

Reporting to the agency early for my 11:00 a.m. appointment, I sat outside the booking room with several other models. The tenseness released just the day before at the lake now returned. The lack of work in Milan at the moment soon became the topic of discussion, with all of us agreeing that the problem ran wide. The jobs continued to dry up as we approached summer, and everyone felt the financial strain. Our self-confidence also began to drain out of us. We mistakenly identified working as being the reason for our confidence, a false veil surrounding our self-worth. *If you're not working, maybe it's because you're not good enough.* Any of us could quickly spiral into the pit of despair at such thoughts.

Later that afternoon, I met with Jean-Luc from Carin Models in Paris yet again. Saying he still would love to represent me in Paris, it momentarily boosted my confidence. Yet, I doubted the time was right to return to Paris. Work there, like in Milan, if rumors were true, had also slowed.

For me, it seemed as if I wanted to stay in Europe, to stay in modeling as long as it wasn't stressful or frantic all the time. This is where my confusion lay. Some models loved the frantic pace and kept going, eventually either making it big or crashing and burning. There were so many of us, so many tall, gorgeous gals and guys from all over the world, competing for the same jobs. We couldn't all make it big. And was that the only reason to continue, to seek top model status? Did I foresee myself modeling forever, consuming my days and nights with this lifestyle? While New York and Paris had been my testing grounds, Milan had become my educating ground, showing all sides, from popular model, all the way to just another one of the hundreds in town.

In the days that followed, I held my head high and attempted to remain optimistic about my career and future. But soon it all started to crumble. While out one day with Sean and Hetty, things began to turn for me. Whenever I said something they considered "too American," both of them would lecture me. They were always quick to tell me the millions of things wrong with my home country. At times, it felt like a verbal assault. Something had to change.

MILAN

On a Tuesday morning, I awoke to find that there were no go-sees for the day. Strikes crippled the city, and I sat wondering if the Italians simply hated to work as they seemed to always be on strike. At a nearby café, Hetty and I sat talking about our immediate future. She suggested we go to Austria to work and tank up on money. I thought maybe I should try Germany since they had liked me so much while in Paris. I knew I had to do something, I couldn't continue sitting and waiting for the tide to turn.

We made our way to the agency, thinking that maybe we could talk to them about our situation. Yet, once there, we felt jilted by their rudeness and dismissiveness to our concerns. Hetty stormed out, but I decided to wait for Lorenzo. I always felt comfortable talking with him about anything. When he arrived, I pulled him aside, asking him about possibly sending me to Germany for a little while to make some money. He disappeared for a few minutes to talk with one of the other agents, then returned.

"At the moment," he said, "there is work in Zurich, Switzerland. I will send you there."

When I arrived back at the apartment, I told Hetty the good news. The agency would send us to Zurich. Excitedly, she nodded, adding that her agency in Austria called. They had already booked her for a three-day job in Vienna. Our spirits buoyed for the moment, and once again we saw possibility.

A short while later, the agency called, telling me I would indeed be going to Zurich, and I would be leaving the next day. With such short notice, I began to panic. I had so much to do! What would I do with all my things? Where could I store them?

EUROPEAN DAZE

We had to vacate the apartment, no doubt so they could fill it with more new models coming into town. Sean, back at his apartment sick with some type of cold or flu, surely wouldn't expect this type of sudden news. I had to tell him in person, not over the phone.

I found Sean in bed, now with a fever and chills. Handing him the aspirin and juice I picked up on the way, I sat down beside him. With so little time left, I had to be quick about it. At first, he became upset but then calmed. He understood. I assured him it would most likely only be for about three weeks or so, then I would return.

By the time I got back to the apartment, Hetty already had all her belongings packed up. I began to do the same until one of our neighbors, Mark, invited us to his daiquiri party up on the roof. I felt I had to go for a short while, if for no other reason than to celebrate leaving Italy. Packing all my things from almost five months turned out to be a challenge, and I stayed up most of the night.

The next morning, I awoke after only a few hours of sleep, my first thought being that today would be the day I moved to yet another country. I had always heard about the beauty of Switzerland, and I couldn't wait to see it, explore it, live in it. I felt a new lease on life.

Hetty and I walked over to our favorite café for one more quick cappuccino before starting out on our separate adventures. I then headed to the agency one last time. Lorenzo handed me my train ticket to Zurich and information on my agency and hotel there. He also led me into the accountant's office, telling them to advance me 800,000 Lire.

MILAN

"Ciao Bella," he whispered, as he kissed me on each cheek.

By the time I returned to the apartment, I had little time to spare. Just making it to the train station for my 1:10 p.m. departure, I raced out on to the platform, easily finding my train and climbing aboard. How different this day was from that first day I ventured into this train station, on the brink of tears, searching for a ticket counter and the first train to Rome.

The train doors shut as I wrangled my bags onto the luggage rack above my seat, located in an empty compartment. Settling into the seat, I could finally exhale and relax.

As the train left the station, left Milan, steadily heading north, the scenery began to unfold. The mountains, the lakes, the towns we passed through, so breathtaking I dared not lean back or close my eyes. I wanted to see it all. Waterfalls gushed with racing water and white foam. Green trees reached high into the perfectly blue sky. At that moment, I realized how wonderful my life was. How had I forgotten that back in Milan?

ZURICH
MAY 25-JULY 9, 1985

By the time the train arrived in Zurich four hours later, evening had already begun its descent. Once again, as with the shrinking of daylight, I felt myself shrinking inside, suddenly fearful of a new city, a new language, and a new market to start all over in. I stepped off the train and wrangled my several pieces of luggage down to the platform. For a moment, I stood frozen, glancing around my new city. Eventually, I nudged myself to get moving and located a small cart to haul my bags out to the taxi stand.

As my taxi approached the Hirschenplatz, a square in the heart of the pedestrian area of the old part of Zurich, I could see crowds of people and musicians gathering. Hesitating at first, I collected my bags and made my way quickly through the wide wooden door of my hotel. Nervously, I wondered if I had made a mistake by leaving Milan, by leaving Hetty and Sean.

The Hirschen Hotel consisted of three different houses, combined into one. Yet it appeared to be more like a pensione, or boarding house, than a hotel. My room, #20, a rectangular room, contained one bed, one small cabinet, a table, and a stool. In the corner sat a pedestal sink and a bathtub, but no toilet. I sat down on the bed. I hated feeling this way. I had felt it three times now: when I arrived in Paris, when I arrived in Milan, and more so now arriving here in Zurich. I began missing Milan and its smog, and I missed Sean.

Cueing up a dose of courage, I forced myself to go out and explore. Before doing so, however, I sought out the toilets, finding them up a few stairs and down another hallway. Once outside, I just started walking. Zurich felt more like a small village than a large city. Cobblestone streets led me away from the hotel, and I followed them for several minutes. The narrow alleys nearby were lined with cafes, restaurants, beer halls, antique stores, and a few art galleries. It seemed almost bohemian. And they all led down to the Limmatquai, the breathtaking riverside boulevard running along the east bank of the Limmat River.

Eventually, I came upon a small bistro that looked non-threatening and took a deep breath as I entered its doors. The waiter spoke English, and I breathed a sigh of relief. The language spoken in this part of Switzerland is German. To the west, it is French, and to the South, closer to Italy, they speak Italian. Fortunately for me, here in Zurich, many also spoke English. Ordering a *thunfischsalat*, a tuna salad, I sat back, surprised at my ability to talk myself out of hiding in my tiny room all night. I sat by the window of the restaurant, enjoying my salad with fresh bread and aqua, absorbing everything around me.

Then it hit me. *I'll be damned*, I thought to myself. *I'm in Switzerland.*

As I finished eating, I attempted to decipher the tab, paying out ten Swiss francs. I had gotten used to using different currencies by now. Although I still converted them into US dollars in my head, I began to understand the amounts in French francs, in Italian lire and now in Swiss francs without having to convert to dollars each time to determine if something was affordable or expensive. It didn't take long to figure out that costs in Switzerland were much higher than in Milan.

Walking slower now, back to the hotel, I noticed a type of 1960s craze trending at that moment in Zurich. Several people I passed wore tie-dyed shirts and mini-skirts and sported long, straight hair. Strains of Jimi Hendrix's "Purple Haze" drifted out of one of the small bars. I entered the hotel and noticed a tall, willowy black man standing at the counter, speaking English to the clerk. Curiously, I had seen very few black people in Paris and in Milan. I wondered why. Walking up to the counter, I glanced over and said, "Hi." He smiled and said hello back.

"Where are you from?" I asked.

It turns out he came from Nassau in the Bahamas and played in a band at the jazz club downstairs. Before rushing back down, he mentioned he would be there all week. I hoped we could talk again before he left.

Returning to my rectangular room, my little prison as I now called it, I sorted through my things. Sean had given me a picture of himself, so I placed it on the table by my bed. I decided to try to read myself to sleep. I had no idea what to expect the next day, or of Zurich itself.

Morning came quickly, and I headed downstairs for breakfast, then returned to my room to gather my things for the day. As I entered the tiny lobby, the clerk handed me a message. Francoise, the head booker with my new agency, Time Models, had called, telling me to hurry it along. Lucky for me, the agency turned out to be right across the square.

As I entered its doors, I was surprised at how small it appeared. The room only held two bookers, both sitting at a round table which took up much of the room. I filled out the necessary forms, then purchased a map of Zurich from them for ten francs. Francoise handed me a list of clients and photographers which not only included addresses and phone numbers, but also the number of the tram to take and which stop to get off at. Zurich didn't have a metro but instead had a phenomenal tram system. You could find a tram stop about every 300 meters, or every 900 feet or so. Already I began to admire how efficient the Swiss seemed. Like a precise timepiece or a detailed Swiss army knife, I felt I was in good hands.

As I studied my map, another model entered the booking room. Ivy hailed from Berkley, California, and stood just shy of my height, with curly, sandy-blond hair and an energetic smile. She too came from Fashion Agency in Milan, but I had never seen her before. Since we had the same two morning appointments, she invited me to tag along with her as I learned the city.

At the tram stop, Ivy purchased a day ticket for five francs, which lasted twenty-four hours. Since I didn't have five one-franc pieces for the machine, I bought a regular trip ticket. I would have to find a way to obtain more coins after the first go-see. As we waited briefly for the tram, Ivy showed me

ZURICH

best ways to use my new map and how to get around the city. Usually, once I arrive in a country, I am on my own, figuring it out as I go. This morning experience with Ivy immediately made Zurich much more inviting and friendly.

The first two go-sees of the day seemed like any other go-see in Paris or Milan. You think they like you but, in all honesty, you have no idea. I began to believe that all photographers and clients attended the same school to learn how to respond to models, to act uninterested even when they were.

For lunch, Ivy and I headed down to the Limmatquai on the river where we bought a sausage, bread, and a coke to enjoy while sitting by the water. With the sun shining overhead, I looked around at the beautiful, clean city. By this time, I had already forgotten dreary Milan.

On my own for the afternoon go-sees, I studied my map and made my way to see someone by the name of Huber, located on Muhlebachstrasse. Huber wasn't even there when I arrived which was not a surprise to me. This often happened in Paris, and occasionally in Milan. I left a card with the assistant and made my way to the next appointment to see H.P. Schneider on Quellenstrasse. He invited me in to sit and chat. I found this interesting as rarely had this occurred in the past. As I left, I felt good about him and whatever jobs he cast for. So good that I skipped the first tram stop, instead choosing to walk and soak in the sunshine and fresh, clean air.

Back at the agency, two more go-sees had popped up on my schedule. A German model, Claudia, also with Fashion agency in Milan, and I headed out together. I had met her model boyfriend, Tyler, at one of my morning go-sees. She told me they always traveled together. I thought about Sean. Would I want to travel with him all the time?

Returning to the hotel, I called Sean from the phone in the hall. We couldn't afford to talk long. Three minutes cost about six francs.

"I miss you," he whispered into the phone.

"I miss you too! I wish you were here with me. We could have so much fun wandering around Zurich. There is this beautiful spot down by the water..." My words trailed off as my heart pounded just thinking about the two of us together in this beautiful city.

"I love you," Sean said with a sigh now.

"I love you too." My heart swelled, and I knew I meant it. I did love him.

By the time we hung up, I felt happy. I walked down one level to meet Lisa, a model from California who I had met earlier in the day. We hit the streets, along with Ivy, seeing Zurich by night.

Ivy had a date with a Swiss man who spoke little English, so Lisa and I decided to stroll along the river. The night, by the river, with the city lights shining, felt perfect. All along the way, people enjoyed their drug of choice out in the open, shooting up heroin or snorting cocaine. Others just smoked their hash. I pretended not to notice.

Stopping at an outdoor café on the Limmatquai, Lisa and I sipped on hot chocolate and talked about our grand adventures back in Milan. Around midnight, we made our way back to the hotel. The square had filled with various eccentrics and several prostitutes. We waded through them all and said goodnight.

ZURICH

I lay in my bed, mesmerized by all that I had seen, and experienced, during my first full day in Zurich. I liked it. All my fear and fretting of the night before had been for nothing.

ZURICH

The Limmat River, and the Limmatquai, soon became my landmark to orient myself in the city. The hotel sat on the east side of the river, between the two bridges that crossed over. Everything else I found in the city was oriented as to where they were in relation to the Limmatquai, and more directly, my hotel.

The waterfront promenades always made me feel as if I were on permanent vacation. Every time I turned a corner and found myself near the water in the days ahead, my mood calmed, and my pace slowed. The city itself beamed, clean and impressive in the summer sun. Zurich was a rich city, a global banking and financial center, much like Milan in Italy, but without that stale, stern business feel to it.

I soon learned that Fridays in Zurich were much like Mondays in Milan—slow with not much going on. After I ate breakfast downstairs with Lisa and Ivy, we walked over to the agency. Our first go-see took us to see the editors for *Blick* magazine, a Swiss German-language tabloid newspaper. Afterward, we headed across town to another go-see. Once there, two men invited us to sit and have coffee with them. Recognizing my name from my card which they had already received from the agency, they spoke to each other in fast German. It seemed my last name, von der Osten, was of great interest to many I encountered in the days ahead. It is an aristocratic name, I often heard, as well as possibly a royal one. Maybe good, maybe not. You just could never tell.

Next, we made our way to see *Schweizer Familie* magazine. The woman there asked if I could return on Monday to show my portfolio to the Art Director for the magazine. Her invitation seemed like a good sign, and I quickly agreed.

In the afternoon, Lisa, Ivy and I walked to an area near the University of Zurich to look at a set of available apartments. Staying at the hotel would be too expensive for the long term. Upon arrival at the address, we recognized it as some type of, for lack of a better thought at the time, psycho clinic.

The apartments were originally built for the people who studied at the University and worked at the clinic. The rooms were large, and there was a community bathroom with showers for all to use. The huge kitchen, much like in a big restaurant, was to be shared by all the residents as well. Small, stainless-steel refrigerators with locks, one for each resident, lined a wall like a set of school lockers. We would also have access to a swimming pool, a tennis court, and a gym on the premises. Yet the clinic itself seemed to surround the living spaces, almost providing a choking, claustrophobic feel.

Somewhat spooked, I stayed silent as the tour ended. *If I live here*, I wondered, *will I go crazy myself and in turn, have experiments conducted on me by mad scientists?* Admittedly, that might make a good book, but it was not something I wanted to experience in order to write about. I also considered the possibility it might be more of an observation experiment with cameras throughout as the scientists or doctors watched our every move. This seemed to be the start of paranoia in me or at least my recognition of it.

The three of us remained quiet, politely smiling and nodding. I think we all just wanted to get out of there in one piece. The gentleman who showed us the apartment singled me out and handed me the key to one of the downstairs apartments, saying if we wanted to move in over the weekend we could. I graciously accepted it, knowing full well I would just have to drop it back off the next week.

With the arrival of June, I realized that I had been in Europe for five straight months. Back when I first arrived in Milan in January, I remember speaking with other models who had already been in Europe for several months. I had been in awe of them, not able to imagine being away from the States for so long. Now, here I was, one of them.

The Hirschen Hotel had a small, enclosed patio, and I planted myself there for a few hours after breakfast on my first Saturday in Zurich. Lisa's roommate, Tanya, arrived back in Zurich from her job in the mountains. She seemed a little on the flighty side but likable. We explored the streets of Zurich together in the afternoon before an allergy attack forced me back to my room. Once under control, I rejoined them for dinner and a quick stop at the Roxy nightclub just across the river. I didn't stay long, but I enjoyed seeing what a club looked like in Zurich. Amnesia in Milan had been the best nightclub for me, but I now felt burnt out from clubbing and decided to make it an early night.

As I sat out on the patio again the following day, reading and writing in my journal, Rick, the black guy from the

Bahamas I met my first night in Zurich, stopped by. We talked for a while then headed down to the riverside for a walk. We discussed racism in general and, particularly, in Europe. I mentioned how one day while in my agency, I overheard one of the bookers talking on the phone, asking the person on the other end of the line if she were black. After a short pause, the booker informed her that there wasn't a market in Zurich for black models and therefore no reason for her to come there. Her voice did not seem apologetic for this, just simply stating a fact. I felt horrified for the model at the other end of the line. Quietly, I had turned and left the office before anyone could see me.

On Monday I returned to the offices of *Schwiezer Familie* to see the Art Director, as promised the Friday before. The magazine, in turn, optioned me for a four-to-five-day job. Options for jobs meant that a client called the agency and placed a hold on you for certain dates. They could create these holds for several different models, then once they decided, they informed the agency who they wished to book. That way, we wouldn't be off working for someone else on those days.

With another allergy attack gearing up, I stopped off at the Apotheke near the hotel. The pharmacist spoke English and recommended some eye drops and pills to combat the allergies. I gladly obliged, not caring how much it cost as long as it provided fast relief. Zurich bloomed with rhododendrons and azaleas, but for me, my runaway allergic reactions likely stemmed from the grasses and birch tree pollen. Attempts to get the itchy eyes under control were imperative as having bloodshot eyes didn't bode well in photographs, nor did red noses from constant running and blowing with harsh tissues.

Returning to the agency, I heard yelling as I turned the corner. It sounded like Ivy, and I froze just outside the booking room. She screamed at the bookers as they repeated that she had to go back to Milan because she didn't have a composite card, and one was needed to work in Zurich. Calling Fashion Agency in Milan, Ivy proceeded to scream at them for sending her to Zurich, knowing full well she didn't have a card yet. I couldn't blame her for being upset. As she stormed out, Lisa and I quietly followed. We listened to her as she packed and then helped her take all her things to the train station. I hoped Milan would be kind to her.

ZURICH

It didn't take long to realize that the agency wasn't exactly as efficient as a Swiss watch after all. They began to remind me of my agency in Paris, always mixing up times or dates, maybe even making them up to seem like we had more appointments than we really did.

Often, I arrived at a go-see at the time specified by the bookers and found no one there. Yet, I didn't yell at them like I did at the agency back in Paris. Emotional outbursts seemed to be kept more in check here, a difference from my early days in Paris, and even occasionally in Milan. It seemed that maybe I had matured in some ways and found better ways to deal with the frustrations. Cultural differences came into play in various ways also. There was no dramatic throwing up of hands here. In Switzerland, and later Germany, I could see that directness of speech and action were more at play than emotion.

After two weeks at the Hotel Hirschen, the agency informed us that we had to move to another hotel. I didn't fret. In two trips, Lisa and I managed to haul all our luggage down the cobblestone streets to the Hotel Otter, on Oberdorfstrasse, south of the Hirschenplatz. The Otter became our new home base. At least we were on the same side of the river, near the Limmatquai, keeping my orientation in the city somewhat intact.

The Otter turned out to be even more like a boarding house, with the owner, Ellen, watching over us and bringing breakfast to our rooms every morning. In the evenings, we gathered downstairs in the lobby where the only television could be found and watched various shows in German, Italian, French and occasionally, English.

Oddly enough, my first job in Zurich actually required me to fly to Dusseldorf, Germany. I apparently had made a good impression somewhere on one of my go-sees, but I had no idea which one. Boarding the plane, I found my aisle seat next to a businessman. As I sat down, I accidentally touched his leg as I struggled to place my carry-on bag under my seat. Embarrassed, I apologized and looked up at his face. He reminded me of the Marlboro man in all those print ads, a slightly older man and attractive, if you like cowboys in expensive suits, that is. He seemed to have a patient, curious way about him as he smiled back. Having spent several months in Italy, I had gotten used to recognizing a man's intentions almost immediately. Not so, I soon surmised, with German men such as the one now sitting beside me.

We talked during the flight, mostly small talk at first. Axel, his name I soon learned, managed an advertising agency in Dusseldorf. Upon landing, he offered me a ride to my hotel, and I graciously accepted.

As Axel pulled his car up in front of the address given to me by my Zurich agency, we both stared out at the building which resembled a brownstone apartment building more than a hotel. A small, unlit sign hung on the side, and we could barely make out the name, Hotel Mondial. I exited the car and walked up to the door. It was locked. I rang the bell several times, attempting to get the hotel manager as it wasn't even 9:00 p.m. yet. With no response at the door, I climbed back in Axel's car.

He drove me to a few other hotels nearby, but they were full due to a conference in Cologne (or as the Germans spell it, Koln) less than an hour away. Finally, Axel made his way to the swankier BörsenHotel. At 130 Deutsche marks a night, I cringed as I handed over the money. Axel waited at the bar in the lobby, and I joined him after placing my things in my room upstairs. He didn't seem to have any ulterior motives for being helpful. I didn't know what to think. Maybe the German men *were* different from the Italians. At least, I hoped so.

After two drinks, Axel said goodnight, and I returned to my room alone. As I attempted to fall asleep, I realized that if I had not met Axel on the plane, who knows where I might have ended up for the night. Another angel put in my path, perhaps? My Mom always helped other people, even when we thought she shouldn't. She would often say, "I just hope that if my children ever need help, someone will be there for them as well." She got her wish, more than once with me. That time in Rome when Emilio and his mom invited me to their house for the night, and now Axel could be added to that growing list.

Morning arrived and, once at Studio Keupen, I admonished the client and photographer for the hotel situation. They played dumb as if they didn't know the hotel locked its doors so early. I gave in, giving them the benefit of a doubt. Maybe, I surmised, they really didn't know that the hotel locked its doors at 8:00 p.m. The hairstylist, Shaun, from London, saved the day by grabbing my arm and pulling me over to the chair. From that point on, the day flew by, with outfit after outfit, and hairstyle after hairstyle. When we finished, I had to dash out, barely making it to my plane with only five minutes to spare.

Axel visited Zurich again a few weeks later for business, and we met for dinner. Afterward, we walked along the Limmatquai. Before parting for the night, he handed me a gift—a bottle of Chanel COCO perfume. Apparently, Chanel was a major client of his advertising agency. At least that is what he told me. I couldn't decipher what he expected from our friendship, if anything. I did not feel an attraction, physical or emotional, for him. Instead, curiosity is what led me to meet him for dinner. Perhaps, I thought, maybe the mixed signals were a part of the German culture as well.

When I returned to Zurich from Dusseldorf, I found Hetty had arrived from Austria. We celebrated by going out for a late-night hot chocolate. I told her about my experiences so far in Zurich, and she told me about her job in Vienna. It felt wonderful to see her again yet also strange as we were now in such a different place.

While Hetty headed out on her first day of go-sees. I relaxed, preparing for another job outside of Zurich. Catching the 6:00 p.m. train to Lausanne, a few hours later I met up with the crew for the job at the first-class Bahnhof Buffet restaurant in the train station. Four models were already there including two Germans, one French, and one Italian. Within the first minute, I could tell the photographer was disappointed that I wasn't German. At the first mention of my being American, he and the clients grew quiet, staring at me before walking away.

ZURICH

Lausanne wasn't our final destination for the night. We climbed in the photographer's car and drove to the small village of Gruyères about forty-five minutes away. Pulling up to the Hostellerie des Chevaliers, we unloaded and were handed our room keys. I would be sharing a room with Sophie, the blonde French model.

The hotel sat just outside the walls of the medieval village of Gruyères where we would be shooting the next day. As I crawled into bed, I vowed to make the best of the situation, enjoy the location, and pretend the rudeness of the clients didn't bother me.

Awaking at 6:30 a.m., I hurriedly applied my makeup and styled my hair for the day. As I wasn't in the first set of photos, I took my time eating breakfast. Looking out behind the hotel restaurant, I viewed rolling hills with cows and sheep leisurely grazing. I half expected Heidi to come skipping down the hill with her pigtails flying. A very different Switzerland from Zurich indeed.

Once inside the medieval city walls, I stayed close by the group, although I rarely talked and they, the clients, rarely spoke in English. I felt relieved when the photographer and models returned, but once the majority of them left, I found myself on my own again. I glanced around the town, branching out a little further each time to see more of the village. Gruyères, known for the production of the cheese by the same name, also seemed to provide its residents with fresh cream every morning. I quickly found a shop serving fresh whipped cream atop a hot chocolate and pastry; mouth-watering pleasures even I couldn't resist.

EUROPEAN DAZE

The spectacular views of the mountains and the quaintness of the village, however, couldn't quell my growing uneasiness. As it turned out, my intuition proved correct. In the afternoon, while I posed on the cobblestone street, near the old castle, one of the clients walked up to me saying, in barely discernable English, that he didn't think I fit the job. Apparently, I later learned, they claimed I didn't look sophisticated enough for the outfits and the ads. I think it was more because I was an American.

I changed out of the clothes, handing them to Sophie who took my place in those shots, then walked around the town. Now that I had been tossed aside, I felt no need to stay close by or put on a good face for them. I bought a few postcards and some amazing milk chocolate candy, and enjoyed what I could of the visit. Yet my irritation with the client and the entire group nagged at me, and I couldn't wait to get away from them all, away even from this picturesque Swiss village.

By late afternoon, I got my wish. With all photos complete, we raced back to Lausanne to catch our trains, each of us going in different directions. As the only one going back to Zurich, I felt relief wash over me as I boarded the train alone.

With this experience, I suddenly felt like I was going backward in my career instead of forward. The client and the photographer hadn't told me what type of look they were looking for so I would know how to do my makeup and hair. Besides, the odd feelings started when they realized I was American and not German. Would my nationality be an obstacle in the future as well?

ZURICH

Attempting to put the Gruyères' experience behind me, I spent the following day going on various go-sees all over the city and sitting at cafes when I had time to spare. Stopping at the agency before the end of the day, I learned that the four-day option with *Schweizer Familie*, a sewing and pattern catalog, had been confirmed. This client at least knew me as an American and wanted me anyway.

I headed back to the Otter. Sean had called to say he would be jumping on the next train to Zurich. Surprised, but delighted, I made my way to the station to meet his 11:00 p.m. train. He looked tired but smiled wide. Wrapping his strong arms around me, I melted into them.

Sean and I spent the following day exploring Zurich, starting with a hot chocolate at the popular Confiserie Sprüngli Café. Finding it overly crowded, we left after just one cup and walked down the Bahnhofstrasse with its fancy designer stores before branching out to the cobblestone streets of Zurich. Eventually, we ended up at the waterfront. Once there, we felt no need to rush or do anything else. Sean remained quiet most of the day, telling me that being out of Milan, out of the meat market, even if only temporarily, made him happy. We enjoyed spending the day alone together. In Milan, we always had other people with us, no matter where we went.

EUROPEAN DAZE

The next day, with Sean already on his way back to Milan, I slowly gathered my things and packed a bag for my trip outside of Zurich for the *Schwiezer Familie* job. I climbed aboard the 6:04 p.m. train to Arth-Goldau, heading in the direction of Lugano, on the Zurich-Milan railway line. Less than forty minutes later, I arrived at Arth-Goldau. From there I boarded the Gotthard Railway, a cog railway taking me up the Rigi, the Alpine "queen of mountains," to the town of Airolo.

In all honesty, I felt quite fed up with the traveling jobs, having to pack up everything and live out of a suitcase. I couldn't help feeling down, maybe because I had just seen Sean. Tears dammed up behind my eyes as I made my way off the train. Fortunately, right across the street from the train station sat the Hotel des Alpes. Even in the dark, I could tell its building characteristically old and inviting.

Once at the desk, I found the other model checking in, a German model named Edith. She spoke perfect English and instantly seemed down to earth and likable. We placed our bags in our rooms then headed back down to the restaurant for dinner. The clients and the photographer were already there holding a table for us. I heaved a huge sigh of relief as I sat down. The previous trip to Gruyères, just a few days earlier, had stepped on my confidence and my tolerance for being treated as an object. Now I felt that confidence, that hope, rising again.

The entire crew climbed in a van the next morning and headed out, scouting locations to shoot the various outfits. Finally, we pulled off the road near a large brook. The bone-

ZURICH

chilling wind whipped through me as I posed alongside the water, just now beginning to slightly thaw. The photographer signaled me before snapping away on his camera, and I did my best to still my shaking, and unfreeze my face into a slight smile. It felt ten times colder here than it ever felt in Milan, even with the snow. It may have been the middle of June, but the Alps didn't seem to notice.

After lunch back at our hotel in Airolo, we again climbed in the van for a scenic drive up the Gotthard Pass. Gotthard is a major north-south route through the Swiss Alps, with the road curving precipitously like a slithering snake. The hairpin turns jostled us around the van, making several of us queasy and uneasy. We thought it would never end.

At the top of Monte Prosa, as the road began to straighten a little, we approached a four-story building set out on a flattened rocky clearing. A seemingly odd find in the middle of nowhere, the San Gottardo Ospizia, a thirteenth-century guesthouse, now a simple hotel, provided a warm restaurant for us to spend a short break while preparing to shoot a few photos outside in the snow. We entered the small restaurant and sat at a table near a window, ordering the hottest coffee they could serve. As I sipped on mine, I glanced out the window to see an adorable St. Bernard puppy playing in the snow, running through it as if it were sand. Now what can be more Swiss than that, I girlishly thought to myself.

For the next two hours, we shot in the snow. Beautiful scenery but shockingly cold, our outfits, although wintery, were nowhere near warm enough to keep us from shivering.

EUROPEAN DAZE

Finishing around 6:00 p.m., before the day's light had completely faded away, we headed back down the curvy way to the hotel for the night.

We returned to Monte Prosa early the following morning, capturing the dawn light. As the photographer planned and shot more photos of Edith and a little Swiss girl, I roamed around the few buildings, playing tourist, and buying more postcards, film for my camera, and a Swiss bell keychain. The muted colors of the snow-covered Alps surrounding us and the drab colors of the hotel seemed to add to the overall stillness. The overall quietness. After posing for a few photos, we gathered once again in the restaurant, this time for a coffee doused with a shot of liquor. That seemed the faster way to warm up, and a good way to end the day.

Laughing and happy, we returned to the hotel down the mountain and found that Stefan, a male model from Sweden, had arrived. The group chose to go out to another restaurant for dinner, but Edith and I stayed at the hotel to have soup. We both felt a cold coming on and wanted to get to bed early.

It turned into a horrific night, memorable still to this day. I awoke around 3:00 a.m. with a massive pain shooting up my right shoulder. I paced the hallway outside my room for what felt like hours. Tears streamed down my face. The pain radiated throughout my entire body and felt worse than anything I had ever experienced before. Around 6:00 a.m. I finally found a way to lie in the bed that didn't make it worse. But at 7:00 a.m. the photographer banged on my door, shouting that we had to get to work.

ZURICH

TOP: Photo shoot beside a brook in the Swiss Alps, near the town of Airolo..

CENTER: Gotthard Pass, a major north-south route through the Swiss Alsps.

BOTTOM: At the top of Mount Prosa, a desolate, colorless rock cropping in the Swiss Alps.

Somehow, I managed to cover up the pain, and the cold that had now sunk into my head and chest. As we all sat together eating breakfast, I remained quiet. Shortly another male model, Kevin, an American, showed up, along with another child model, a Swiss boy. Exhausted, I made way out to the van and through the day without complaining. Several cover-tries took place, and this time, mine made the cover of *Schweizer Familie's* fall and winter 1985 issue, along with the little girl sporting pigtails and a smile.

Ahead of schedule, a few of us managed to catch trains back to wherever we came from that night. Edith headed back to Munich. The hairstylist and I headed back to Zurich.

I spent the next two days in bed at the Otter. My shoulder pain came from a pinched nerve, and I was told it would take three months for it to subside. My cold sucked any life left out of me, and I focused on getting well before the weekend. Sean's friends, Taber and Ian, were arriving in Zurich, and I wanted to be well enough to show them around.

When the weekend arrived, Hetty and I met Taber and Ian at the train station and treated them to a group dinner with Janice, a model from Boston, and Karen, a model from Hawaii, at the Spaghetti Factory. The reasonably priced restaurant offered spaghetti in seemingly endless variations and had become one of our favorites. Afterward, Taber, Ian and I stopped in the Bistro, the restaurant I had had my first dinner in the night I arrived in Zurich, for a coffee and dessert. We talked and talked about Milan and about Sean. We all knew things were changing. I felt caught in the middle of the old and the new, with Taber and Ian on one side, and my new friends Lisa, Janice, and Karen on the other.

My new friends in Zurich differed greatly from my old friends from Milan. What I liked most about them was that we had real conversations. We didn't just sit around bragging about our latest tear sheets or who we worked with last week. That superficiality had been left in Milan. All of them were a few years older than me and had been in the modeling world much longer. They didn't appear to be concerned about superstardom but were more laid back, enjoying what life had to offer, appreciating this grand opportunity to see the world. I admired them.

ZURICH

Monday arrived and along with it my job for Sulzer on Weinbergstrasse. The client required I have my hair and makeup done in a natural style and my nails painted a pale pink. The job turned out to be for an advertisement for ice cream and might make the cover of a restaurant's new menu. I held various sundaes up in front of my lips, smiling with my eyes. For two hours we played, at least that's what it felt like. The client seemed pleased with me and mentioned she might very well use me again for another job soon. I hoped so.

Before heading back to the agency, I stopped at the TWA office nearby to check on my round-trip ticket, purchased by Fashion Agency for my flight to Milan back in January. It had an open return, and I needed to know the expiration date. Admittedly, I felt rather weary about taking a TWA flight again because, at that very moment, one of their planes sat hijacked on the tarmac in Beirut with several American hostages onboard. This became a new reality in the world, and it directly affected my world as well.

Soon armed with the knowledge that my ticket wouldn't expire until early January, I felt relieved that I didn't have to worry about using it right away. Now that I had already been away from the States for so long, another six months didn't seem that challenging or foreboding.

Working again on Wednesday, I made my way to Paul Erhardt's studio. The editorial job was for *ModeBlatt*, a magazine showcasing clothes and patterns that you could sew at home. This seemed to be a common type of magazine among the Swiss. With another model from Canada, we filled the day caking on makeup, and weaving our way through traffic as the photographer shot photo after photo. The outfits were warm, and mine included a red, two-piece knit dress and another fuchsia colored sweater dress. Fortunately, the heat of June in Switzerland didn't match the sweat of June in Florida.

I returned to Paul Erhard's studio again a few days later to work for the same client. First, we shot a cover try, but I didn't count on it making the actual cover. Photographers often do this in an attempt to impress the client with their work, and hopefully add a cover to their own portfolios. As before, we shot in the streets as well as in the studio. For both days, I was paid at an editorial rate, which again meant that I might get good tear sheets for my portfolio, but not much money. This was mid-June, and the client mentioned that the spread would be out in the September issue, just a few months away. As always, I would have to wait and see.

ZURICH

Although I had been in Zurich for almost a month and had worked several jobs, I still had to obtain Swiss working papers. This was my first experience in having to obtain the papers myself, and I had to do so by returning to Milan and visiting the Swiss consulate there.

On a Sunday, I boarded the 9:04 a.m. train to Milan and settled in for the long ride. Sean met me at the station, and although glad to see him, I wasn't happy to be back in Milan. It seemed as soon as I arrived, a black mood descended over me once again. We dropped my bag off at his pensione and then met up with his friend, Jerry. As we headed to dinner at Rhiskios for a little garlic spaghetti for old-times sake, we ran into Ivy. She said that upon returning to Milan a few weeks ago, she switched agencies and now had lots of work. I was happy for her. Things can change in an instant in the world of modeling. We had all seen it many times.

The next morning, I entered the booking room at Fashion Agency, and they greeted me as if I had been gone forever. I felt confused. Didn't they know I was only back for a few days? As I gathered up my waiting mail, including a care package from my parents, Lorenzo walked through the door. He greeted me with a kiss on each cheek, pulling me into his office. He had just returned from New York and couldn't wait to tell me that my agency there, Legends, was finally getting their act together once again. I was relieved to learn this as I had not heard from Legends in months.

This bit of good news buoyed my spirit as I headed back out into the streets of Milan. I met Sean, and we picked up a panini to enjoy in the park. He seemed rather grumpy all day, so once back at the pensione, while he took a nap, I sat by the window and opened my parents' care package. It felt like Christmas! Out poured Aunt Jemima's pancake mix and syrup, a box of Sweet-n-Low, a few of my summer clothes, a pair of shoes, two books, and my favorite purse.

The following morning, I arrived at the Swiss consulate at my scheduled time. With all my forms already filled out by the agency in Zurich, it only took about an hour, and I had my official working papers.

Back at Fashion, I met with Lorenzo again. Although he seemed to be asking me if I would return to Milan at the end of August, it felt more like an order. I nodded my head yes, but truthfully, I had no idea where I would be in August, much less September. I switched the conversation over to Munich and how I wanted to go there for a while to meet with photographers and clients. He agreed, saying he would call the agency there and let me know soon.

Once back in Zurich, I found that many of my options had dropped and the work had slowed. I had been rather lucky the past several weeks but now knew it might be a good idea to move on. Zurich is a small market and not one in which to overstay your welcome.

ZURICH

Temporarily putting all thoughts of work aside as the Fourth of July arrived, my friends and I decided to celebrate the distinctly American holiday with an American brunch. We met at Janice and Karen's tiny apartment before noon. The feast included French toast and pancakes doused in the Aunt Jemima syrup my parents had sent, along with fresh orange juice and a big fruit salad.

I missed celebrating these holidays back at home in Florida with a big barbecue, my Mom's homemade ice cream, and fireworks spilling out over the Halifax River not far away. Overall, what I missed most about home was all the great meals out on the back porch of my parents' one-hundred-year-old house. This had been the gathering place for family and friends and for celebrations. These continued of course, just without me.

That evening, Taber, Ian, and I took Hetty to the station to catch her train back to Vienna. Earlier in the day, we had sat together alone and talked, reminiscing about our days in Milan. We considered meeting up in Spain to work before the end of the year as we had heard that Barcelona had a lot of work. She gave me her designer off-white coat that she had gotten when she was in Japan. I always loved that long coat. I hoped this wasn't a final goodbye. Maybe we would meet up in Munich in another month or so.

Ian and Taber left the next day, returning to Milan. I wondered if I would ever see them again also. Feeling rather sad, and a bit nostalgic for those days in Milan with the gang, and not wanting to be alone, I stopped in the agency. A note waited there for me, from Talents Agency in Munich. They were ready for me.

With my spirits lifted, I threw myself into packing up most of my things over the weekend, now up to six bags to carry around. Sean had been booked for a one-day job in Zurich on Sunday so came up the night before. Meeting him at the train station on Saturday evening, I dressed up and wore Hetty's Japanese coat. He arrived, telling me I looked fantastic and how he had fallen in love with me all over again the minute he saw me. Once back at the Otter, however, the good mood quickly evaporated as he immediately started in on his political diatribe, this time about the hijacking in Beirut, berating the horrible Americans. Funny thing though, Sean dreamed of moving to New York, yet he acted as if he hated Americans.

With the mood still tense, I steered the conversation over to us and our relationship. The talk had been a long time coming.

"You know I love you, right?"

Sean moved in closer but didn't say anything.

"I love you, but I just don't think I'm in love with you. Does that make sense?"

He didn't move away but instead looked down at the floor. If he knew this conversation was coming, he didn't let on.

"Well then, do you still want to be with me?" Now he looked up, into my eyes.

"Yes, of course. I…" My words fell off, and I found it hard to look into his eyes at the same time as trying to convince him this was for the best.

"You know," he started. "I've noticed a lot of changes in you since leaving Milan."

I didn't know exactly what changes he was referring to but didn't feel that this was a bad thing.

ZURICH

"I was lonely in Milan, and so were you. Maybe our relationship grew out that. Now that I'm out of Milan..." I couldn't finish the sentence. I had never had to talk with anyone about my feelings before, and I surely didn't want to hurt him.

"Things between us moved too fast for me. I've never had a relationship like this before."

It wasn't just that I had never had a real relationship before, but the confusion I felt about modeling and how to go about succeeding, I constantly told myself that in this business, you can't afford the luxury of falling in love, much less maintain a serious relationship. It's just too hard. You had to concentrate on your career. Everyone had a different market, and I had to keep moving to find mine. Sean needed to do the same.

We talked for over an hour. It began to seem that Sean had been part of Milan, and now that Milan was behind me, so too might whatever we had had there. We both felt relieved that we talked and got everything out in the open. Maybe some of our differences were just too hard to span.

The next morning, after Sean left for his modeling job, I sat drinking my coffee. Loneliness swept over me. Since our talk, naturally everything suddenly felt different between us. Later that evening, I met him at the train station, and as we said our goodbyes, neither of us knew when we would see each other again. With my going to Munich, and he most likely returning to London soon, it might be a while. First, Kristen, Ava and I had been separated, now the Milan gang might well be separated as well, for a long time. Maybe forever.

When the new week started, I pushed my loneliness aside and called Talents Agency in Munich, asking if I could come the next day. Why wait? They, thankfully, said yes. I called Lorenzo in Milan to tell him my plans to head to Munich. As long as I kept moving, loneliness could be held at bay.

For my last evening in Zurich, I ate dinner at the Bistro by myself, one last time. I had the tuna salad, bread, and aqua, just like that first night I had arrived in Zurich, nervous and timid. Afterward, I made my way to the Gran-Café on the Limmatquai, treating myself to a *Coupe Danemark* (ice cream with a warm chocolate sauce). It just didn't taste as good alone, however.

As morning approached, I focused all my attention on the day ahead. After storing four of my bags with the hotel, a service I gladly found they offered, I headed into the agency. They owed me several francs, and I needed to collect before traveling to Germany. Afterward, I stopped at the bank to exchange a few francs to Deutsche marks, and the rest into good old American dollars. The exchange rate for US dollars was always better than the exchange rate for other currencies, so I kept as much as I could in dollars and exchanged them as needed.

With the hotel bill paid, extra luggage tucked away in storage, and goodbyes said to the agency, I boarded the train, bound for Munich. My time in Zurich had been like an exciting, sexy, exotic rebound affair after my messy break-up with brooding Milan. Now with that out of my system, I could focus on what came next.

ZURICH

Swiss fondue dinner with Zurich friends
(l-to-r) Karen, Janice, me and Lisa.

EUROPEAN DAZE

TOP: Advertisement for ice cream.

BOTTOM: Photo shoot for a magazine on the streets of Zurich.

MUNICH
JULY 9 - DECEMBER 7, 1985

My first view of Germany entered through the large square windows of the northbound train. With the sun shining overhead, I saw a small town spread out before me where young and old alike gathered by a lake, swimming, pedaling paddle boats, picnicking and laughing. Thoughts of running through the green grass barefooted, throwing off my clothes and diving into the lake suddenly came over me. This is what you do in the summertime. As the train moved past, I settled back into my seat, speechless at the beauty of southern Germany as the train continued its trek, now veering off slightly towards the northeast.

As the train approached Munich, however, my thoughts returned to the focused seriousness of arriving in a new place, all alone, once again, and having to find my way. The trip from Zurich had taken almost five hours, and the time for daydreaming had passed. The Munich Hauptbahnhof train station, a mammoth steel structure, appeared clean and orderly as I made my way down to the platform, dragging my two bags behind me. Another new city, yet, for some reason, it didn't feel strange or foreign at all. I slowed my pace, eventually finding the taxi stand outside. Climbing in, I gave the driver the address, Schellingstrasse 24. He simply nodded, and we were on our way.

Pensione Frank, another boarding house type accommodation similar to Zurich's, only much larger, played host and revolving door to dozens and dozens of models. After checking in, I made my way up to the second floor to a small room with two double beds. I would be sharing the room with a Dutch model by the name of Annika.

Setting my bags to one side of the room, I sat down on the bed closest to the door, giving myself a moment to take it all in. I heard a rap at the door. As I turned, Edith, the German model who I had worked with in Airolo in the Alps just a few weeks before, barged in. Expecting to see Annika, she stopped short, then grinned. I smiled back. I had planned to call her the following day to let her know I had arrived in Munich. We headed downstairs to the small pizzeria for dinner.

If you have never stayed in a pensione, imagine it as a small college dorm, where each room contains two to four beds and very little else. The bathrooms and showers are usually on the same floor, but as my luck would have it, at the Pensione Frank they were at the other end of the hallway—a long walk in the middle of the night.

No one got the royal treatment here, that's for sure. Downstairs, on the main floor, was the breakfast room, where we gathered every morning. A television room sat adjacent to the breakfast room, and several models often lounged in there. The biggest problem I found with these living arrangements, especially at the Pensione Frank, was the utter lack of privacy. It seemed that the majority of models in the pensione were American models. Loud, obnoxious Americans at that.

MUNICH

The small pizzeria restaurant below the pensione became a popular place for anyone who stayed at the Frank. The owner, Italian of course, constantly talked and would come out and flirt. What is the saying? You can take the man out of Italy, but you can't take the Italy out of the man?

My new agency, Internationale Talents Modelle, sat on Ohmstrasse not far from the pensione. From the moment I entered the booking room, I could feel the excitement and energy filling the air. This, I thought, is how an agency should be. Four bookers talked on their phones at once, as one spun the lazy-Susan tray center of the round table, snatching out a file and slamming it down in front of her. Another one of the bookers spoke sternly into the phone, punctuating the air with her pencil.

An older lady, with short set hair, saw me first and put her finger up, asking me to wait. I nodded and turned toward a bench to sit down. Heidi Themlitz, the owner of the agency, joined me shortly, recognizing me from the photos sent by Lorenzo. I felt an instant rapport. She gathered up a Talents portfolio book for me to place my photos and tear sheets in, along with a voucher book to take to jobs, and a brochure listing eighty-eight studios and photographers, along with their addresses and telephone numbers. Another booker, Patty, walked over to introduce herself and hand me forms to fill out for the agency. Next, I was shepherded into the accounting office to meet Dagmar. Everyone seemed happy, positive, and shockingly organized.

EUROPEAN DAZE

While at the agency, I met an American model who had also recently arrived in Munich. Coming from Spain, Lisa Bevis radiated with positivity. She invited me to join her and her boyfriend Rafa, a Spanish photographer, for a coffee before our go-sees. I gladly accepted. We sat talking for a while, and I learned she and Rafa met in Barcelona and decided to travel together, working on their respective careers.

Lisa, a few years older than me, seemed much like my friends back in Zurich. She regaled me with tales of her travels, all over the States and Europe, first as a mime act. She said her mother had put her in theater classes when she was young because of her extreme shyness. Once she found mime, she burst out of her shell and has been performing in one way or another ever since. From trapeze stunts, fire-eating, street theatre, singing in a punk band, and now to modeling, the world really did seem to be her oyster.

Over the next several days, I kept busy, making my way to go-see after go-see, getting acquainted with the city and with the clients and photographers. At a go-see with clients at the agency, they took one look at my Chameleon tear sheet (from Milan), smiled, then closed my book, moving on to another model. It seemed they were looking for someone more conservative looking. Going outside of the city, to Martinsried, I received a completely different reaction. Peter Kaiser, the photographer, and his clients looked through my book slowly as if analyzing each photo and tear sheet.

The more time I spent out on the streets of Munich, the more people I saw who reminded me of my family on my father's side. The German side. Apparently, many of the Germans felt

MUNICH

the same way about me, often telling me I looked German, some even saying I resembled their kinswoman, actress Natasha Kinski. I felt flattered, and to an extent proud, of my German heritage. I felt surprisingly comfortable in Munich, almost at home. Never had I felt like this in Paris, Milan, or Zurich. Maybe the Germans were more like myself, a little more reserved and serious, but friendly in a way I considered normal. I wanted to settle down here, concentrate on work and make enough money to live on for a while without worry.

MUNICH

Life at the pensione soon became fraught with too much noise and immaturity. The male models raced around banging on everyone's door at 3:00 a.m. or yelling at the top of their voices out in the hallways. One of them, a thirty-year-old American with a master's degree, must have thought he was eighteen or nineteen again. He seemed to be the ringleader. Many of the girls were just as obnoxious, and I did my best to steer clear of most of them, marking myself as an outcast. Our room, or rather, Annika's room, became the central meeting place for everyone in the pensione.

I did my best not to spend much time there and would meet Lisa and Rafa, or Edith, for dinner, leaving them to their parties. I knew I had to get out of there as soon as possible. Talking with Heidi at the agency, she said she would be on the lookout for an apartment for me to rent. Meanwhile, my first option turned into a confirmed job for *Freundin* magazine. I had two jobs for hair lined up, including one for Trendline hair products, and another for a shoot entitled "What to do with my hair on a Saturday night." I also had an editorial job confirmed with *Quick*, a weekly German-language illustrated news magazine. The German clients and photographers I met during my first few weeks seemed to be excited to work with me. I felt the same about them.

EUROPEAN DAZE

In between go-sees one day, I stumbled upon an English bookstore and roamed around inside. I settled on three books, one of them being *A Pocket History of the United States*. I wanted to catch up on my history and be able to talk more intelligently about my own country with others such as Sean, especially when he began blasting America's actions of the past. I was finding out that knowledge can serve more than one purpose.

Speaking of Sean, I tried calling him only to find he had left Milan and wouldn't be back until September. I didn't know where he was. Maybe London, Zurich, or Paris? August is the month many Europeans spend on vacation, and I heard work slowed, nearly coming to a standstill, for most markets during the month. Germany, however, remained busy.

A few days later, Sean called from Zurich. He was on his way back to London and wanted me to know he missed me and still loved me. I didn't know how to respond. I couldn't even bring myself to say I missed him. He said he might be back to Zurich sometime in August. Maybe we would see each other then? Maybe, I said.

As the days went by, Annika moved out of the pensione, and I had to move to another room, sharing with three other models. Fortunately, Heidi called from the agency, telling me she knew of an apartment where two rooms were being rented out. I jumped at the chance. The scheduled time to see the apartment fell between 9:00 and 10:00 p.m. on a Friday evening. I walked up the Leopoldstrasse, a broad avenue running north and south, and turned left on Franz-Joseph-Strasse. One block in sat a four-story building on the corner, a neo-baroque building with bay windows, balconies, and a garden gate. I entered the double wooden front door and made my way up the wide wooden stairs to the fourth floor.

Hartwig, the owner of the apartment, met me at the door. Wiry, he stood about my height, with dark eyes and shoulder-length black hair. His face, although aged more than my own, seemed boyish as he grinned a wide grin. He welcomed me in, and as I made my way past the living room, he introduced me to his Royal Bavarian Pullen, an enormous sectional sofa. The apartment felt large and roomy, grounded by old wooden floors.

Hartwig's bedroom sat just off the living room. Across the hall sat the kitchen, a separate room tucked in between the two bedrooms for rent. The back bedroom seemed to be three times the size of my room at the pensione, and the front one looked to be a little smaller. I immediately wanted the back bedroom and all its space. A mattress lay on the floor, with no bed frame. A large wardrobe closet pressed against the back corner. Even though there was only one bathroom, it was large, and I didn't feel uncomfortable in the slightest sharing it. Hartwig led me into the kitchen, a room as big as my bedroom at the pensione, with full-size appliances and a comfortable rectangular table. Pouring us each a glass of wine, he invited me to sit.

Hartwig spoke fast, as excited, and passionate about his work as ever I had seen anyone. He told me of his travels in the United States, seeing more states than most Americans, including me. A documentary filmmaker and cameraman, he told me of his travels to India, Nepal, and Sri Lanka for work. He had recently returned from Thailand. While away for such a long period of time, the apartment had sat dormant, and now it needed painting and remodeling. Friends of his had stepped up to help out and would be coming and going during the next several weeks. I needed to know that if we decided to be roommates. We talked for over an hour, but my decision had been made the moment I entered the apartment. Now if only he approved of me. Upon leaving, I skipped all the way back down the Leopoldstrasse.

Two days later, on a Sunday, I moved in.

Showing off the old kitchen in the apartment on Franz-Joseph Strasse. In the back is a door to the tiny balcony where we spent many mornings drinking coffee and tea, and eating breakfast.

MUNICH

I had arrived in Munich during the time of two Germanys – Federal Republic of Germany (West Germany) and German Democratic Republic (East Germany). (German reunification wouldn't occur until five years later.) Munich, of course, lay in West Germany and served as the capital of Bavaria, which sits in the south, just above the top edge of the Alps. Although a financial and global city, containing the headquarters of such corporate giants as BMW and Siemens, I didn't find it as formal as Zurich or as fast-paced as Milan.

The city itself contained a mixture of the old and the new. Many historic buildings destroyed during World War II had been rebuilt, many to the same look and specifications of the former ones. The old town, or *Altstadt*, centered around the Marienplatz, a large square containing the town hall and its famous Rathaus-Glockenspiel. This huge mechanical clock, encased in the 260-foot tower, is a work of art unto itself, with some forty-three bells chiming and thirty-two figures coming to life, three times during the summer—11:00 a.m., noon, and 5:00 p.m. The rotating and chiming show, depicting scenes from Munich's history, lasts for about fifteen minutes. The area surrounding the square is pedestrian only and often crowded with students from the nearby university along with hundreds of tourists.

Munich consisted of forty-one boroughs (much like the five boroughs of New York City). The pensione, the agency and my apartment on Franz-Joseph-Strasse were all part of the Schwabing borough, just northeast of the city center. A historically bohemian neighborhood, Schwabing had a history of providing shelter to artists and writers such as Rainer Maria Rilke and Thomas Mann.

Walking and public transportation were by far the best modes of getting around the city. With the U-Bahn (underground railway or metro/subway) and the S-Bahn (suburban trains), Munich has one of the best systems in the world. My new apartment sat between two metro stops, Giselastrasse and Münchener Freiheit. Metro lines U3 and U6 ran through these two stations and took me most places I needed and wanted to go. For instance, three stops south, on either the U3 or the U6, and I would be at the Marienplatz. It was that simple. And to find the addresses I needed to go to on my go-sees and jobs were just as easy, as a station always sat nearby. There were also convenient trams and buses when needed.

The Leopoldstrasse, (the common link to the agency, the pensione, and my new apartment) ran slightly to the west of perhaps one of the largest and most beautiful parks in the world, the *Englischer Garten* or the English Garden. Bigger than Central Park in New York, it provided a little of something for everyone, including numerous bicycle and walking trails. Full of old-growth trees, winding streams, meadows, hills, and monuments, you could spend hours there and still not see it all.

Through the middle of the park ran a stretch of the Isar River. On one side of the river you can lay out in the nude, on the other you can lay out topless or in clothing. The relaxed attitude toward the human body, and nudity, in Germany, and most of Europe, continually surprised me. I stayed on the non-nude side, of course though, and the only reason I lay out topless was to keep from getting tan lines that might show in photographs. I needed an even tan.

On my first day in the park, at the urging of Edith and a few other models, I walked down to the bank of the river and slipped into the rapidly moving water. Instant shock shot through me at the water's coldness. Gasping, my body felt numb as the water carried me down to the bridge and the small landing where I could climb out. That was the first and last time I tried that.

There were several biergartens (beer gardens) in the park as well. The largest one was located at the Chinesischer Turm, a five-story pagoda shaped tower. This tower became one of my landmarks to orient me in the city.

Other beer gardens and beer halls flooded the city as well, and my favorite order became a beer and a humongous pretzel. Another common food I enjoyed were sausages, or rather, *wursts*, such as bratwurst and weisswurst (white sausage), served with a sweet mustard. As for the beer, both men and women alike ordered up the huge liter mugs, or ein mass (*ein pitcher* in English), of beer, myself included, with the choices being Dunkel (dark beer), Helles (light or pale beer), or Radler, a half lemon soda and half beer concoction. I soon found that a Radler, after a long bike ride in the park, to be part of my favorite pastime.

One week after moving in, Hartwig threw a housewarming party for the re-opening of the apartment. At first, I felt nervous. Hartwig's guest list included photographers, videographers, artists, and business people. Although I could invite as many people as I wanted, I chose very few. I didn't want all models there.

The night before the party, Hartwig's friends brought in additional furniture and set it up throughout the apartment. A friend of his arrived from Berlin, bearing Russian champagne which we sampled. The taste, so smooth and clean, dazzled me.

The night finally arrived and along with it, several bottles of wine lined up on the table in the kitchen, along with a keg of beer set up in the corner. All guests were told to bring wine glasses to use then leave behind as a housewarming gift. The first guests arrived at 8:30 p.m.

I started with wine to loosen up and relax my nerves. I soon found most everyone spoke at least some English and were open and kind, all there to have a good time. Most had traveled extensively, and I felt comfortable around them. And the best part was that so few of them were models. I did have a few moments with forward men, one in particular, Manny, telling me in English, "I would like some contact, would you?"

"Uh, no," I replied.

After that, he seemed the perfect gentleman. I also met a man by the name of Hans, an advertising photographer who knew my friend Edith. I had invited Edith, and she eventually showed up. Towards the end of the night or early morning, Hans, Edith, John (an American singer), and I decided to check out a nightclub nearby called Domiciles. We only stayed a short while before walking back to the apartment. By now it was 5:00 a.m. and people still mulled about. I had had enough and slipped behind my bedroom door, closing it firmly before crawling in bed.

When I awoke, I adjusted my eyes to the day and saw that someone lay sleeping on the floor of my bedroom. It was Armin, a friend of Hartwig's I had met earlier in the week. I stepped over him as I made my way out into the hallway.

As I headed toward the kitchen, the smell hit me head on. I stopped at the door. At least a hundred dirty glasses sat on the table and counter. Spilled wine and beer dotted the floor. I made my way to the sink, starting the long, arduous task of washing the glasses and bringing some kind of order to the room while doing my best to vanquish the stench. Hartwig's parties, as I had now learned, were no joke.

Hartwig worked constantly and was rarely ever at the apartment in the following weeks. His girlfriend, Hannah, occasionally stopped by to wait for him at night. Hannah's English wasn't very good and neither was my German, but we got along. I felt she might be more serious about Hartwig than he was about her, but that was none of my business. I liked them both.

Meanwhile, daily go-sees continued. I ran into Lisa Bevis at the agency one morning, and she introduced me to Celine, a model from San Rafael, California. She and I had briefly met at Count Umberto Caproni's estate outside Milan back in the spring. The three of us made our way to a casting for a commercial for chocolate bars called Banjo, each auditioning in front of a video camera.

Returning to the agency, Heidi and I sat together, going through my photos and tear sheets, deciding which ones to include on my new model composite card. My Munich agency seemed much more respectful of its models and appeared more organized. I could work anywhere from here through direct bookings. With this, and the apartment, I knew I would be staying for quite a while in Munich.

Later that evening, Celine stopped by the apartment to look at the second room for rent. I had mentioned it to her earlier in the day. Perhaps ten seconds after arriving, Hartwig and I knew we had found our third roommate.

The next day I worked a job for a large department store's sales advertisement along with Jane, a model from South Africa. Several inches shorter than me, with long blonde hair, Jane was fun to work with. After posing for several photos out on the streets of Munich, a male model showed up. He had only been hired for an hour to do a cover shot with us. As we finished up for the day, the rain began to fall. The client hurried us out of the studio and to a Vietnamese restaurant down the street, treating us all to dinner. We had not stopped for lunch during the day but instead snacked on fresh fruit. Once again, a difference from the French and the Italians who stopped for lunch come hell or high water.

A day later I ran into Jane, and she told me that the client, who had been so nice to our face, had called her agency complaining about her and refusing to pay. A few days later the same client called my agency and didn't want to pay my full rate. The photographer vouched for me, however, and even brought me back another day for work. The reality of the business is that some clients will dislike you no matter what you do, and others will love you. You couldn't take it personally.

Everything was going well, and I was happy in Munich. As I sat on the large sectional sofa in our living room one evening, sipping on a glass of red wine, the phone rang. It was my agent Lawrine, with Legends Agency in New York. We spent several minutes catching up, comfortable with each other as always.

Although I knew there had been some troubles back in New York, I didn't know exactly what they were, and Lawrine didn't share anything about them. Soon she began asking me if I thought my portfolio was strong enough to bring back to New York in September. I wasn't sure but told her I would send her a copy of everything I had at the moment. That way she could see for herself and offer her professional opinion. I didn't feel like I was ready to return to New York, but I realized that I should go back as soon as possible. I needed to work harder and be more responsible for my modeling career. But, something nagged at me. I wanted to delay it as long as possible.

EUROPEAN DAZE

Posing on the streets of Munich for a sales ad.
(I am on the right.)

MUNICH

By the end of July, I felt almost German. With my go-sees done for the day, I joined Hartwig for a little grocery shopping. As we strolled the aisles, he occasionally picked something up and bit into it. Appalled and embarrassed at first, I quickly succumbed and did the same. As we headed outside, we saw pots of gladiolas and decided to buy a few to decorate the apartment. A group of models passed by, including a few I knew from Pensione Frank. We spoke casually for a few minutes, and I could see the curiosity in their eyes before walking away. I felt completely different now that I was away from the model dorm and living what felt like a more authentic German life.

Back at the apartment, we cleaned off the tiny balcony just off the kitchen, arranging a small metal table and two chairs, all that would fit in the small space. Lisa, Rafa, Celine, Hannah, and Robert, a good friend of Hartwig's, joined us later in the evening. We sat in the living room, sipping wine and eating popcorn sprinkled with garlic salt and Parmesan, laughing, and joking, before Hartwig disappeared into the kitchen to cook dinner.

By this time, Hartwig and friends began calling me *Babsy*, apparently a nickname for Barbara in German. I wasn't sure I liked it but knew it was better than being called Barbie.

EUROPEAN DAZE

August arrived and, along with it, a job for a clothes commercial. I waded my way through several models dancing for the camera, making my way upstairs for makeup and hair. When the action shot down below completed, ten models left, leaving only four of us—two Germans, one English, and myself. I stood at the base of the stairs outside and was the first to move for the camera. All I had to do was take off my jacket, but only after the camera panned in for a close-up of my face.

A few days later, Hartwig and I decided to drive out into the countryside. He tossed me the keys as we walked to his old BMW. I hadn't driven a car in over seven months but bravely climbed behind the wheel, feeling completely at ease. Off we went to Herrsching, southwest of Munich, which sits on the east bank of the Amersee Lake, providing a beautiful location for a walk. Later, we drove to Andechs Abbey, a hilltop Benedictine monastery and church, with its own brewery and beer garden. It had been built in 1454. As we sat in the biergarten to eat, we naturally ordered up a mug of the monks' special brew.

With me driving again, we made our way back to Munich, stopping off at Café Fahrenheit for a coffee and sambuca before joining Celine and a few friends back at the apartment for dinner. We had planned to go out and do our laundry in the evening, but stayed in instead, watching one of Hartwig's documentaries about American Indians, based on the English book *Touch the Earth*. The film contained footage from eleven different States, from the Grand Canyon to New York. I sat wide-eyed, enjoying every second. Glancing over at Hartwig and Celine, I could see they had fallen asleep. I continued watching to the end, then gently woke them. It had been another good day.

On the first Monday of the new month, I jumped on the early morning train out of the Hauptbahnhof, Munich's main train station, for the two-and-a-half-hour ride west to Stuttgart. A manufacturing hub, Stuttgart hosted the headquarters for such German companies as Mercedes-Benz and Porsche, and as it turned out, many photographers and fashion clients. Once I arrived, my directions from the agency led me to the Castle Solitude, a short taxi ride away. As the taxi pulled up just outside the castle, my first thoughts were not of magnificence or awe as it sat smaller than I had imagined. Yet as I stepped out and walked closer, I couldn't help but feel giddy inside.

Constructed in the 1760s, Castle Solitude, or rather, Solitude Palace, had been abandoned and only recently renovated by the government. As I walked around the pearly white building, I caught sight of a fashion shoot and made my way over.

The wind whipped around the castle all day, making any decent hairstyle almost impossible. The remedy soon became scarves and hats, of which the stylist had several. There were four models for the shoot, two of which seemed to shun me the minute I arrived. Fortunately, the third one seemed friendly. That's how it was in Germany. Many of the German models didn't want to associate at all or took some time to warm up to you.

With a sprinkling of rain now joining the wind, we called it a day. I grabbed a taxi to Hotel Ketterer Stuttgart which sat in the heart of the city, tucked in between a church, a museum, and a theater. Historic in its own right, opened in 1933 before World War II, it nevertheless felt modern and cozy. And across the street, believe it or not, sat a McDonalds. I couldn't resist. After indulging in a burger and fries, I returned to my cozy room.

Filling the bathroom sink, I placed a few pairs of underwear in the soapy water. I had waited too long to wash clothes back in Munich, and this trip to Stuttgart caught me off guard. Just that morning as I sat down to breakfast with my roommates, the phone rang. Long ago I learned that when the phone rings in the morning, it's usually the agency and you're almost late to something. Heidi hurriedly gave me directions for my job that day in Stuttgart. I had one hour before my train left the station. Learning my lesson, I felt sure I would wash clothes on a more frequent basis going forward.

As the rain continued to fall on the second day, we had no choice but to shoot the remaining photos in the studio. I had been looking forward to going on location again, but it wasn't meant to be. Because of my young look, I had to wait for the set of clothes requiring a youthful appearance. For once, I wished I could do the more sophisticated shots. I did my best to stay busy as I waited, writing in my journal, finishing up a letter to my parents, and arranging my appointment book. Yet I felt bored. All the waiting and waiting seemed a waste of my time.

Around 3:00 p.m. I began my set of photos, finishing up an hour and a half later. We raced for the 4:57 p.m. train, barely making it aboard before it left the station. I found the dining car and enjoyed a beer before heading down the cars to an empty compartment. Sitting inside, as the train made its way to Munich, I thought of my good fortune in finding the apartment, and two roommates I actually liked. My agency in Munich, and most importantly, Heidi, seemed behind me and pushing me out to clients, believing in me. With a sigh of contentment, I closed my eyes.

A few days later I returned to Stuttgart, via train, for another client. We had foolishly been out the night before, dancing, until 2:30 a.m. When my alarm didn't go off the next morning, Hartwig barged into my room, shouting me awake. I grabbed everything in a panic, and we jumped in his car for the short ride to the train station. Boarding the 6:51 a.m. train a minute before it left the station, I made my way to the tiny bathroom to wash my face and hair in the sink. A few hours later, the train arrived in Stuttgart. The photographer's assistant stood at the end of the platform, holding up a sign with my name on it. I couldn't help but laugh.

Four male models had already arrived and were shooting outside. It turned out I was to be a prop for a men's catalog shoot. I knew two of the models, one from Milan and one from Munich. Before and after a big lunch, I shot photos with each of the male models, no doubt one would make the cover.

EUROPEAN DAZE

My job in Stuttgart, as a prop for a men's catalog shoot.

MUNICH

Work for me continued. It seemed I finally felt comfortable in front of the camera. I had never been good at free posing, moving this way and that, without overthinking it, without wondering what to do with this arm, or if that arm angled awkwardly. Suddenly at a job one day in Munich, it all clicked, and I moved with ease as the photographer snapped away.

At my next job, for Head sportswear, however, that didn't seem to matter. The photographer decided, after several photos, that I was too tall for the shoot. This didn't deter me in the slightest by now. The following job would prove why. The client, Sportive, put me in ten shots for tennis wear on location at a set of tennis courts. Next, they found a canoe and took us out into the boonies, the wilderness, where we shot several more photos in hiking clothes. A few days later I would be working for a different client, wearing various wigs. The good always outweighed the bad.

By now, I had three model portfolios, and I often sat and rearranged the photos and tear sheets in each of them. It seemed hard to believe that this time last year I had none. While I couldn't find all my tear sheets and catalog publications, I found enough to fill my portfolios. It's doubtful that many of the catalog photos would make it into my book to show to clients anyway, so I didn't worry about them. Many went without my even seeing them.

Often, I would arrive back at the apartment, exhausted from the day, only to find odd people milling about. Friends of Hartwig's often stopped by, including ones from London and from Johannesburg. On one such night, I arrived home after a long day on location to find an Indian guy in the kitchen cooking a big meal. The girl with him had stars in her hair and white paint on her face. Hartwig was nowhere to be found. I took one look at them, then headed to bed. In the morning, I walked into the kitchen, finding it to be a smelly pigsty. I refused to clean up the mess and left for the day.

Perhaps my favorite pastime while in Munich became sitting at outdoor cafes and people watching. One of those cafes, Tony B.'s, sat on the corner of Leopoldstrasse and Kaiserstrasse and you could say I became somewhat of a regular there. Another favorite way to spend my free time involved going to see movies at the Europa Theater, near the Hauptbahnhof. The theater would put out flyers of their movie schedule, and I always kept a copy on hand. We did have a television at the apartment, and occasionally a show in English would be on. Usually though, movies, even the old movies, such as *Flight of the Phoenix* starring Jimmy Stewart, would be dubbed in German. I didn't mind as by now I had picked up enough German to figure out what was going on.

The English Bookstore continued to be my personal sanctuary. I rarely ever ran into other models there and enjoyed taking my time looking through all the shelves and shelves of good books.

MUNICH

The English Garden provided ample space to lay out on a sunny day, read a good book and take a nap. It also had phenomenal bike trails, and I knew I had to find a bike. Luckily, a German guy who lived downstairs from us had one for sale, and I soon became the owner of a pink bike. The first day I got it, Hartwig, Celine and I took a five-hour bike ride through the park, stopping off here and there at one of the biergartens for a Radler or Weissbier. This soon become a weekly activity. I even began riding my bike to jobs close to the apartment.

Shopping in Munich seemed much more enjoyable than anywhere else I had been so far. I frequented the closest grocery store, and the fresh fruit and vegetable market nearby. Most of the shops closed at noon on Saturdays and would not reopen until Monday. And many times, milk would be sold out by the time I got to the store. It seemed the milk tasted different in Europe, especially in Germany. I drank it every day as well as having it in my cereal. One of my big weaknesses became the *Shoko Muesli* cereal, which made the milk almost chocolate. Another particular item I grew fond of was quark, a concentrated milk in the form of cheese curds, similar to plain yogurt. I mixed it with regular muesli or fruit, and it soon became my morning go-to breakfast.

Hartwig cooked often and was quite good. On a few occasions, he turned pumpkin into delicious meals. I had never eaten much pumpkin, and when I did, it usually came from a can and usually made into a pie. Now, however, I was being introduced not just to pumpkin soup, but also to a stew with pumpkin instead of potatoes.

EUROPEAN DAZE

For anything non-food related, I could most likely find it at the Hertie Department Store where they sold almost everything, from clothes to home goods. I also found a Woolworths in Munich and didn't hesitate to shop there whenever I needed something quick and familiar.

MUNICH

Toward the end of August, I decided to return to Zurich for a few days. I had left four bags of my belongings there and needed to retrieve them now that I had my own place. Also, Sean was in Zurich, and we hadn't spoken much in the past month. I knew our meeting would be somewhat awkward, and neither of us would know how to act when we saw each other. During our time apart, we had both dated other people, or rather, I had gone out with just one, a model I knew from Paris, but Sean had apparently been with several.

When I first arrived in Munich, and a few weeks before moving out of the pensione, I ran into a male model I had met in Paris a few days before flying back home to the States for the Christmas holiday. Bill Golden had sexy good looks, not the ordinary handsomeness of other models. His curly blond hair and swimmer's physique caught my attention one night at an agency party.

Bill had been discovered by famous photographer Bruce Weber on the docks of his hometown, Key West, Florida. From there it had been a whirlwind of an experience, jetting off to New York and now Europe. We had Florida in common, but also something more. We enjoyed talking, mostly about the simpler things in life. When we saw each other again in Munich, we both remembered how we felt during those long conversations back in Paris and started them again. We spent hours walking around Munich. We dreamed about returning to Florida where I would maybe open a bed and breakfast, and he would have his own boat for fishing charters. I had never had these types of discussions with Sean. All our plans had revolved around modeling.

I felt an attachment to Bill unlike any other. At times, I know he felt the same way toward me. Yet, as his career accelerated, to the point of being one of the top three male models in Europe, he pulled away. He had that same thinking I had while dating Sean in Milan. To be successful in modeling, you had to be free to follow it wherever it took you. Relationships could bog down your ability to keep moving. Or at least that is what I told myself.

I would see him for the last time later in the year when he stopped by my apartment on Franz-Joseph Strasse. It was a short visit, and he seemed troubled and indecisive. It seemed he now was so caught up in the model world, he lost that part of himself that enjoyed the simple things in life. When he walked out the door, I knew I would never see him again, but I found that I was okay with that.

A month or so later my friend Edith told me she saw Bill at a bar in Hamburg and he obviously was living the life of a partying playboy. For what it's worth, I never saw him that way and never wished him any harm. But I did let go of any idea of us together, in Europe or in Florida.

As for Sean, I had heard rumors of the women he had been with, including someone I thought of as a friend. He had heard about Bill. Now, with both of us here in Zurich, Sean and I didn't know where we stood with each other. I checked into my room at the Otter and met up with my old girlfriends, spending most of the following day with them.

Before heading back to Munich, Sean and I walked along the Limmatquai, mostly in silence. Finally, he spoke, telling me I was in the driver's seat as far as our relationship was concerned. My wise friends told me to forget him and move on. Celine would later tell me to forget him and find a nice German man to date, forgetting all male models completely. Maybe they were right. None of them were dating models and seemed much happier.

On the train ride back to Munich, I continued thinking about Sean and our time in Milan when my thoughts were suddenly interrupted as a middle-aged Turkish man entered the compartment and sat across from me. We politely said hello and chatted a bit of small talk. But once he found out I was American, his whole persona changed, and he decided he would pay me for my services. Many foreigners believed that all American women were loose and ready to party with anyone, anywhere, anytime. This man unnerved me.

As I planned the best way to get up and leave, with all my luggage, and find another seat, three younger guys, students from Portugal who spoke perfect English, entered the compartment and sat down. The Turk quietly stood up and left, but kept pacing outside the compartment, staring in at me. Once the train arrived back in Munich, and as I approached the taxi stand outside the train station, the students from Portugal raced up. They had watched the Turkish man follow me and wanted to make sure I got in the taxi safely. I had never had this happen before while in Europe, and it honestly took me by surprise. I would have to be more careful.

MUNICH

The start of September found my home state of Florida bracing for Hurricane Elena and me heading back to Stuttgart for yet another job. Celine had already left for Lausanne, Switzerland, for two weeks to do fashion shows, and Hartwig worked constantly. The weather in Munich began to change, moving away from the sun of summer, and metamorphizing towards winter.

In Stuttgart, I worked again with Jane, the model from South Africa. When we returned to Munich, she introduced me to her German boyfriend, and they gave me a ride back to my apartment in his flashy Alfa Romeo Spider. Jane had changed dramatically in those past several weeks since we first worked together. Her personality seemed to slide into the typical model attitude of pretentious importance. Had mine changed as well?

Although I said I would never cut my hair as short as it was when I was in Paris, I eventually gave in and let a friend at the English Haircutters salon do just that. My agent, Heidi, had been asking me to do this for the past four weeks, but I had refused. Returning to the agency, my mood dampened, however. Heidi did her best to convince me that it was a better look for me. Yet, the shortness of it made me feel ugly and naked. Depression began to sneak up on me again, as it had in Paris, then Milan.

Fortunately, Janice, Karen, and Lisa arrived in Munich for the weekend. They had never been to the city before, and I couldn't wait to show them around. After eating lunch, I decided to introduce them to the English Gardens. As we approached the river, I grinned as I looked across to the other side. An older man with a big stomach, naked as can be, ran back and forth along the bank. Suddenly all laughing stopped as they caught their first glimpse of him. Janice shielded her eyes, refusing to look his way.

The next day, up early, we set out on our adventure to Salzburg, just across the Austrian border, less than a two-hour train ride away. We were only going for the day, so we wanted to make the most of it. To hide my boyish haircut, I wore Sean's black beret that I had long ago "borrowed" from him—and still have to this day.

The four of us walked all over the old city, seeing the gardens, churches, Mozart's birthplace and family house. We then took a cable car, the Festungsbahn, up to the Hohensalzburg Castle, a huge medieval fortress hovering above the city. So many tourists, most of them Americans, lulled about and we sought to get away from the crowds as much as possible.

What I knew most about Salzburg came from one of my all-time favorite movies, *The Sound of Music*. With the crowds and so little time to explore, we managed to enjoy what we could of the sites where Maria von Trapp (played by Julie Andrews) lived. In the geometric Mirabell Gardens, near the Pegasus

Fountain where Maria and the children danced and sang *Do-Re-Mi*, we stopped to pose for our own photos and memories.

As the long day began to wane, we stopped at a café for dinner. It had been a perfect day with good friends. Before heading back to Munich for the night, we saw Karen off on her train to Zurich. She had a job filming a commercial and was anxious to get back there to prepare. A short while later, Lisa, Janice and I boarded our own train back to Munich.

MUNICH

Anytime you think of Germany in the Fall, undoubtedly the national event of Oktoberfest, one of the biggest festivals in the world, comes up. As luck would have it, I found myself right smack in the center of the 175th celebration of the annual event which arrived mid-September in Munich.

My inaugural visit to the festival occurred one night with Celine, Hartwig, and Hartwig's friend, Robert. There were so many beer halls with bands playing in each one. We drank big liters of beer and ate huge, hot pretzels. We sang, in German, along with the other 4,000 people in one big beer hall. I was wise enough to stop drinking after my second liter of the Special Oktoberfest Beer, which had a slightly higher alcohol content, or else I wouldn't have been able to stand up by myself.

A few days later, Janice, Karen, and Lisa came back to Munich, and we saturated ourselves with beer and good cheer at the festival, spending most of that time in the Hippodrome beer tent. A day later Janice and I returned, buying corny Bavarian hats to wear. We sat by a German man and his eight-year-old daughter, who often took a swill of her Dad's liter of beer. Behind us sat a group of Japanese men, and Janice quickly taught me a few words in Japanese so I could surprise them. They videotaped us all, even when we climbed up on the bench to sing and clap to the band. A short time later an eighteen-year-old American studying in Florence joined us.

We switched tents and had another beer before heading home to the apartment for the night.

After my friends had gone back to Zurich, I again returned to Oktoberfest with Celine and Hartwig. This time we met a group of Australian rugby players and joked around with them most of the night. Oktoberfest turned out to be a smorgasbord of different nationalities, all having fun together.

The next day I felt rough. A week of Oktoberfest had caught up with me, and I wanted to do nothing but crawl under the covers and sleep the day away. My roommates had other plans, however. Hartwig had to go to Nuremberg to complete a filming project and, somehow, he convinced us to go with him. We piled into the old BMW for the 170 km (or 103 miles) drive due north. Even with my head pounding and my beer-induced exhaustion, I knew I had to see as much of the city as time would allow.

Hartwig set up his camera amidst the stone towers and fortifications of the Old Market, and we left him there to wander around. Medieval architecture surrounded us, almost overwhelming our senses. Kaiserburg Castle rose above the city, and I tried to imagine what it would be like to live there. I became furious with myself for staying out so late, for drinking so much on a night before a visit to such an important place.

I had vaguely heard of the international trials held in Nuremberg at the end of World War II to bring Nazi war criminals to justice. Although I felt at home in Germany, knew it to be my ancestral home, and loved its people, I never once felt aligned with the Nazis. They were invaders of what I knew and loved about Germany and its people. It never occurred to me that there could have been a few of my ancestors among them.

At the beginning of October, Hartwig left for Yemen in the Middle East for a month to film a documentary. I had a trip on location coming up in Tunisia on the African continent. As I waited for the trip, I tackled my boredom by roaming around the bookstore and exploring the streets of AltStadt. By this time my writing had gained steam, and I started my fourth journal, writing about my daily occurrences, thoughts, feelings, frustrations, thrills, scenery, as well as short stories and poems.

Music also cheered me on, just like it had back in Italy. At the Marienplatz I could buy any type of music and selected ones by Falco, an Austrian singer ("Rock me Amadeus" and "Der Kommissar"), Depeche Mode, a British group ("People are People", "Blasphemous Rumors", and "Master and Servant"), and Modern Talking, a popular German duo ("You're my Heart, You're my Soul" and "Cheri Cheri Lady"). But my all-time favorite became Don Henley and his song "The Boys of Summer." I played that song over and over again until I wore out the cassette and had to buy a new one.

Reading the *International Herald Tribune* became a habit, and I sought it out whenever I could. From it, I learned a great deal about the world around me and about the past. For instance, one day I sat at a café reading about the Cuban missile crisis back in the 1960s when President Kennedy had been in office. It seemed the fashion world no longer could contain my curiosity and single-minded focus. There was just too much more out there, too much more to learn.

EUROPEAN DAZE

Enjoying special Oktoberfest brew in Munich.

MUNICH

As my trip to Tunisia grew closer, I began to prepare. Much had recently happened in the world, including the hijacking of a small Italian cruise ship where an American in a wheelchair had been killed. A short time later, the top headline in the *International Herald Tribune* screamed out "U.S. Jets Force Hijackers to Go to Italy." I felt a sting of pride at my countrymen taking this action, although I kept it to myself. Not everyone in Europe agreed with the strong-arm tactics of the United States.

With all the uncertainty going on in the world, I grew slightly nervous about my upcoming trip, as did my parents. I did my best to assure them I would be fine. Occasionally I would put on a British accent to avoid conversations that I knew would begin with "You Americans," followed by some critical analysis of how all Americans handle things, delivered in a patronizing tone. Learning to avoid certain conversations became a skill I needed in the new realities of the world around me.

The day finally arrived, and for the first leg of the journey, I flew to Frankfurt to meet up with the group. The photographer and client greeted me warmly, but then grew quiet. I knew then that they thought I would be German and were now reconsidering their choice. Two German models and another American model soon joined us, and I felt relieved.

We made our way to the counter of Tunis Air. Out on the tarmac, luggage had been set out in separate sections. We had to walk out, one by one, and identify our luggage before they would put it on the plane. Once we landed in Tunis, we had to get off the plane while they refueled. The other American model, Shannon, and I stuck close together. We remained quiet and attempted to look European. After re-boarding, the final leg of the flight over to the island of Jerba went quickly. As I passed through passport control, the clerk growled at me, stamping my passport before tossing it back.

Tunisia seemed like an odd place to go on location. Jerba, a small island sitting just off the coast, apparently had become quite the vacation spot for Europeans. So much so that a fancy, all-inclusive Club Med had been established on the island and staying there made the location much more palatable. You almost didn't know you were in a different region of the world.

As it was late when we arrived, we agreed to meet for breakfast the following morning, and all of us headed to our separate rooms for the night. Locking my door, I placed a chair up under the doorknob for additional assurance, before crawling into bed exhausted.

We spent the first day acclimating to the island with the photographer scouting locations and checking on lighting. He had been here before, so he didn't seem too concerned with the overcast start. The stylist, Sylvie, quickly took control of the clothes. Barbara, the German model, with short dark hair slicked back, proved to be the sexiest of the group and Sandra, the second German model, was more like the sweet best friend. Shannon, on the other hand, was the most outgoing one. As for the photographer, even with our questionable meeting back in Frankfurt, he and I soon clicked.

Shannon and I got to know a few of the French G.O.'s at the club and hung out with them at the shows and disco. G.O. stands for *Gentil Organisateur*. They are the ambassadors of the Club Med spirit. In all honesty though, it just looked like a fun summer job. Two of them were water ski instructors during the summer and snow ski instructors in the winter in St. Moritz, France.

After a week on the island, and several photos on the beach and in the desert, we headed back to Germany. I was glad to return to Europe. Shannon flew back to Munich with me to stay at the apartment for a few weeks before returning to New York. Our week had been fun and productive, yet I doubted I would get many tear sheets for my book from it. As it was for a catalog, I doubted I would even see the results a few months from then, if ever.

On returning to Munich, I found I had three days of work in Nuremberg for one of the biggest clients, Quelle. The first day I took the train early in the morning. Arriving at Studio Intensiv, I worked with four male models, three of whom I knew. After two shots, I headed back to Munich. The next Saturday, I returned to Nuremberg by train and this time worked with three female models in addition to the four male models. Both days had been fun, with large lunches and sipping beer while waiting in the dressing room. For the third day of work, I rode up and back with another model in her car.

EUROPEAN DAZE

Halloween was just around the corner, and I was determined not to spend it the way I had back in Paris, wandering around the Bonne Nouvelle looking for a late-night test photo shoot. Having convinced Denny, the manager of a trendy restaurant club to throw a Halloween party, we focused on our costumes.

Celine, Shannon, and I dressed ourselves in aluminum foil, applied silver makeup to our lips, cheeks, and eyelids, and sprayed our hair silver. We were going for the spacewoman look. We grabbed a taxi to 1-2-3 Nightclub, meeting up with Darlene, another model from Florida and Silka, a German model, outside the club. They were dressed as newspapers. As always, we made a scene by dancing on the tables. The party didn't stop there though. We made our rounds to the other clubs we knew, including Domiciles and P1, with our foil outfits now starting to rip and fall off, revealing either black tights and snug camisoles underneath or, in my case, a short black dress.

The next night Celine talked me into going back to 1-2-3 with her. Although we had planned only to have dinner, other friends showed up, buying champagne and tequila slammers for everyone. One model I didn't know climbed up on the table and started dancing, knocking glasses off, and shattering several. I swiped my hand across my lap, not realizing glass was on it, and nearly sliced off my finger. Denny took me into the back, applying pressure to stop the bleeding and after almost an hour, bandaged me up. Denny was a quiet, kind man closer in age to Hartwig, but with a heart of gold.

This is how November rolled in. I went on a hot tea and water fast for a few days, wanting to get all of the alcohol of the last few months out of my system. The first snow fell, and I began getting excited to go home to Florida. But as I had a month of winter ahead of me, I needed to stay warm. I had somehow misplaced my coat, the one I bought back in Paris, and now needed a new one. While out shopping with Celine one day, I came across a beautiful long, black, wool cape. It cost 600 Deutsche marks (or about $200), but I knew I had to have it. Never had I owned anything like it before. Never had I spent so much on myself before.

I began to think about home more and more now, and excitedly started Christmas shopping for my family. This seemed to hit a raw nerve with Hartwig. He apparently didn't have a close family and didn't understand why I wanted to buy gifts for them. Our apartment life seemed to be getting a bit tense as the year grew closer to its end and Celine and I would be moving out.

Sean and I had sporadically kept in touch all this time, but with no great involvement by either of us. In early November, he called from Italy, saying he would be going back to London to work and save money so he could go to New York in January. I wished him all the best luck in the world. We didn't know when we would see each other again, if ever.

As I headed out on my go-sees a few days later, a wave of anxiety washed over me. At one particular casting, there were so many models that I suddenly couldn't breathe, as if I were being suffocated by all these tall creatures dressed in black. It was then I realized I desperately needed a break from the model lifestyle.

EUROPEAN DAZE

About this time, I received a letter from Lawrine in New York. It seemed strange that she mailed a letter instead of calling me on the phone. She wrote that the delay in writing to me had been caused by her travels for promoting the agency, most recently in London. She had received the tear sheets I sent to her and agreed that I needed stronger ones. We should meet, she wrote, and decide our next steps. Several agencies in London had shown interest in me, and she wanted to talk with me about that. She also thought it a good idea for me to spend January in New York. Problem was, I didn't want to. With my move to Zurich, then Munich, my focus had begun to shift from modeling as a single-minded career path to a mode for making money so I could stay in Europe. In other words, it became more of a job than a career. And the closer I got to my goal of making enough money to extend my stay in Europe, the further I got from New York and its pull.

MUNICH

My roommate, Celine (r), and I dressed in aluminum foil for a Halloween party at a favorite restaurant and bar.

MUNICH

With mid-November came more snow. I awoke to find everything outside covered in a white blanket, with the snow still coming down. Before making my way down to the Marienplatz to a candle shop to buy beautifully carved candles for Christmas presents, I stopped off at the Post to send a sixth box of my belongings to Florida. Back in October, I had started the process of shipping boxes home. With several bags of clothes, approximately forty books, and various other items, there was no way to take it all back on the plane with me. And I didn't want to leave them in Munich. I still had a box of belongings in Paris and hated to think I would lose more of my personal belongings. It would take about a month for each box to get there, by ship. That had been the most affordable option.

Hartwig returned from Yemen, and for his thirty-sixth birthday, he threw himself an Arabian dinner party. I didn't feel up to it, and although I was there, I didn't socialize much and called it an early night. October had gotten somewhat out of hand with the partying, and I had had enough.

With the snow continuing to fall, and winter blowing its cold air, I curled up most nights in my room, the warmest room in the drafty apartment, reading my books and writing. My next job took me to Hamburg, in the north of Germany.

EUROPEAN DAZE

In the snow I made way to the airport for my 9:00 p.m. flight and, upon arrival, found my way to the Parkhotel Alster-ruh, a small hotel with water views of what I soon learned to be the Osterbek canal.

The following morning, I made my way to Studio Brem to work for *Brigitte*, the largest women's magazine in Germany. The job turned out to be a spread for physical exercises, shot in ultraviolet light. We spent the entire morning waiting for a gym instructor to arrive. It was almost 1:00 p.m. when he walked through the studio doors. The wrist and ankle weights we were to use had been spray painted neon orange (so as to glow in the dark), but still hadn't completely dried. This delayed the shoot even more. Finally, at 4:00 p.m. we began shooting the photos. When we finished four hours later, I took a taxi back to the hotel and although tired, I couldn't sleep. I seemed to be transitioning from the thought of Europe and work to home. I felt in a limbo stage between the two.

Working for *Brigitte* magazine again the next day, I arrived at Studio Thomas to work with photographer Isla Thomas. This was a fashion shoot, and we started shooting around 12:30 p.m., working until after 5:00 p.m. On my flight back to Munich, I felt pleased with my last two days and hoped to work with the photographers again in the future. And I looked forward to spending more time in Hamburg. But for now, I needed a break. I needed home.

Back at the apartment, I continued my packing, sending four more boxes home to the States, making that ten boxes total. I also continued my Christmas shopping, making my way down to the Marienplatz to buy a carved candle for my

MUNICH

grandparents in Alabama and a cardigan sweater for my Dad. With the snow cascading the city, I wandered around the English Gardens taking pictures with my new Nikon 35mm camera which I finally bought to replace my old disc camera.

The days seemed to go by slower and slower now. Celine and I spent time enveloped in the sofa of the living room, sipping on hot tea or wine, talking about our months in Munich and what we wanted to do next. Soon we would be separated, and there were no guarantees on when we would see each other again. I had felt this before, almost a year ago, when Kristen and Ava, my Paris roommates, and I went our separate ways. I had recently heard from Kristen that she changed agencies in Paris, from First Agency to Clip Agency, and that things were going well. Ava, I would soon learn from her letter waiting for me back in Florida, had moved on to London, then New York but now sat at home in Georgia trying to decide what to do next.

As I continued going on go-sees in Munich, Celine left for a week to a ski resort in Austria, for a catalog job. Thanksgiving arrived, but since I was alone in the apartment, I didn't celebrate. Although glad to be going back to Florida soon, I knew I would miss Munich, miss Germany. Not once did I ever feel like a stranger in a strange land here. Yet, I knew, if I returned, it wouldn't be the same. I wouldn't be moving back to this apartment, with Hartwig and Celine. Change, it seemed, became my only option.

December finally arrived, and I did my best to prepare for the busy week ahead. Just the thought of it stressed me to the point I couldn't relax or sleep. I spent the first three days wrapping everything up, sorting out the bills with Hartwig, and sitting down with Dagmar in accounting at the agency. To use my return ticket to the States on TWA, I had to fly out of Milan or else there would be an additional $400 charge. It turns out any change in destination would have to go through the purchase location, New York, which in turn had to get in touch with the purchaser in Italy. For $100 I could fly to Milan and avoid all that hassle.

My original plan had been to take the train to Zurich on Friday, then on to Milan for the night. That way I could simply wake up in Milan on Saturday morning and casually make my way to the airport. But, as usual, a curveball is always thrown in the best-laid plans. I had to work in Hamburg on Friday.

Early Friday morning, Celine and I took the bus to the airport. She flew to Frankfurt for work while I flew to Hamburg. The job turned out to be for a hair campaign for Wella, the same client who had given me my first job back in Paris. After shooting my one photo, the photographer and crew decided they liked me so much they wanted me in the group photos as well. We finished in time to make the 6:30 p.m. flight to Munich, placing me back at the apartment around 9:00 p.m. with a nervous stomach. *Now, as long as all goes well tomorrow*, I thought, *and if Italy will cooperate, I should be fine*.

Saturday, December 7, barged in after only a few hours of sleep. Up at 4:00 a.m. I lugged my two bags and one carry-on down the four flights of stairs and climbed in the waiting taxi. At the airport, I calmly made my way to the Lufthansa counter to check in for my flight to Milan, only to find it had been held up due to the weather in northern Italy. I was already on a tight

MUNICH

schedule, having to fly to Milan and switch airports to catch my flight to New York. My stomach tumbled, and my head began to throb. Gratefully I soon heard the calling to check in for my flight. I raced up to the counter and quickly made my way onto the small jet, so small in fact that if I stood straight up in the cabin, I would knock myself out. I now understood why the plane might have issues flying into the bad weather in Milan. Sighing, I crammed my long legs and body into my seat and closed my eyes, praying over and over again, "Please, please, please."

As the jet neared the Italian border, it became a volley between whether we could land at Linate Airport as scheduled or have to land at Malpensa Airport due to the weather. I hoped for Malpensa since that is where my flight to New York would be flying out of. At the last minute, however, the weather cleared enough for us to land at Linate after all. Momentarily disappointed, I soon switched back to my focus on getting my luggage, hoping I could get through Italian customs quickly, and high-tail it over to the other airport. Once we landed, the six customs agents seemed to like my tired smile and only rummaged through one of my bags. I did my best to joke with them, thinking this might make it all go faster. It didn't.

With little time to spare, I raced outside, found a taxi and settled in for the short ride. As the taxi drove past the Duomo, then up Corso Sempione, I felt as if we were traveling down memory lane. I couldn't believe an entire year had passed and that I had actually lived here. It felt so long ago.

The rest of the morning passed without any difficulties or delays, and once on the flight to New York, I sank wholeheartedly into my seat. I didn't have to do anything for the next six hours. I blankly stared out the window for the first hour, in a transition of sorts. It felt surreal. I couldn't believe I was sitting on a plane bound for the States. It finally began to hit me that I was really going home. I had been in Europe, away from my family, for an entire year.

Landing at Kennedy Airport several hours later, I made my way to the luggage claim then through US Customs. From the moment I stepped off the plane in New York, I felt assaulted, and an overwhelming feeling of repulsion swept over me. The people all around me talked so loudly, so rudely. Everyone raced around the airport in a self-important air. It startled me, back into the reality of New York City itself. *Could I ever live here again? Would I even want to?*

When I finally boarded the flight to Orlando, exhaustion overtook me again. But, I was finally on my way home. The people I would see next would be my family. Glancing in a mirror, I noticed my eyes were as red as the heart of a ripe watermelon. I sank into the seat and stared out at the clouds until a short while later, the plane began its descent. Finally, a day starting in Munich and passing through Milan and New York was over. I was home.

HAMBURG
JANUARY 15 - MAY 1, 1986

Icelandair Flight 664 flew through the night, crossing the Atlantic Ocean with barely a notice from its passengers. I sat by the window, with the middle seat open and an older woman sitting on the aisle. Except for the rude German woman sitting behind me and the loud, obnoxious American student towards the back of the plane, the calming flight soared, taking me back to my beloved Europe.

As the plane touched down in Luxembourg, I had a few hours wait until my puddle-jumper flight on LuxAir over to Frankfurt, then a connecting flight on to Hamburg. Dreariness and rain surrounded the small airport, and the people appeared to move in slow motion. They stared at me as if I had something sticking to my face. I swiped my hand across it several times as if to wipe away their stares. A man sitting at a nearby table smiled and leaned over to chat. From Luxembourg himself, he told me people here weren't used to seeing my type. I smiled politely. *I have a type?*

Returning to Germany had been my agents' idea. Lawrine in New York and Heide in Munich both weighed in, confirming I already had jobs lined up in Europe in the new year. This time, Hamburg appeared to be the right place for me.

Upon arrival, I made my way to the temporary agency apartment, and as I walked in, my eyes surveyed the room.

EUROPEAN DAZE

Clothes lay over chairs, dust was piled high on the side tables, and dirty dishes filled the sink. Two models rushed past me, leaving me alone in the apartment. I found the smallest bedroom and lined up my suitcases with no intention of unpacking them. Celine would be in Hamburg in another week, and we would find a new place to stay then.

Studio Wolfgang Klein sat only two blocks away from the pigsty apartment and my first job of the new year would be for *Journal für Die Frau* magazine, for beauty. It might even make the March cover. With the effects of jet lag showing on my face, the makeup artist and hairstylist at the studio accepted the challenge to make me camera-ready. A few hours later, we completed the half-day shoot, and I quickly made my way to the agency.

Christel Flath, an unassuming beauty with short dark hair and soulful eyes, smiled as I entered the room. With no rush, we sat down to review the paperwork. Christel led the Hamburg branch of the Talents agency and seemed to enjoy getting to know each of her models. She also mentioned an apartment I might be able to rent. With the address in hand, I wasted no time in calling to schedule a time to see it.

The apartment sat on the fourth floor in a brownstone on Eppendorfer Baum, in a clean, quiet, residential neighborhood. The owner had gone to Jamaica for three months, and her sister managed the rental while she was away. The apartment had a fully stocked kitchen, living room, dining room, large bedroom, and bath. It only took a few seconds for me to decide to take it. Anything to get out of the dump I currently had to stay in.

HAMBURG

Later that evening, back at the messy apartment, Thomas, an American who was one of the roommates, walked into my bedroom. He needed me to pay 100 Deutsche marks for the rent. Apparently, the two of them were broke; work just hadn't come their way yet. I handed the money over to him, hoping he would leave. Desperate people, I learned, make poor roommates and worse friends. I often found there were two extremes in modeling: those who worked a lot and always have a surplus of money, and those who didn't work as much or didn't know how to save and were always broke. I fit somewhere in between, never a huge surplus but usually enough to pay my debts, enjoy a little comfort, have some fun, and save a few dollars for a rainy day.

Working again the following day, posing in bathrobes for three long hours, along with three male models, I took it all in stride. In the evening, I headed back to the airport. Before leaving Europe last December, I had been booked for a job on location in Nice, France.

With snow pouring out of the sky, my flight to Frankfurt had been delayed. This worried me because I had a tight schedule for a connecting flight to Nice. When I did finally arrive in Frankfurt, I only had ten minutes to get across the huge airport. I stopped at the first Lufthansa counter I came to, and they called ahead to the gate for my flight to Nice, telling them to wait for me. At passport control, I raced to the front of the long line, a horrified look on my face, and the guards allowed me to break in front. As promised, the door to the plane remained open, and I flew through it. I buckled myself into the seat, and shortly after takeoff, ordered the first of two beers.

Nice, a resort town on the French Riviera, normally would be exciting. But visiting in the dead of winter, with overcast skies and empty beaches left it more subdued. Our hotel, the Hotel Continental Massena, proved upscale, however, with its stocked mini-bar and snack basket, all compliments of the client. After devouring a meal from room service, I climbed in the huge tub for a long, hot soak, sipping on a gin and tonic while nibbling a piece of dark chocolate.

The next morning, the stylist for the shoot called to tell me I didn't have to work that day but had a fitting scheduled in the evening. I slowly got dressed and headed out to see Nice by day. The sun hid behind clouds but warmed me nevertheless as I walked along the shore. Sitting on a bench, looking out across the ocean, I recalled how my Mom often mentioned that, while at the beach, she sometimes looked out across that same ocean, thinking of how I was just on the other side. Now I was thinking the same thing.

It wasn't until late the next afternoon that we finally began to shoot the clothes commercial. And because of the late start, several of us missed our flights, including my 5:30 p.m. flight back to Hamburg. My agency was furious about this as they had called the film crew earlier in the day and told them I had to be on that flight. To appease them, the clients rushed to get me on the last flight to Paris where I would stay overnight, then catch a flight back to Hamburg early the next morning, allowing me to arrive at my editorial job for *Petra* magazine only an hour late.

HAMBURG

Later that same day, Celine arrived from California. We picked up the keys to the new apartment on Eppendorfer Baum and happily moved in, lugging our luggage up the four steep flights of stairs.

Work continued with a group shot for *Nicole* magazine and a cover try for *Brigitte* magazine, followed by a day of go-sees all over the city. It had been a whirlwind of a first week back in Germany, back in the modeling world. And we had the weekend to catch up on sleep, get ourselves organized and learn a little about our new neighborhood, and our new city.

HAMBURG

Hamburg, a major port city, sits in the north of Germany, connected to the North Sea by way of the Elbe River. Hundreds of canals streak through the area. Extensively damaged during World War II, the rebuilt city maintains its old-world ambiance, unlike anything else I experienced in Germany up to this point. My ancestors came from the northern parts of Germany, and there were clearly differences in the people here and those in the South, in Bavaria, much like those from the north and south in the States.

For the first time, I didn't lay out the city in my mind, nor seek out a landmark to orient myself. I trusted the U-Bahn, which had a stop a long walk away from the apartment. Addresses for photographers and clients, 118 of them, were not as easy to find as they had been in Munich, and I often found myself walking in circles.

At the beginning of my second week back in Germany, I hit the ground running. My editorial job for *Petra* magazine lasted almost all day. The photographer shot the entire spread in black and white. In the evening, I once again made my way to the airport for a flight to Cologne (Köln). From there, I took a taxi to the Komsul Hotel in the nearby city of Bonn, the capital of West Germany.

EUROPEAN DAZE

In the morning, I reported downstairs, meeting with the photographer before taking the short ride over to Studio Robinson, a huge, drafty warehouse. Shortly, two other American models arrived, followed by four German models from Köln and Dusseldorf. These German models were different, not as sure of themselves, and weary of us Americans. I did my best to bridge this gap, but they seemed a bit less worldly than my counterparts in Munich and now Hamburg.

After everyone had their hair and makeup done, we poured ourselves into long red skirts and jackets, accompanied by three-inch red heels. It was to be another group shot, with a wealthy businessman, for *Stern*, a weekly general interest magazine. As we waited for the businessman to show up, the photographer tested the lighting, and the makeup artists went around touching up our faces, telling us not to frown or laugh too much. Finally, eight hours later, the businessman strolled into the studio.

We crammed together in various poses and facial expressions, acting as if we were all fighting to get to him, as the photographer snapped away. Thirty minutes later, we were done. Ten minutes later, three of us raced to the airport, barely missing our 7:00 p.m. flights. We sat at the bar, drinking beer, until the next flight two hours later.

Overall, Hamburg itself didn't hold the excitement of Munich. Not only did the people seem different, the atmosphere felt different, more proper, and old, like a middle-aged millionaire in contrast to the teenager feel in Munich.

HAMBURG

Celine and I wandered around our new neighborhood and found a small Greek restaurant and an Italian one named New York, New York. These became our go-to restaurants, mainly because they were so close to the apartment. Otherwise, we cooked our own meals, including hamburgers and potatoes. We had gotten used to this while living in Munich with Hartwig and didn't care to eat out every night.

By now I had been back in Europe, back to modeling, for four weeks. Fortunately work continued, with several jobs again being for hair, such as an advertisement and promo for Gard hair products. I also continued doing catalog work, including one for golf fashions. Many days I worked two jobs, one in the morning, and another in the afternoon, usually around 2:00 p.m. Occasionally, I had editorial shoots, the more active, better tear sheet possibility jobs. In one, for *Bild der Frau* magazine, I posed for an Indian-style editorial spread, wearing saris and choli tops, and posing in odd ways. I also frequently flew back to Munich for a one-day job, including one with a feisty cat that obviously didn't want to be photographed.

On a Sunday evening, towards the end of February, I flew to Dusseldorf. I hadn't been back there since my first job in Zurich, back in May of last year, when I met Axel. I still heard from him occasionally but chose not to call him this time. From the airport, I took a taxi into the nearby city of Essen, about thirty minutes to the north, to Hotel Bredeney. On Monday morning, I walked across the street to the headquarters of Karstadt, a German department store chain. From there, we traveled to a museum for a full-day catalog shoot.

EUROPEAN DAZE

When I returned to Hamburg, the blues overtook me again. Was it the cold, dreary weather, the business of modeling, or maybe a mix of both? I worked the following day, this time with a fifteen-year-old model from Texas. Why was she in Europe alone? Why didn't she want to attend high school like normal teenagers? It appeared her parents were all for her pursuing a modeling career and gladly let her stay out of school. After the shoot, I decided to walk the thirty minutes back to the apartment instead of jumping on the U-Bahn. I needed to clear my head and try to figure out what would make me happier. When I arrived back at the apartment, I told Celine about my day. My mood sunk low. She suggested we check out the nightlife, something we had not yet done.

We dressed up and took a taxi to a club called Madhaus. Hailing itself as a disco, its true vibe was hard rock. Crowded, we quickly noticed how everyone wore plain dark clothes while we were sporting more colorful, fashionable outfits. We didn't fit in so we headed over to Gala, another club we had heard about which played music we could dance to. Once finding it, we danced until 5:00 a.m. We still didn't fit in and knew we stood out, but by then, just didn't care.

The next day brought the start of the month of March. Since it was the first Saturday of the month, stores stayed open until 6:00 p.m. and we dragged ourselves out of bed and made our way down to Jungfernstieg, a popular urban shopping promenade. With our heads pounding, we shuffled slowly around the shops. In one of the old buildings we found a Burger King, of all things, and quickly got in line. Overly crowded, we couldn't find a seat, so we took our meal outside, sitting on the stone steps. All those who passed by stared at us, frowning as they did so. We gathered this wasn't something commonly done here. We seemed to have a hard time fitting in anywhere in Hamburg.

After a little more shopping, we stopped at a café for cappuccinos and as we sat talking, an older man, possibly in his early to mid-thirties, leaned over to our table. Had we been at Gala the night before, he asked. We nodded. Apparently, we had stood out, not just because of our clothes but our faces and actions as well. He slid his chair over to join us. Although German, Walter told us he lived most of the time in London, working as a journalist.

A few days later I went to work at PPS Studio which was located in an old drafty and dark WWII bunker. As I prepared for my first photos, an alarm screamed throughout the bunker, sounding like one of those air raid alarms you hear in old war movies. Chills shot up my spine. Although it had only been a test by the owners of the building, it set me on edge for the rest of the day.

The job itself was for Otto, the largest catalog in Germany, and focused first on swimsuits, followed by cardigan sweaters, an unusual combination for one shoot. There were three other models for the job also, one American and two Canadians. The Canadian models had grown in number, and I found myself working with them more and more. In between photos, during the long waits, our conversations ranged from mother-daughter relationships, God's test of the human race, to the all-important boyfriend problems.

Finishing by late afternoon, I made my way to a video casting for a coffee commercial. I never liked going to evening castings, and this one was no exception. Once there, they told me my look wasn't commercial enough. Could it be the hair, or my face? Meanwhile, Celine heard back from an agency in London, where she hoped to work. They rejected her because her look was too commercial. So, there we were, one of us too commercial looking and the other not commercial looking enough.

On the following Thursday, I finally got to work with Peter Pfander, a popular photographer in Hamburg. The job turned out to be for *Maxi*, a fun, stylish women's magazine. I laughed as I walked into the studio, seeing Cissy, a model also with Legends Agency in New York. She and I had run into each other in every country so far, including Tunisia. The male model of the day turned out to be Robert Iannucci, Mr. Calvin Klein himself, who I first met back in Paris in 1984. I called him that because of his sexy Calvin Klein Jeans ad, shirtless and full of chiseled muscle.

In the evening, Celine and I met Walter at a trendy café, where we chatted for over two hours. We both believed Walter to be a spy. He had lived in the Middle East and spoke fluent Arabic. He also had a strange acquaintance with a male model from Finland named Sachary. Did he work with Walter as a spy? Maybe I had been reading too many Robert Ludlum books lately, or maybe, just maybe, I was right.

HAMBURG

Feeling a bit sluggish, Celine and I decided to join a gym, thinking it might motivate us. Sport Live had an impressive workout area with all the latest equipment. It also had a quaint café which not only served alcohol to its members but also allowed people to smoke. After a workout with Sven, our trainer, we often enjoyed the whirlpool, the sauna, and the small pool, all of which were co-ed. Naked bodies lurked about everywhere. The Europeans never ceased to amaze me when it came to their comfortability with nudity.

The workouts soon began to clear my head and increase my energy, and also started to show in my body type. About a month after regular workouts, I went on a go-see at *Für Sie* magazine about an option they had placed on me for a job. They said I had a super body—not so skinny as those other sickly models. This took me aback slightly. It seems that underneath this slender body I had muscles which had been waiting to be developed. With the miles and miles of walking since the days in New York and Paris, my legs had increased in size, shaped by muscles I didn't know I had. And now muscles in my upper body, including abs, were making their debut as well. This could become a real problem. Didn't clients prefer sickly skinny models?

EUROPEAN DAZE

On our good days, Celine and I often stopped off at Karstadt Department Store, buying different shades of nail polish and other small items which made us happy. We also found a music store where I purchased cassettes such as the new one by Mr. Mister which contained the songs "Kyrie" and "Broken Wings." My favorite, however, soon became the new song by Jennifer Rush, "The Power of Love."

I continued to write letters home to my parents and wrote sporadically in my journal. I had asked my mom to gather information on the University of Miami as I thought I might return to college in January with plans to be a teacher and a writer. Again, I managed to find a store that sold books in English and devoured such paperbacks as Robert Ludlum's *The Matlock Paper*, Frank Yerby's *The Foxes of Harrow*, and classics such as *The Good Earth* by Pearl Buck and *Watership Down* by Richard Adams.

I also continued to read newspapers, including *USA Today*, as well as American magazines *Time* and *Psychology Today*. One day I came across a German magazine, *Tempo*, which had a picture of a regal looking fellow and his dame on the front cover. His name was Hubertus von der Osten. Maybe we were related. I bought a copy to send to my Uncle Herb who had been compiling family records and the only one in the family who still spoke and read German.

From what I could tell from my simple translations, the article told of Hubertus' profound lust. In a return letter from my uncle, he confirmed that the article, and the magazine itself, were a bit racy, so much so that he refused to show it to other family members. He also complained to my dad about me being under bad influences in Europe. The article had simply been about how aristocratic youth were defying their aristocratic families, a rebellious streak. This type of article appeared normal in Germany, and I couldn't believe my uncle made such a big deal about its inappropriateness.

Mid-March arrived and along with it the arrival of Kay Mitchell, the head of my New York agency, Legends. I had not seen or heard from Kay in over a year. I took a taxi to her hotel, Hotel Elisia, and sat down at the table in the lobby restaurant. An awkward, forced conversation ensued, and I found her to be even more strange than the time I met with her in Milan. I wonder what she thought of me. Had she spoken with Lawrine about me lately? With no answers or encouragement from her, it seemed like a relationship on its last leg.

A few days later I turned twenty-one. The day began with my working with Peter Pfander at his studio. Christel, from the agency, dropped by to surprise me with a beautiful bouquet of flowers and to say happy birthday. Back at the apartment, I opened a package from my parents. Inside was a beautiful bracelet and earrings to match a necklace they had given me for Christmas and two books. Also, tucked inside I found a box of Cream of Wheat, the one with individual packets. I had craved this for over a month now and squealed in delight.

Celine treated me to dinner at our Italian restaurant nearby where I had the eggplant parmesan, and although it was good, it didn't compare to my Mom's version of the dish. We headed back to the apartment and watched a world ice-skating couples' competition as we drank a bottle of champagne. Not the ideal twenty-first birthday celebration but enough.

EUROPEAN DAZE

Early the next morning I caught my flight to Dusseldorf. When I arrived at the studio, I could tell it was going to be a long, slow day. No one moved swiftly or energetically, and the other model, who didn't seem overly smart, flitted about in between her naps. I didn't shoot until after 1:00 p.m. then again at 3:30 p.m. With orders from the agency to leave the studio at 5:00 p.m. no matter what in order to make the 6:00 p.m. flight back to Hamburg, I packed up my belongings. The furious photographer and client bereted me as I did so, and I told them to take it up with the agency.

Working again the following day but in Hamburg, I arrived at the studio and made my way to the makeup artist's chair. The stylist walked over as I sat down, hovering over me, and speaking in German to herself before walking away. The photographer arrived, took one look at me, and started shouting because my hair had grown longer than shown on my composite card. Finally, the client showed up, stopping short when she heard me say hello. It was written all over her face. I wasn't German.

I continued on, doing my best to ignore them all as I got ready for the first photo. Conversations continued behind me until the only positive person in the room, the makeup artist, touched my arm softly. The client had decided my calves were too big and the job had to be canceled. The assistant photographer walked up, asking in a soft voice with a slightly embarrassed look on his face if he could take a photo of my legs. I figured they wanted this for proof to argue their case with the agency so they wouldn't have to pay. I let him take the photo. Whether reality or the angle the assistant photographer

HAMBURG

held the Polaroid camera, it came out perfect. The stylist ranted in German as she glanced at it, and I smiled as I gathered my things and left without saying another word.

While I had been in Dusseldorf, Celine's friend, Natalie, arrived from California. The three of us decided to visit Berlin and dragged ourselves to the Hamburg Airport early one morning. The Pan Am flight took off at 7:00 a.m., arriving in Berlin an hour later. We hadn't planned out our visit, so we simply made our way to Hotel California on the famous Kurfürstendam, a large avenue comparable to the Champs Élysses in Paris. The hotel, while not the fanciest in the world, provided a space at an affordable price. We had heard about it from other models and managed to snag a room for the three of us.

We ventured back on to the busy Kurfürstendam and found a cute café to sit in and decide what to do during our time in the city. We had arrived on a Tuesday, so the city buzzed. As we walked around, we came upon a magazine shop and decided to take a quick look inside. As models, we commonly stopped to look through the latest issues of magazines to see if we were in them. I immediately found Celine's photos in *Vital* magazine and found myself in *Petra* magazine. We were surprised and laughed, all the while critiquing them. A few seconds later, Celine found me on the cover of *Diana* magazine and, I must say, it wasn't flattering. I cringed.

Meanwhile, Natalie fumed, finding us arrogant snots for focusing on ourselves in this way. Of course, she didn't share our enthusiasm. How could she know how important this was to us? We waited so long to see if our photos even made the magazines.

In the afternoon, the three of us arranged to join a bus tour into East Berlin. By this time, Berlin had been divided into east and west since the end of WWII, during the resultant Cold War. As we entered Checkpoint Charlie, the guards searched the bus and slid mirrors under the carriage. No one smiled. Within a few minutes, we were cleared, and our tour guide boarded the bus. He spoke English like someone from Brooklyn. As we drove into East Berlin, the city looked dreary. Already an overcast day, the clouds darkened at times, making the city seem even more lifeless. There were no bright colors anywhere, no people out walking, no dogs running about. Nothing but drab buildings and a feeling of air pressing down on us and the city.

As the bus slowed, then stopped altogether, the door opened, and we marched off, gathering near two tall, angled, red granite monuments. These beautiful, slanted walls sat at the entrance to Treptower Park, the entrance to the Soviet War Memorial. The Hammer and Sycle, symbols of the Soviet Union, were engraved upon each of them, and they loomed high over the statues of two kneeling soldiers. As they hovered above us as well, the guide beamed with great pride as he told of the Soviet soldiers who fell in the Battle of Berlin in the spring of 1945.

Curious, the three of us wandered away from the group, looking beyond the granite walls. Suddenly, the guide magically appeared in front of us, as if corralling us and leading us back to the group. He continued to keep an eye on us as if we might run away. Yet, why in the world would we even want to stay in such a sad place? Heralded back on the bus, the next stop was a tiny restaurant, if you could even call it that. They undoubtedly wanted us to spend money. Not finding anything appealing on the menu, we settled for coffee.

One thing you couldn't help but notice was the many soldiers everywhere, all carrying rifles. We saw no pets being walked, no children skipping on the sidewalk. A short while later, as the bus drove back through Checkpoint Charlie, we sighed with relief, happy to be out of that dark, desolate place and back into bright, flashing, exciting West Berlin. The two halves of the city were like night and day, a very dark night, and a very bright day.

We spent our last day in West Berlin wandering around the city in rainy weather, stopping off at cafes, walking through parks, glancing through stores. At one point we entered a bar to have a drink. As I looked around, noticing we were the only women in the place, and the men didn't even look our way, I punched Celine's shoulder. We were in a gay men's bar. In the evening, we decided to check out the nightclubs and walked around practically all night, stopping in one club after another. None seemed our type, and most of them were empty. Finally, we found one with music we could dance to and stayed for a while. At 4:00 a.m., we climbed in a taxi and headed to the airport.

Back in Hamburg, Celine went straight to an early casting while Nicole and I went back to the apartment and crashed. I had to work in the afternoon. The trip had been too short and not well planned, but at least we could now say we had been to Berlin.

EUROPEAN DAZE

My roommate, Celine (l), and I at the Soviet War Memorial in East Berlin.

HAMBURG

Getting ready for dinner with Kay Mitchell, the owner of Legends, my agency in New York. Kay was in Hamburg for a few days and we discussed future plans and possibilities. It was a relationship on its last leg.

HAMBURG

April arrived and with it came much change. The owner of the apartment returned to Hamburg, and we had to move out, and in with a German family for a few weeks. Before the two weeks were up, Celine had flown to Barcelona, Spain to try her luck there for a month. With my trip to the Canary Islands for work rapidly approaching, I packed my belongings again and stored them with our friend Walter, the spy.

The trip would be taking me first to Frankfurt, then on to Madrid, Spain where I had a long wait for a flight to Lanzarote, one of the islands. Much had happened in the world recently, and it wasn't all good. I would write about it in my journal:

> The Libyans are furious with Spain and England for their participation in the recent bombing of Libya. Not too long ago a bomb exploded on a TWA flight, killing four Americans, including a baby. Then there was a bombing at a disco in Berlin, killing two people including an American soldier. This all led back to Libya's leader, Gaddafi. Americans carried out a second air strike on Libya as a result. President Reagan acts! Everyone seems to be in a panic. Many riots and demonstrations have taken place all over Europe, here in Hamburg as well as in Barcelona where Celine is. They are all furious with America. I called Sean in

London last night. The British are not only furious with America but with Prime Minister Thatcher due to her cooperation with President Reagan. People all over Europe are scared! I'm keeping a low profile and not voicing my opinions. It's safer to keep quiet. I met Walter for coffee yesterday. I saw so many people who looked like they could be Libyans. Walter agreed. He's a pretty big-time journalist and seems to know a lot of "scoops". He claims Syria is the real culprit, but America wants to get rid of Gaddafi so bombed Libya instead. It's a scary situation!

When I arrived at the Frankfurt airport, the photographer and client seemed confused when I didn't speak fluent German. Couldn't the agency make it clear I wasn't German beforehand? Suddenly, it occurred to me that maybe the problem lay more in the fact I was an American, at a time when America seemed an enemy.

The four other models for the trip arrived shortly, gratefully interrupting the silence. Eva and Karin were German, Ruth hailed from Austria, and Susanne came from Denmark. I was the only American.

Eva, with long dark hair topped by a straw hat, seemed to be the tough girl of the group. Katrin, with her short blonde hair and perpetual smile, had an outrageous, over-the-top personality and spoke perfect English, including slang, after spending a summer in California. Susanne, sporting long sandy blond hair and bangs, with a more girl-next-door look, seemed quiet and distracted. Ruth, with short dark hair, spoke little English and appeared rigid, yet she had kind, dark brown eyes. We all boarded our flight to Madrid, and after a four-hour wait there, climbed aboard the final flight to Lanzarote.

The Canary Islands sit just off the west coast of North Africa below Spain and Morocco. Of the seven islands, Lanzarote lies closest to the continent. As the client checked us in, the five of us models wandered out to the pool patio of Hotel Las Cucharas in the Costa Teguise Resort, to enjoy a welcome drink. We were staying in villas, large villas with two floors to include a kitchen, living room, bedroom, and bath on the first floor, and a second bedroom and bath on the second floor. For some reason, the client had roomed me with Ruth, the one model who spoke the least English. She chose the upstairs room, so I had the entire downstairs mostly to myself.

Before settling in, the photographer and client established a schedule of sorts. We didn't have to meet for group dinners so we could eat at any of the restaurants in and around the resort. As for breakfasts, we needed to purchase our own food at the store nearby to enjoy in our villas before work each day. With initial ground rules established, the five of us models decided to go out to eat together at one of the quaint restaurants nestled among shops on a promenade. We had six days of shooting ahead of us and might as well get to know each other a little better.

On our first day of work, I waited around, not shooting in the morning. After lunch, the photographer shot photos of Eva and Katrin, and the rest of us stayed nearby. My roommate, Ruth, decided she would spend her time waiting on the roof, in a patio type area, sunning herself in the nude. She asked me to call her whenever we were ready to go out on location.

EUROPEAN DAZE

When I got the word, I walked over to the villa, calling to Ruth twice. Racing back to the group, I climbed in the van, and we waited several minutes before the photographer ordered the driver to leave Ruth behind. A screaming fest, in German, erupted inside the van. We can't just leave her behind, they all seemed to be saying in one way or another. I sat there quietly. *Hadn't I done what she asked? If she chose not to hurry, why should we wait?* Suddenly, one of the other models, Katrin, switched to English and yelled for me to go and get her.

Thinking everyone had agreed, I jumped out of the van and raced back to the villa, turning the wrong way, and having to backtrack before finding it. Ruth looked at me quizzically, as if she had no idea that we needed to hurry. By the time we returned to the parking lot, the van had already left. Furious with Ruth, furious with the other models who told me to go get her, I ranted and raved out loud. Fortunately, Ruth didn't understand a word I said.

Still steaming, I vaguely heard a horn beeping and turned to see the van grow closer. The client had come back for us. I didn't say a word but climbed in. Once at the location, I began applying my own makeup for the shoot. The other models—Eva, Karin, and Susanne—all talked to me at once. That's when I lost it and told them, "Next time, you fucking go, but do not ever again tell me what to do!" I rarely ever cursed but when I did, I meant every word.

As I finished my makeup, I listened to music on my Walkman. I didn't care if I spent the entire week alone without socializing at all with the others. At a break in the shoot, I approached the photographer, telling him my side of the situation. He smiled, telling me how glad he was I came to him directly to talk about it. We were shooting outside a restaurant, and he purchased a gin and tonic to calm my nerves. All seemed well between us.

While I waited for my turn to shoot, eight little girls ran up, pleading with me to put makeup on them. I pulled out a few things, applying lipstick with a brush to their puckered lips, and flitting blush on their tiny golden-brown cheeks. They posed and giggled, excitedly speaking to each other in Spanish. That was one of the best moments of the trip. This calmed me down more than the alcohol.

While at a photo shoot on the island of Lanzorote in the Canary Islands, a group of young girls pleaded with me to apply makeup for them.

Lanzarote, windy and leaning toward the chilly side, nevertheless felt like an island, like a step closer to Florida. It was the middle of April, and the temperatures fluctuated crazily between lows and highs. I hadn't brought many warm clothes, but, fortunately, the shoot itself consisted mostly of winter clothes which I could borrow if needed.

Work took up the majority of our days, and Katrin and I soon became the two models in almost every photo. We worked harder than I had ever worked on location before, early morning to last light of day. Although feeling honored to work so much, we weren't pleased that the other three models had so much free time.

After one long, hot day, no one wanted to go out but the two of us. Stopping at the first small restaurant bar on the promenade, I ordered a Kahlua with cold milk. The waiter, shaking his head at such a combination, looked at me incredulously, commenting, "Only in America." The photographer's assistant, feeling the work pressure himself, soon joined us. We joked and laughed, making the long day a bit more bearable.

Once the shoot wrapped up, we packed our bags and returned to the airport. Flying first to Las Palmas, located on one of the other islands, then to Frankfurt, we all split up and went our separate ways. I flew back to Hamburg and Walter met me at the airport. I only had three more nights left in the city, and I spent my time wrapping everything up with the agency and collecting the money in my account, which had grown considerably during my time in Hamburg.

Back in Europe for almost four months now, work had been abundant, but good tear sheets for my portfolio were not. Conflicted, I walked outside only to be assaulted by the icy wind. Northern Germany wasn't helping to clarify my goals and future plans as I had hoped it would.

Before departing for the Canary Islands, I had purchased a ticket to fly to London for a few days, then on to the States by way of Boston and Tampa. I wanted to stop in London to see Sean and visit a few of the agencies there before flying home. I had already spoken with Lawrine back at my agency in New York, and she gave me the names of the London agencies to visit. We also discussed my plans to return to New York in September. Maybe I could go there for a few weeks to see if any interest and work developed. Celine and I also considered going to Australia to work later in the year and had recently received a notice from the agency there, excitedly asking us to come in the fall. Could we really go to the land down under?

As for my return to Florida so soon, I decided I needed to take a break and wanted to clear out my head so I could think straight and plan my next move. I also wanted to check on my family. My mom had recently moved my grandparents to Florida from Alabama to take care of them. Everyone in the family seemed mad at everyone else, and all seemed to be in chaos. Not sure how I could help, I just knew I needed to be there, at least for a while.

As April ended, I flew to London. Sean met me at the airport, and I stayed at Ian and Taber's flat. Sean now had a new girlfriend, so naturally, I couldn't stay with him. This didn't bother me. The minute I moved out of Milan, our relationship changed. I didn't see it as a failure on my part or his. I felt grateful for the time we did have together and was happy for him.

EUROPEAN DAZE

Dragging myself out onto the streets of London the following morning, I visited one agency, Laraine Ashton IFM. I instantly didn't care for them, and to be honest, I didn't care much for London overall. I skipped meeting with any of the other agencies. Meanwhile, Walter had flown back to London, and we met for a few hours before my flight to the States. He showed me around Piccadilly Square before driving to Harrod's luxury department store where I purchased a pair of sandals made with real animal hide (which I still have to this day). In my mind, however, I was already on my way home.

TOP: While back in the States, we celebrated Mother's Day at a restaurant in Ponce Inlet (FL). Here I am (far left) with my mom, my sister Trudy, and brother Kurt.

BOTTOM: While home, I was also able to spend a little time with my grandmother, Barbara Allen Jackson, who had just moved to Florida.

MUNICH
II
JUNE 8 - DEC 7, 1986

F light information blared from the speakers, first in German, then French, then finally English. As I entered the charter hall, a blonde sitting with a small group at the rear of the last gate caught my eye. Sophia, a sexy Swedish model I knew briefly from a few hours of work at a shoot a month or so before, illuminated the hall.

Back in Munich for only a week after returning from my visit home, I hoped this second trip to Tunisia would re-kindle the fire in me to move forward, to get back in the game. Benger, a major sports brand out of Austria, had booked me for the week-long trip. As I approached the group, I could see them all laughing. Apparently, they had all worked together before, and I instantly felt like the odd man out.

The direct charter flight to the island of Jerba took just under three hours. I took the time to observe the others and wrap my mind around the upcoming week. Sitting beside the stylist and her girlfriend, a fact both tried to conceal, I listened to conversations between Sophia and Helmut, one of the clients. They obviously had a thing for each other. Sophia spoke English well, and her accent oozed even more sexuality as she grinned and stroked Helmut's arm.

Club Meninx sat along the coast of the Mediterranean Sea, a more relaxed and quiet resort than the Club Med I had stayed at on my previous trip. Wasting no time, we all changed into our swimsuits and shorts and met on the beach. The clients stared at Sophia and me, no doubt assessing our bodies and deciding which swimsuits and clothes we would wear. I felt anxious. Over the last several months I had given in to a paranoid insecurity, like so many of the models around me. One of the worst things a model can do is lose confidence in herself. So, I did what any self-respecting model would do, I faked it. I faked my self-confidence.

The heat magnified here, and the wind blew stinging granules of sand at my face and legs. I moved under a shelter, dozing off until one of the clients, Fritz, came over to check on me. A doughboy type guy with curly, reddish hair, mustache, and a fun, mischievous smile, I couldn't help but like him.

On the first full day on the island, while the others scouted locations to shoot the photos, Sophia and I remained poolside, sipping on colas. A tall guy with long, rangy black hair walked up. Speaking in undeniably American English, he asked if we were there working. At first, I didn't think much of him, not overly attractive or enticing. He introduced himself as Kraig, the male model who had missed our flight the day before. As he sipped on a cola beside us, he regaled us with stories of his California lifestyle of drugs, sex, and surfing.

The resort, much smaller than the Club Med, also had fewer restaurant options. Sophia and I made it to breakfast the following morning, barely in time to order coffee. It tasted like mud. Large flies swarmed all over us, making us squirm. We headed to the beach to lay out in the sun, but the wind again threw stinging sand at us. Meeting up in the stylist's room in the afternoon, we discussed the type of shoot this would be

MUNICH II

and what they expected. It didn't take long to establish the work schedule, all based on the natural light available. We were to work from 5:00 a.m. to 8:30 a.m. every morning, then again in the evenings from 5:00 p.m. to 7:30 p.m. This meant we had free time between 9:00 in the morning and 4:30 in the afternoon. Not a bad schedule, to say the least.

Because I easily tan, my skin's golden-brown hues impressed the clients. However, Sophia needed to catch-up since we would be doing several photos together. So, while she tanned, I stayed out of the sun, spending my time in the shade and swimming in the pool. The next morning, I awoke at 4:30 a.m., met everyone at 5:00 a.m. and we headed out to a location—a wide beach with towering sand dunes. For three hours, we shot singles and doubles, all for swimsuits, including bikinis with lacy bandeau tops, mine in lime green and Sophia's in fuchsia.

Once back at the resort, Sophia and I sat out by the pool most of the afternoon. Around 3:00 p.m., the two clients, Helmut and Fritz, arrived with a bottle of champagne and several glasses. As the clock struck 5:00 p.m., we again met and traveled back to the same morning location to shoot summer clothes instead of swimsuits.

Dinners at the resort were less than desirable, with a soup starting off each meal. The ongoing joke for the week soon became we were having the same soup every night, just in a different color. It had no discernable taste so we kept adding salt, wine or whatever we could find to spice it up. I quickly learned to fill up on the much more desirable lunch buffet each day.

EUROPEAN DAZE

For the second day of shooting, we again met in the early dawn hour and this time headed into the small downtown. Every shot seemed to take forever as the photographer fidgeted with his camera and adjusted to the light. After several singles, doubles, and a few triples, we headed back to the resort, and the same routine followed as the day before, including the 3:00 p.m. champagne.

An interesting thing started to develop. Kraig seemed to grow frustrated at the flirting between Sophia and Helmut. He obviously had his eyes on her as well. I found being the observer delightfully entertaining. After a long, at times frustratingly slow, evening shoot, the entire group decided to go out dancing and drinking, even jumping in the pool for a swim in the early morning.

The next day we all felt equally rough, with only a few hours' sleep. Yet we managed to meet at our designated time and headed out. We were in this together. This time the location for photos turned out to be a large set of rocks. It also now appeared, after the night of dancing, Sophia and Kraig were an item.

We followed the same routine for the next two days. Shooting early in the morning, laying out by the pool most of the day, sipping on champagne in the late afternoon, then shooting more photos in the evening before long nights of dinner, dancing, and drinking. I was having more fun than I had had all year.

On Sunday, our last full day on the island, we completed the work and headed into the city for dinner. Sophia and Kraig hung all over each other, deeply sad the week neared its end, and they would have to go their separate ways. Meanwhile, Frigish, the photographer, seemed to latch on to me. Now with the photos complete, he decided to show me how much he liked me. Although flattered, I turned him down. This wasn't how I did things.

The week had been perhaps the best job on location, the best trip, the best group of people I had ever experienced during my time as a model. This is what made it all worthwhile. A group of people, working and playing together. It wasn't about the tear sheets any longer.

When I returned to Munich, I moved into a tiny studio apartment in a student residency I had arranged prior to the trip to Tunisia. A dorm type room, it nevertheless felt cozy with a twin bed, desk, table, kitchen, and a full-size bathroom. After living out of a suitcase for the past three weeks, the relief of being able to unpack everything excited me. The room sat on the fifth floor and fortunately the building had an elevator. I didn't mind living alone. I knew Munich would never again be the same as when I lived with Hartwig and Celine on Franz-Joseph-Strasse. Those moments were fleeting at best, like everything else in this line of work.

EUROPEAN DAZE

TOP: Sophia (r) and I poolside for the daily 3:00 p.m. champagne.

BOTTOM: Sophia (r) and I at the resort club, ready for another night of drinking and dancing.

MUNICH II

It's a wrap!
The Tunisia crew on the beach after the last photo.

TOP ROW: (l to r) Me, one of the clients, the stylist, and Sophia, the other model.

BOTTOM ROW: (l to r) Frigish, the photographer, Helmut, and Fritz (two of the clients).

MUNICH II

The hot, muggy summer days continued, and I made my way up the Leopoldstrasse to the Holiday Inn for a cattle call for a hair advertisement. A room full of hopeful models sat in the lobby, in complete silence, as if too scared to talk. At another casting, for eyeglasses, I sighed as I sat down in front of the photographer and client. I didn't hold out much hope in getting the job as someone had once told me my face was too small and my nose too thin to model fashionable eyewear. I went through the motions anyway and surprisingly, every pair I tried on for the client fit perfectly. The client mentioned they had ordered the collection in a small size, to fit perfect little model noses. I got the job.

The month of July sped by, with various jobs in the city and many more go-sees and castings. I met up with a few models I knew at the theater or at cafes. Yet I felt bored. I honestly didn't care to immerse myself again in the model world although it easily could have been done. The excitement, the newness of the experience had waned. Maybe if I had gone to a new market, a new country, my excitement would have returned.

At the agency, I received a telex from Chadwicks Agency in Sydney, Australia. It included information on obtaining tourist visas and about sending tear sheets and composite cards prior to our arrival. Talking with Celine in Spain, we decided not to pursue the Australia trip after all. It might prove expensive and non-producing as far as tearsheets and money were concerned. I wrote out a telex asking Chadwicks if we could postpone our trip until at least January. I hoped we weren't giving up an opportunity of a lifetime.

My next trip occurred at the beginning of August, with a British Airways flight to London, then on to Leeds, England. From there I made my way to Bradford, a textile boom town. Just across the street from my hotel sat the headquarters for Empire Stores, the oldest mail order catalogue company in England. For a day and a half, I tried on outfit after outfit. They were only fittings; the real shoot would occur in London a week later.

Returning to Heathrow Airport in London the following week, I jumped in a taxi to the Bedford Corner Hotel on Tottenham Court Road, where I met up with the other models for the shoot. Diane, sporting boyishly short, reddish-blond hair and wide hips, had flown in specifically for this job from Missouri. Undine, a German model with blonde hair, lived in Hamburg.

After meeting downstairs for breakfast, the three of us walked the short distance to the studio of photographer Colin Thomas. We felt an instant rapport, and the shoot got off to a great start. My first set of pictures involved an hour of twirling and leaping. The photographer talked constantly as if cheering me on. The client, Melody, and her assistant, Ann, were the dream duo. We also had Mary, the stylist, and Dottie, the hair miracle worker, rounding out the group for the week. Dottie swarmed around us, with hairspray in one hand and a brush in the other, not leaving one hair out of place.

MUNICH II

Although the first day had gone so well and sped by, the second day dragged in comparison. The spread, for jeans and leather, required more detail and perfection in the way we moved. In one shoot, the pair of jeans clung to my legs like a second skin and the leather halter and jacket hugged my upper body. I felt like Olivia Newton-John as Sandy at the end of the movie *Grease*. When the shoot ended, the stylist handed me the tight jeans as a gift. This had never happened before. Contrary to what family and friends believed, clothes modeled are not given to the model. At least, not in most cases. The comradery in the studio made the days fun and lighthearted, not like work at all.

After three full days of shooting, Diane, Udine and I decided to treat ourselves to a show. Stopping off at the Dominion Theatre on Tottenham Court Road, we purchased tickets to the night's performance of *Time*, a rock musical starring Cliff Richards. That night, as we found our seats in the theater, lights flashed all around as the music grew louder and louder. I sat at the edge of my seat like a little girl at her first Rockettes show. The storyline went something like this: a world-famous rock star and his trio of backup singers are suddenly taken through the time zone to a different universe, while time stands still on Earth. They are in a universal trial with three judges and Akash, the ultimate word of truth portrayed by Laurence Olivier. They have to defend the Earth and its peoples and prove they are an asset, not a threat, to universal peace. Pretty heady stuff.

Now mesmerized by live plays, we decided to attend another one the following evening. The client's assistant, Ann, joined us at the hotel and the four of us walked to the Prince

Edward Theatre to see the musical *Chess* about the World Chess Championship between a Russian and an American. After winning, the Russian defects to the West and falls in love with the American's girlfriend. The next year at the Championship, he defends his title against another Russian and in the audience is his Russian wife. In the end, he decides to return to Russia with her. Who knew you could make a love story out of playing chess?

Too excited after the show to return to the hotel, we found a small restaurant to share a pizza. The four of us chatted noisily before two guys collapsed at the next table. One had his shirt open and smelled like vomit. The other one, reeking of body odor, looked over at us, staring for a moment before saying, "Yeah, there's some nice English cunt out tonight." I first glanced over at Diane, and as I turned back towards him, about to tell him what I thought of his classless comment, I caught sight of Ann. As the only English woman at the table, her eyes pleaded with me to stay quiet. I stopped myself and looked away. Needless to say, we didn't stick around for coffee and a chat.

On our last day in London, we stopped by the studio to check if any reshoots were needed. None were, so we said our sad farewells. Off we went, by taxi, to Kings Road, then later back to Covent Gardens to shop before our flights. Undine and I got a taxi to Heathrow Airport while Diane headed to Gatwick Airport to catch her flight back to Missouri. Both of them were returning to their homes, to their husbands. I returned to Munich alone.

MUNICH II

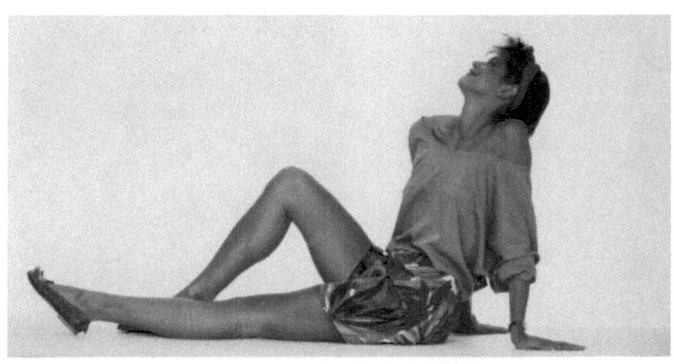

Just another day at work. A fun photo shoot in London for Empire Stores in August 1986.

MUNICH II

Work continued, with a trip to Stuttgart for thin summer clothes shot outside on a cold and windy day, followed a few days later by a trip back there for a mattress and bedding advertisement. The first job for a magazine, at low editorial pay, for *Prima* magazine, involved a stylist and client who picked and picked at the clothes, obsessing over perfection until I thought I would scream. A trip to Innsbruck followed, modeling skiwear with a Swedish male model. The two-day job modeling fashionable eyeglasses finally arrived, and all went well, as did a job for the client Triumph, for their catalog in Finland.

Fashion shows had never been my market, or rather, not one I pursued wholeheartedly. Besides the one at the nightclub in New York and the one at the art museum in Paris, I had not done any other shows. However, that didn't stop my agency from booking me for a set of shows around Germany.

Fashion Lights International Fashion Show Production Company presented a new fashion label by Austrian designer Helmet Lang, in a tour of five German cities. We traveled by way of a big tour bus, from city to city, spending Monday in Munich, Tuesday in Stuttgart, Wednesday in Hannover, Thursday in Dusseldorf and finally, Friday in Cologne.

No choreography for the shows evolved, and it became more of a free-for-all. The only guidance given was whoever felt it at the moment would let their coats fall down their shoulders and start the procession of models down the runway. To me, this felt like a disaster in the making. What if two of us got that feeling at the same time and both started towards the runway from our spot on the stage? It happened only once to me, and I didn't even see the other model, but I hear we almost ran smack into each other.

Back in Munich, a photo shoot for ski goggles and eyeglasses took me on location to the old-world town of Garmisch-Partenkirchen which I instantly fell in love with. So much so, that I returned the following weekend to leisurely walk around and enjoy. Sitting slightly to the southwest of Munich, with the Zugspitze, Germany's highest peak, towering overhead, I meandered around the town for hours. Historic buildings lined the narrow cobblestone streets, three or four stories high, with wooden shutters highlighting pastel shaded frescos.

With my father's constant reminding to make time to see the famous Ludwig castles in Bavaria ringing in my ears, I headed south again the following weekend. This time to Schloss Linderhof, or Linderhof Palace, southwest of Munich, near Ettal Abbey. The smallest palace of King Ludwig II of Bavaria, it captivated me in a way few things had so far in Europe. I joined a tour of the interior of the palace, and we descended into the Venus' grotto, underneath. On the water sat a small, shell-like boat. The tour guide revealed that the King often sat in the boat, drifting for hours and hours as he daydreamed. The Grotto felt magical and private, and I didn't want to leave. Trancelike, I barely heard the guide describe a stage nearby where the king's favorite composer, Richard Wagner, performed for the King and his guests.

After ascending and making my way outside, I found a seat on the low wall surrounding the fountain in front of the palace. As the water spewed upwards, then back into its cradle, awe overcame me at the grandness of the palace and the grounds surrounding it. It reminded me that history is real, and although appalling in places, it is absolutely mesmerizing in others.

The next week I made my way south of Munich a third time, to visit Neuschwanstein, perhaps the most famous of the Ludwig castles. As I approached the castle of fairy tales from below, my mind stumbled in comprehending the site before me. *Is it real?* As if a mirage in the distance, the castle loomed large, and I pinched myself to see if I was awake. A mist of mystery descended all around me. When I finally emerged from a dreamlike state, as if awakened from a dream in which sleepwalking had taken me into the past, I felt I had been transported to a different world. I couldn't recall specific details of the rooms of the castle or its gardens, only of the otherworldly experience of being somewhere out of time.

Meanwhile, back in Munich, back in the model world, I had been invited to attend a party at Café Munich for the American rock band ZZ Top. An oddly sterile, and surprisingly boring event, the three band members sat at a table in the front of the room while everyone else sat at round tables in front of them. It felt like a wedding setup but with no bride and groom, only three men wearing jeans, two of which sported beards practically down to their waists. Again, I couldn't get too excited over the prospect of seeing famous celebrities. They didn't seem extraordinary. They didn't intimidate me nor did they display any larger than life tendencies. From what I could tell, they were just three guys as bored as I was, fulfilling an obligation someone else set up, and thinking about how glad they would be when it was over. Surprisingly, there weren't many models at the event. Apparently, only a few had been invited by the agency, and somehow, I had made the list.

MUNICH II

Photo shoot for ski clothes and eyewear in Innsbruck, Austria.

EUROPEAN DAZE

Goofing off between photos in Stuttgart. Although I lived in Munich, I would often take the early morning train to Stuttgart for work.

MUNICH II

Photo shoot in Munich for fashionable eyewear. I had previously been told I couldn't model eyeglasses because my nose was too small.

MUNICH II

By mid-October, I grew restless again. My agency suggested I return to Hamburg for a few weeks, and I jumped at the chance. Even though I had left that city feeling depressed back in late spring, I now welcomed the opportunity to see it once again. Stopping in the little cafes I had enjoyed either alone or with Celine, I felt happy to be back.

In the agency, the bookers were excited to see me, telling me how good I looked. I had lost a little weight and let my hair grow again. Sitting with Keske, the accountant, we went over my account, which held over $2,000 free and clear for me, mostly from the London shoot. She also helped me prepare a letter and bill to send to Berlin so I could get paid for the fashion shows I had done recently for Helmut Lang. Although they initially said they would pay us in cash after the last show, that didn't happen. Now we had to go through formal channels for payment.

Meanwhile, in the real world, terrorism had again shown its ugly head with a recent hijacking of a Pan-Am flight. Departing from India and bound for Frankfurt, Pan-Am Flight 73 made one fatal stop, in Karachi, Pakistan. Militant hijackers boarded the plane. Of the over three hundred passengers, forty-three were either injured or killed, including Americans. I had been so fortunate in all my travels up to this point. I hoped my luck would hold out a little longer.

A week later, while purchasing a ticket for the U-Bahn, I noticed an Arab couple and their two children struggling to figure out how to buy tickets. I walked over and smiled, showing them what they needed. The father spoke English and told me he was from Iran, and his wife came from Iraq. They were trying to get to London but had been held up in Hamburg because of a problem with their papers. As we made our way down the stairs to the train, I didn't think anything of it. Then he asked the question.

"You speak very good English. Where are you from?"

Before thinking, I responded. "I am from the States."

The man grew silent, and his pleasant, grateful smile faded. The train arrived, and we all boarded. Crowded, we stood facing each other. His face grew contemplative as he continued to stare at me. His wife tended to the children, never once meeting my eyes.

As the train began to move, he mumbled something about America under his breath. He then mentioned the recent hijacking of the Pan-Am flight, and I told him how horrible I thought it was, to which he replied firmly,

"Americans deserve to die. You have too much freedom."

Taken aback, as if slapped, I had never felt such hatred and emotion from anyone before. I didn't shy away from him and refused to believe he truly meant it. Our respective governments showing arrogance and unprofessional diplomacy didn't warrant the deaths of innocent people.

He recanted his statement a short while later as we bantered back and forth. Yet, although he may have been okay with me, the idea of America never would be. So began my education in US-Middle East relations, and one not easily forgotten.

MUNICH II

I returned to Munich at the start of November to a small apartment near the student residency I had stayed in previously. I liked the neighborhood and was glad to be back in familiar territory. It seemed I began just going through the motions, the excitement and motivation of the model lifestyle having long left. Sure, I could string this along for a while longer if I truly wanted to. I had seen others do it, postponing any other type of major life decision. I was only twenty-one, but many models I had met along the way were now in their mid-to-late twenties and were still moving around in the business.

A package arrived from home bearing homemade fudge, jams, and jellies. And of course, boxes of Cream of Wheat. I felt homesick, not just for Florida but for big meals on my parents' back porch, for walks on a real beach, and a swim in the ocean.

Celine finally arrived back in Munich for a few weeks. She had gone from Barcelona to Madrid and now had a charming Spanish boyfriend. When he came to visit her in Munich, he lavishly spent money on her, doing his best to convince her to live in Spain with him full time. I knew where this was leading, and it was not to Australia in January as we had tentatively planned.

After six months back in Europe, work slowed, so much so that while at a photo shoot one day, everyone joked I might be the only working model in Munich. It seemed like a good time to go home for the holidays.

Once back in the States, I flew out to California after Christmas to visit Celine in San Francisco and to also see my brother, Kurt, who had moved out to San Diego over the summer. He had driven cross country, with his golden retriever, Chivas, riding shotgun. Meanwhile, my sister, Trudy, had completed training to become a cross-country truck driver and now spent her days driving an eighteen-wheeler from coast to coast. It seemed we had all gotten out of Florida, one way or another.

Plans were in place for me to return to Europe for jobs already scheduled. I would then decide what to do next. I lingered in limbo stage, not wanting what I had but not exactly knowing what should follow. Throughout the entire modeling experience, I had had no mentor, no guide. My agency in New York, dealing with their own business-related issues, turned us loose in the world. Every model handled it differently, no doubt. One had tried New York again, only to find low interest and mounting expenses and returned home. Another returned to college, leaving her modeling experience behind completely. Several still hung on, barely making enough to live on, and getting older by the day.

1987
THE BEGINNING OF THE END

Pulling on the black catsuit, I stood, allowing the stylist to tug at the zipper, locking me in. The representative from Cartier approached, latching a heavy diamond necklace onto my now covered neck, followed by a bracelet on my left wrist and a diamond ring on my gloved finger. She snapped her fingers, and a man dressed in a dark suit walked up. He nodded at me, and I nodded back. My security guard for the evening. Before leaving the back-staging area, another Cartier representative sprayed me with the perfume we were there to promote, *Panthere De Cartier By Cartier For Women*. Along with two other models, I pulled on a black eye mask, hiding my identity, and entered the crowded room.

As I sauntered cat-like around and through the sophisticated crowd, a million-dollar gal for the night, I enjoyed the anonymity of my role. I could be someone else entirely for a few hours. Walking past men in tailored suits and women in shimmering cocktail dresses, I leaned in to show them the jewelry up close before moving on to the next, leaving behind a waft of perfume to garner their senses.

With the entire room now circled more than once, I made my way to the back room again. The same woman who had placed the jewelry on me now silently removed it, putting each piece back in its protective case. I changed into my leggings and an oversized sweater, and on my way out picked up two of the gift bags given out to all the guests, containing samples of the new perfume, while the crowd continued sipping on their champagne.

I had returned to Munich in mid-January and into another tiny agency apartment, sharing with a model from Denver and her white cat. The first major job of the year had taken me to Salzburg, for ski wear. The next took me to the Cartier event. Celine and I had decided to cancel our trip to Australia. Neither of us felt committed to the trip, or it seemed, to the modeling world at large.

In an effort to again jump-start my interest, my agency persuaded me to go to Vienna, Austria for the month of March. I agreed and packed up my belongings once again. Arriving by train late at night, I took a taxi to an address far outside the center of the city. My instructions were to talk with the owner of a small pizza restaurant on arrival, and he would provide the key to a studio apartment above the restaurant. I entered the door, asking the first waitress I saw about the key.

Shortly a man came out, asking abruptly in broken English, "What do you want?" And not in a friendly tone. I tried to explain to him about the agency telling me to meet up with him for a key.

"Ah," he finally said and disappeared into the back for what seemed like forever.

When he returned, he handed me the key and pointed to the stairs outside. I grabbed my luggage and climbed up, opening the door to find a filthy square box of a room, bed unmade, food cartons lying about. No doubt this room had been used for some type of sexual tryst not long before I arrived. No wonder the restaurant owner acted so annoyed. Obviously, someone had been staying in it, maybe even unknowingly to the agency. Too late to look for another place to stay, I bolted the door before picking up the trash and taking the sheets off the bed. I found a blanket in the closet and would sleep on the mattress with it as my only cover. Welcome to Vienna.

A tram ran just outside the studio apartment, and after briefly studying the map at the stop the following morning, I climbed aboard. At least it would take me into the city for less than the cost of a cab ride.

The agency, The Boys and The Girls Modeling Agency, sat on Passauerplatz, near the heart of the city. As I entered the booking room, the three bookers stopped what they were doing and glared at me, without saying a word. I spoke first, introducing myself and mentioning that Heide, my agent in Munich, had spoken with them about me. They seemed not to know anything about it, or me, and talked as if this were my fault; their rudeness and unprofessionalism being the complete opposite of my agencies in Germany. Nevertheless, they had me sit down and handed me the necessary paperwork to begin go-sees in the city.

Later in the afternoon, before returning back to my shoebox of filth, I stopped in a store to purchase cleaning supplies. If I had to be here for a few weeks, I wouldn't let it be in such a horrendous place.

Even with my lackluster attitude, I soon found the city of Vienna entrancing. Beautifully old, with history carved into every building, I wandered around in the freezing cold, silent even in my thoughts. My favorite building, the Votivkirche, a neo-gothic church of epic proportions, with its double spirals reaching for the sky, mesmerized me for hours as I wandered the neighborhoods surrounding it. I preferred observing the buildings of Vienna from the outside, admiring their architecture, including that of the Opera House and the Neue Hofburg, rather than taking time for a tour of the insides.

During one of those long walks around the city, I met a man by the name of Hans, a German representative serving with the CSCE Delegation currently in meetings in Vienna. CSCE stood for the Conference on Security and Co-operation in Europe, and from what I could gather, included thirty-five countries, and also involved the Soviet Union's General Secretary of the Communist Party, Mikhail Gorbachev.

Hans, a hyper man, talked fast, whether by nature or by nervousness. Obviously a scholar and a politician, he looked the part. Although I felt no physical attraction towards him, my mind liked the broadening it received in his company. I believe he found it his mission to entice me into intellectualism. I tiptoed in, as if a child on the verge of adulthood, placing one toe in the unknown water at a time, testing its temperature and enjoyment potential.

Hans showed me the city, explaining a little history as we went along. He took me to wonderful restaurants for incredible meals. We walked around endlessly. On one particular day, he took me to the film museum, which at the time showcased a set of old American movies. We saw *The Belle of New York* starring Fred Astaire and *The Roaring Twenties* with Cagney and Bogart. I fell in love with them all.

1987

During my three weeks in Vienna, I only worked once, and it happened on my twenty-second birthday. A three-hour job for fashion for a catalog, it wasn't much to write home about. It was, regrettably, as dull as I found most of the people in the city to be. Regardless, I made the most of turning twenty-two. Two model friends, Anja and Kelly, came over to my shoebox apartment, now immaculately cleaned and organized, for dinner and movies. I had managed to rent a VCR and a few videos for my big celebration. Kelly and Anja, along with her sweet dachshund Shatzi, brought the cake.

Before leaving Vienna, Hans gave me two gifts, both books. The first, a small orange paperback entitled *William Shakespeare: The Sonnets, Die Sonnette*, included the sonnets of Shakespeare in English and German, side by side, compiled by Philippe Reclam. The card from Hans read:

Happy birthday Barbara!

I hope this little book will inspire you for learning German.

Hans

The second gift, entitled *Ninety-Nine Novels: The Best in English since 1939, A Personal Choice* by Anthony Burgess, presented short summaries of novels, from James Joyce's *Finnegans Wake* (1939) to *Ancient Evenings* by Norman Mailer (1983). This time, instead of a card, he wrote on the first page of the book:

For Barbara,

To whet her appetite.

1987

I returned to Munich in late March, unpacking my suitcases in another tiny studio apartment, this time located within the Rationaltheater, a somewhat controversial cabaret-type theater which provided temporary residency for its actors. It was expensive, and I knew I needed to find another place to stay, or maybe even another country if I wanted to continue modeling. A recent meeting with an agency in Greece had the agent practically begging me to come there. I didn't feel enticed in the slightest. I felt homesick. Homesick for a home.

Contacting Lawrine in New York, I mentioned my potential plan to come back to the States and asked if she had any contacts in Miami, Orlando, or Atlanta. Maybe I could continue working from one of these locations while I attended college. She said she would look into it for me. Meanwhile, I did another hair advertisement for L'Oréal hair products, as well as a two-day job in Nuremberg for a major German catalog.

A trip on location took me to Antalya, Turkey, during the last week of April. When I climbed aboard the Turkish Airlines flight, I hadn't made up my mind about returning to the States and to college. Not overly excited by another trip, I would wait to see if it jump-started my desire to model and to travel.

EUROPEAN DAZE

Arriving in Istanbul a few hours later, I sat down on a hard, plastic seat in the large terminal. For five long hours, I watched others as they walked around, including members of the US military. Seeing them in uniform made me think of Syria which lay to the southeast, and Libya which lay to the southwest of Turkey, both international hotspots at the time. Finally, my flight to Antalya departed, bringing me to my final destination just before midnight.

After a restless night, I made my way to breakfast to meet up with the group I would be working with for the week. As I walked up, smiling, and greeting them in English, they quietly stared at me. They hadn't known I was American. Again, another instance of clients assuming I was German based on my name, von der Osten. My cheery, good mood evaporated, and I plopped down, stone-faced, beside the two German models, Jeanette and Karl.

With the awkward breakfast out of the way, we climbed in a van for a ride to the mountainous area nearby to look for suitable locations to shoot. As rain poured down on us, we stopped in an old country bar to have a warm cup of tea. Old men filled the bar with not one woman in sight. Apparently, I would soon learn, the women were too busy working the fields, even in the rain. The men allowed us to enter and we all sat together, with very little talk. As we silently drove back to the hotel, golf ball sized hail beat down on us.

The next day, as the sun came out, we returned to the mountain area, posing by a slow flowing river. It felt like work with strangers. On the third day, a Sunday, we shot photos in the city, near the hotel all morning. Antalya, a mixture of sandy beaches and traditional Turkish culture, was an ancient Roman port at one time, and its character seemed timeless. The Turkish people themselves proved to be truly lovely. They were friendly and helpful, almost to an overwhelming degree.

For lunch, we headed outside the city. Tiny, unstable tables sat out in the grass, surrounded by a field of beautiful flowers. The roadside stand belonged to an uncle of one of our drivers for the week. The driver's aunt and cousins sat under a canvas, making what they referred to as Turkish pizzas. Everything was done simply, methodically, slowly. The driver seemed to have a slight crush on me and had his cousin string together a wreath type crown of yellow flowers for me to wear. I felt honored.

The following morning, we shot photos at the nearby harbor before taking the afternoon off to roam the street bazaar. Gold and leather items flooded the stalls, all at mostly affordable prices. Although I stayed away from those, I had become enamored with the tiny, narrow Turkish tea glasses and found a set along with several types of tea. This thrilled me in a way the leather thrilled the others.

Returning to the countryside for the final day, I posed for photos in the grasslands as goats grazed nearby. Relieved that the job was complete, we arrived back at the hotel to find it overrun with security details and local police. The President of Turkey had come to Antalya and was staying at the hotel. We were invited to attend a cocktail party with him and his entourage, followed by dinner.

I flew back to Istanbul, then on to Munich, early on the last day of April. Work slowed in Munich again, and many of the models began to panic. I called and spoke with my agents in Zurich and Hamburg, only to find work slow there as well. I considered going to Madrid but just couldn't rally myself to do so. I had also long ago determined that the frantic pace of New York, Paris and, to a lesser degree, Milan, were not for me, regardless of whether I stayed in modeling or not. I had my theater apartment until the end of May. I would decide by then what to do next, doing my best to keep an open mind. I had one foot in the circle, and one foot out, with the inner foot drawing closer and closer to the edge.

1987

TOP: Photo shoot on location in Antalya, Turkey by a river. Sitting on the rock in the center of the photo are Karl and Jeanette, both German models.

BOTTOM: Photos in and around Antalya. (l to r): (1)Karl and I jogging across the street; (2) sitting in the countryside while goats grazed nearby; and, (3) at the harbor posing with Jeanette in the old theater ruins.

TOP: Old Roman harbor near our hotel in Antalya, Turkey.

BOTTOM: Traditional Turkish women making Lahmacun (Turkish pizza) outdoors. These ladies were relatives of one of our drivers for the week.

EPILOGUE

As I write these words, I am sipping on a German Radler, staring at the empty bottle of French *Beaujolais Nouveau* from last fall, now serving as a vase for a pair of pink roses. Next to it sits a miniature bronze Colosseum which I picked up in Rome those many years ago during that chaotic shoot for *Italian Vogue*. In the background, "Boys of Summer" by Don Henley softly plays, my favorite song from my first summer living in Munich. My Mom's eggplant parmigiana bakes in the oven behind me, and my collection of journals, letters, postcards, photos, and tear sheets sit in a bin next to me, ready to be stowed away.

At the end of that May in 1987, I returned home to Florida. I was ready to leave my European days, or rather European daze, behind, and return to college. I still felt I needed to hang on to modeling, however, as it had been a surprise deviation in my life, and it shouldn't simply be tossed aside. Seeking out opportunities in nearby Orlando, I soon landed on the cover of *Central Florida* magazine. All the local models, those who had never signed with a New York agency or traveled in Europe, excitedly showed up every day for the photo shoots, thrilled to be in the local magazine. I didn't possess that thrill. That's when I knew it was over. The time had come to close that chapter of my life and write a new one.

EUROPEAN DAZE

The amazing opportunity I had been given, to model all over the world, a dream of so many but lived out by so few, wasn't lost on me. I believe this is why I had such a long-drawn-out time making a decision on whether to stay in modeling or not. It felt wrong to squander such an opportunity, but it also felt wrong to live a lie, the lie being that modeling was important to me. It just wasn't. Others, I know, found it a career, a life choice, an all-consuming lifestyle. And for them, that is fine. Sometimes though, just because you can do something doesn't mean you should, or have to.

My indoctrination into the modeling world, beginning in New York, and then in Paris, propelled me forward. I worked hard at the beginning; aiming to be a successful model. Milan is where the turn began, from a follower willing to do whatever it took for a modeling career, to an independent thinker. Then, starting in Zurich, and on into Munich, I discovered that I preferred being around different types of people, and not just models and photographers. My focus shifted from an all-consuming career in modeling to an enjoyment of life's simpler pleasures, such as bike rides in the park. Truth is, however, if you don't take modeling as a career seriously, you're unlikely to succeed. I didn't take it seriously, but I didn't feel like a failure either.

I had no doubts that I had it in me to succeed at modeling, to reach a higher level. Signs of this had shown up during various shoots, particularly in the shoot for wedding dresses in Rome. Admittedly, prior to that, I had, at times, felt like an imposter. The longer I stayed, however, I knew differently, and it became less and less about what I could do, and more about what I wanted to do.

EPILOGUE

Upon returning home, I felt no need to explain myself and my decision to anyone, nor to discuss the role of a model and what did or didn't happen. I had discovered something very powerful about myself: an inner strength to find my way through any circumstance in life, all thanks to those incredible days in Europe.

Regrettably, I fell out of touch with everyone from my modeling days. My first roommates in Paris had gone in different directions. The last I heard, Ava had returned home to Georgia after giving New York another try. As for Kristen, I only knew she had changed agencies in Paris, and things began looking up for her. It wasn't until 1990, while glancing at a *Parade* news magazine, an insert in most newspapers at the time, that I learned of her status.

On the first page, in the question and answer section, sitting next to a photo of a woman with short dark hair and enormous pouty lips, a reader had asked how the model of the year, Kristen McMenamy, had made it to the top. There it was. Kristen, not just a supermodel, but the 1990 model of the year, six years after our time together in Paris. She had cut off her long, beautiful red hair and dyed it black, reinventing herself. But most importantly, she continued to believe in herself and her dream. No one was more surprised than me. No one was more pleased than me.

I heard a few more times from Robbie Grey, still with the band Modern English, and a few more times from Umberto Caproni, the Count I met in Milan. Celine and I kept in touch for a while. She happily found a career in fashion in California. Hetty, I believe, became engaged to a musician in Vienna. As for Sean, he fulfilled his dream of going to New York, marrying an American, and living in the States permanently.

For me, upon returning to the States, it was as if I left that world behind, and all the people along with it. Yet friendships forged in the streets of Paris, Milan, Zurich, and Munich too were fleeting. Maybe they were meant to be that way.

As for beautiful, exotic Maria, the reason this all began, I never saw her again. I did try calling and wrote to her while overseas, but never heard back. It would be months, maybe a year, after being in Europe that my sister mentioned she had married and moved out to California. I imagine, still to this day, that the pain, disappointment, and sadness for her was just too great. I still think of her. She was the coolest chick I ever met.

EPILOGUE

The last modeling job of my career, in Orlando, Florida, 1987.
Cover Photograph by Patti Bose (pattibose©1987).

EUROPEAN DAZE

Personal collection of journals, photos, tearsheets, postcards and various memoribilia from my European days.

EUROPEAN DAZE
MUSIC PLAYLIST

EUROPEAN DAZE
MUSIC PLAYLIST

I Melt With You
Modern English

Drive
The Cars

I'm Never Gonna Dance Again
George Michael

Black Cars
Gino Vannelli

Hurts to Be in Love
Gino Vannelli

The Riddle
Nik Kershaw

Wouldn't It Be Good
Nik Kershaw

Cherish
Kool & the Gang

Rock Me Amadeus
Falco

Der Kommissar
Falco

People are People
Depeche Mode

Blasphemous Rumors
Depeche Mode

Master and Servant
Depeche Mode

EUROPEAN DAZE

You're my Heart, You're my Soul
Modern Talking

Cheri Cheri Lady
Modern Talking

The Boys of Summer
Don Henley

Kyrie
Mr. Mister

Broken Wings
Mr. Mister

The Power of Love
Jennifer Rush

You can find this playlist on Spotify, at this link:

https://spoti.fi/2GqfoVs

EUROPEAN DAZE
RECIPES

Earlene's Eggplant Parmigiana

Although I tried various versions of Eggplant Parmigiana throughout my travels in Europe, especially Italy, I found my Mom's to still be the best.

Ingredients

    1 large eggplant (1 ½ lb.)
    3 eggs, beaten
    1 ½ cups dry bread crumbs
    1 cup olive oil
    2 tsp. dried oregano leaves
    2 tsp. salt
    ½ lb. sliced Mozzarella Cheese
    ½ cup grated Parmesan
    Marinara Sauce (homemade or jar)

Directions

1. Preheat oven to 350° F. Lightly grease a 9x9x1¾ baking dish.
2. Cut eggplant crosswise into ¼" thick slices. Dip into beaten eggs, then into bread crumbs, coating completely.
3. Slowly heat oil in skillet. Sauté eggplant until golden brown (2 minutes). Drain.
4. In prepared dish, layer half the eggplant, 1 tsp oregano, 1 tsp salt, half the Mozzarella Cheese, half the sauce, and ¼ cup Parmesan. Repeat.
5. Bake, uncovered, for 25-30 minutes, or until cheese is melted and eggplant is tender.

Serve with a salad and a bottle of an Italian wine, such as a fruit-forward Barbera red wine, or a good White Zinfandel.

Spaghetti Aglio e Olio con Peperoni
Garlic and Oil Spaghetti with Pepperoni

My friends and I often ate a restaurant in Milan that served a pungent garlic and olive oil spaghetti with a dose of pepperoni thrown in. Once back in the States, I devised my own version of that memorable (and smelly) meal.

Ingredients

- 1 lb. uncooked spaghetti
- 6 cloves garlic, thinly sliced
- 1/2 cup olive oil
- 1 6-ounce pepperoni stick, grated or
    1 package sliced pepperoni, chopped
- 1/4 teaspoon red pepper flakes, or to taste
- salt and freshly ground black pepper to taste
- 1/4 cup chopped fresh Italian parsley
- 1 cup finely grated Parmigiano-Reggiano cheese

Directions

1. Add a small amount of olive oil to skillet. Warm at medium-high heat. Add grated or chopped pepperoni and cook until it begins to crisp and the edges curl, usually a few minutes.

2. Combine thinly sliced garlic and olive oil in a cold skillet. Slowly toast the garlic over medium heat, about six minutes or more. Reduce heat when olive oil begins to bubble. Stir garlic until it is golden brown, about another 5 minutes. Remove from heat.

3. Bring a large pot of lightly salted water to a boil. Cook spaghetti in the boiling water, stirring occasionally. Drain and transfer to a bowl.

4. Combine red pepper flakes, black pepper, salt, olive oil, garlic, and pepperoni with pasta. Sprinkle the Italian parsley and half of the Parmigiano-Reggiano cheese in and stir to combine.

5. Top pasta with the remaining Parmigiano-Reggiano cheese and serve.

Pair this dish with an Italian Pinot Noir or Sauvignon Blanc

Schweizer heiße Schokolade
Swiss Hot Chocolate

My favorite pastime while in Zurich was to sit at a café on the Limmatquai and sip on hot chocolate. Once back home, I found a way to bring that experience to my day anytime.

Ingredients

- 3 ¼ cups whole milk
- ½ cup sugar
- 8 oz. Swiss dark chocolate* (at least 70%), finely chopped
- ¾ cup heavy cream
- ½ tsp. pure vanilla extract
- Pinch of sea salt (optional)

Directions

1. Add milk and sugar to sauce pan over medium heat. Stir until sugar is dissolved. Bring to simmer then remove from heat.
2. Add chocolate, stirring until melted
3. Stir in heavy cream, vanilla, and sea salt.
4. Pour into mugs and top with unsweetened whipped cream. Add chocolate shavings for additional decoration.

*I am partial to Lindt Swiss Chocolate, so try Lindt Excellence 70%

German Radler

This popular German drink originated back in the early 1900s in Bavaria.

Ingredients

To make your own Radler to enjoy on a hot summer day, here are a few suggestions but obviously you can adjust the ratio of beer to soda to suit your own personal tastes.

1 can (12 oz) of Minute Maid Lemonade

                OR

1 can of lemon-lime soda

1 can (16 oz) of Weissbier (wheat bear) or your favorite German beer*

Directions

Blend equal amounts of both ingredients in a glass.

* Best if using a lager but can also use a pilsner if you prefer.

I often enjoyed a Radler on warm summer days during bike rides through the English Gardens in Munich. These concoctions are called shandy in northern Germany.

Antalya Lahmacun
Turkish Pizza

While in Antalya, Turkey for a photo shoot, one of our group's hired drivers invited us to his Uncle's place for lunch. We were plied with Turkish pizzas, or Lahmacun, made by his aunt and cousins under a canvas awning. These are thin pieces of dough (or flatbread), topped with minced meat, usually beef or lamb, and vegetables and herbs. It can be rolled up to eat like a burrito. Experiment with it, adding your own combinations. Below is a simple guide, one I created and add variations to every now and then.

Ingredients

½ lb. Homemade pizza dough, or a ready-made dough, at room-temperature

¾ lb. of ground beef (or other meat of your choice)

1 tsp turmeric

½ tsp cumin

1 tsp paprika

1 tsp dried mint

Pinch of cayenne

1 tomato, roughly chopped

1 shallot, roughly chopped

Small bunch of fresh parsley and cilantro

1 bell pepper (green or red, or half of each)

2 garlic cloves, roughly chopped

Salt and pepper, to taste

Directions

1. In a large bowl, add the ground meat and spices. Mix together well.

2. Blend the tomato, bell pepper, shallot, garlic, and herbs together, until it resembles a "salsa"

3. Remove and drain. Add this mixture to the raw meat and spices and mix well. Season with salt and pepper, if you like.

4. Divide your pizza dough into four equal size pieces, rolling them into a ball each. Using a rolling pin, roll each ball out as thin as you can. Spread approximately ¼ cup of the meat and vegetable mixture on top of each piece of dough, gently pressing it into the dough with your hands.

5. You can either bake it in the oven at 450 degrees (F) for 5-7 minutes or cook it on the stovetop in a non-stick skillet over medium heat. Drizzle a small amount of olive oil in the skillet, place the dough in the skillet and cover for about 5 minutes, making sure the dough and meat cook all the way through.

6. Top the crust with tomato slices, fresh parsley, and a squeeze of lemon juice..

BARBARA VON DER OSTEN lives in Florida and is the co-author of the book *LST 388: A World War II Journal*, based on her father's journal entries from World War II. After spending her early years modeling in Europe, von der Osten returned to college, earning a degree in International Affairs before moving to Washington, D.C. to work for a government consulting group. Tired of living inside the beltway, she eventually moved back to Florida. She continues to enjoy traveling and has now added scuba diving to her adventures.

www.ingramcontent.com/pod-product-compliance
Lightning Source LLC
Chambersburg PA
CBHW020348080526
44584CB00014B/937